Corporate Globalization
through Mergers and
Acquisitions

GENERAL EDITOR: LEONARD WAVERMAN

Corporate Globalization through Mergers and Acquisitions

The Investment Canada Research Series

The University of Calgary Press

Published by the Univerisity of Calgary Press in cooperation with Investment Canada and Canada Communication Group - Publishing, Supply and Services Canada.

ISBN 1-895176-12-3
ISSN 1188-0988
Cat. No. Id 53-11/2-1991E

Canadian Cataloguing in Publication Data

Main entry under title:

Corporate Globalization Through Mergers and Acquisitions

(Investment Canada Research Series, ISSN 1188-0988 ; v.2)
Issued also in French under title: La Mondialisation des sociétés par les fusions et acquisitions.
  Includes bibliographical references.
  ISBN 1-895176-12-3

   1. Consolidation and merger of corporations — Canada 2. Conglomerate corporations — Canada. 3. International business enterprises — Canada. I. Waverman, Leonard, 1941-
II. Series.
HD2746.5.C67 1991   338.8'3'0971   C91-091787-6

Translation into French by Translation Bureau of The Secretary of State of Canada

Publishing Co-ordination: Ampersand Communications Services Inc.
Cover & Interior Design: Brant Cowie/ArtPlus Limited

Printed in Canada

∞ This book is printed on acid-free paper.

Table of Contents

Preface

MERGERS AND ACQUISITIONS grew to wave-like proportions in the 1980s, before breaking to a much quieter level of activity with the onset of the 1991-92 recession. Another wave in the not too distant future is predictable, however, as corporate restructuring to meet the requirements of global competition is never complete. Indeed, the many dimensions of globalization appear to encourage joint ventures and other forms of strategic alliances — causing the merger of once serious rivals in a common fight for market share. Future merger and acquisition activity is unlikely to be fuelled by junk bonds and levered buy-outs, as the financial community and investors are extremely wary today of shell games. Rather, solid business and economic considerations will guide corporations in their efforts to become global players.

In addition to its mandate to promote foreign investment, Investment Canada carries the responsibility of ensuring that major foreign takeovers are of net benefit to the country. In order to conduct its regulatory responsibilities in a manner sensitive to global competition, the agency must constantly endeavour to understand the rapidly evolving coprorate forms for meeting this competition. This, then, led the Agency to launch an intensive research program on "Corporate Globalization through Mergers and Acquisitions".

In March 1990, distinguished academics and professionals from Canada and abroad were invited to prepare papers on this topic. The papers were presented at an Authors' Conference in Toronto on November 29 - 30, 1990, and later revised in light of comments by discussants and participants. The revised papers, together with the Rapporteur's report, are presented in this volume, the second in the Investment Canada Research Series. Leonard Waverman, Centre of International Studies, University of Toronto, served as General Editor and his introduction immediately follows.

The Investment Canada Research Series has been developed with three main objectives:

- to advance research on international investment in Canada and abroad based on the highest academic scholarship;

- to foster a better understanding among Canadians of globalization and the vital role played by international investment; and,
- to identify investment policy and research issues requiring the attention of governments and particularly of Investment Canada which has responsibilities for promoting, reviewing and monitoring international investment.

The research assembled in this volume is mainly the product of work undertaken by outside researchers. However, Investment Canada staff managed the project, wrote one of the papers and throughout offered comments on the other papers. As is the case with the Investment Canada Working Paper Series (these papers available on request from the Agency), the views expressed in these research studies do not necessarily reflect those of Investment Canada or the federal government.

I would like to take this opportunity to thank all participants in the research effort, and especially Leonard Waverman, for their work. I know that it will be of interest to a wide range of Canadians and will serve to encourage the development of further research in an area where it is much needed.

MICHAEL WILSON
MINISTER RESPONSIBLE FOR
INVESTMENT CANADA

Introduction

THE FOREIGN INVESTMENT REVIEW AGENCY (FIRA) was established in 1975 to review whether the acquisition of Canadian companies and the establishment of new businesses by foreign investors were of value to Canada. At the time, Canada held nearly one quarter of the world's total stock of foreign direct investment (FDI) and foreign investors (principally Americans) controlled the majority of assets related to petroleum and natural gas, mining and manufacturing. FIRA was succeeded in June 1985 by Investment Canada, whose task was both to encourage FDI and to continue to monitor foreign acquisitions of Canadian businesses to ensure that transactions were of "net benefit" to Canada. During FIRA's regime, foreign control of Canadian business fell sharply. Part of this reduction in foreign ownership was due to FIRA, but part was also due to other Government policies (such as the various programs designed to increase Canadian control in the petroleum and natural gas sector); part was due to the changing global economic environment and the diminishing role of the United States as the world's economic leader (see Graham and Krugman, 1989); and part was due to the rise of Canada as the home base for a growing tide of multinationals (see Rugman, 1987).

The international environment has continued to change. Domestic capital markets have become much more interconnected; the nature of borrowing has undergone significant transformations (junk bonds and their ilk); and a major merger wave has passed through North America. All this has made "globalization" the new buzzword to describe many business activities.

It is clear that FDI in Canada and Canadian FDI abroad are parts of a larger global issue. One cannot examine inward and outward FDI in Canada without examining the international context and the forces creating these real capital movements. These forces are not well understood or researched. Little data exist on the extent of cross-border merger and acquisition (M&A) activity, and how such activity relates to "globalization". Is M&A activity high in Canada relative to other countries? Are there specific explanations of these phenomena, such as tax differences or general explanations such as "corporate strategy"? Do M&As create "value"? Do cross-border M&As differ significantly from domestic M&As? What public policy concerns, if any, are generated by transborder M&As? There are many, many unanswered questions.

It is to the credit of Investment Canada that the Agency commissioned publishable academic research to examine these forces and all of the authors whose works are contained in this volume are grateful to the Agency.

The final paper by Edward Safarian, the Conference Rapporteur, summarizes the papers and provides his insights on policy; there is, then, no need to summarize the papers in this introduction. What would be useful for the reader, however, is to understand why the topics were chosen and how they fit together. A brief digression is first required to examine the enterprise that engages in FDI, the multinational company.

As soon as a company engages in FDI, it has become a "multi-national" — a firm operating in more than one country. The forces of corporate globalization are then the forces which make for multi-country firm operations. Why do multinationals (MNEs) exist? Clearly, they are not new. Krugman (1990) argues that they may indeed have been more important in the earlier years of this century than now. Economists have developed a number of hypotheses to explain the growth of MNEs, the sectors in which they will operate, and the countries to which they will be attracted. The most sophisticated of these hypotheses and one addressed by nearly every one of the authors in this volume, is the "transactional/locational" hypothesis (called T-L). This hypothesis is as follows. Firms are collections of specific assets. Some of these assets are priced in markets and provide few spillovers to other activities (say, a knitting machine). However, some of the firm's assets may be intangible and difficult to price in markets — the value of the firm's patents, its stock of goodwill, the advertising and brand names that spill across national borders, even the talent of highest management.

Some firms have specific intangible assets that they can use in a number of markets — a patent, for example. If a firm wishes to sell its patented product in another country, it could export its product, but transportation costs or other barriers (tariffs, the need to have localized design) make it more profitable for the firm that owns the patent to produce in the foreign country. The firm could produce overseas by licensing its technology to a foreign entrepreneur, but then the firm (patent holder) is at risk that the licensee will acquire all the information developed by the firm and/or that the licensee will adversely harm the firm's interests (opportunism affecting the patent holder's ability to appropriate the pecuniary gains from the patent). The value of the patent to the patent holder is then maximized when the patent holder becomes an MNE and invests (foreign direct investment in the foreign country through an acquisition or greenfield construction). Therefore, the T-L approach suggests that the MNE form of enterprise — ownership of assets abroad — developed so that the parent could appropriate the economic rents on these intangible assets, returns that would be at risk with arm's-length contracts where the rights to these intangible assets were put in third party hands. This T-L approach can also be used to explain *vertical* cross-border M&As, the purchaser finding transaction costs lower in purchasing assets rather than in engaging in long-term contracts (Gorecki, 1990).

This T-L approach, while at the base of any economic analysis of corporate globalization through mergers and acquisitions, is not the whole story. Acquisitions occur through waves and it is unlikely that the development of firm-specific intangible assets occurs with similar waves. Hence, attention is also placed on other determinants of M&As. One clear potential determinant is inefficient management in the acquired firm, management which is not maximizing shareholders' returns and is thus open to a hostile takeover designed to replace the managers. This motive is called the market for "corporate control". (It is unclear, however, that managerial inefficiencies occur in waves as well and thus the "market for corporate control" may not explain merger waves.) It is not evident that foreign managers have the best information on which domestic managers are misbehaving, so that the market for corporate control might be a better explanation for domestic rather than foreign takeovers (of course, if foreign acquiring firms are already operating in the market, they may have a high degree of knowledge about the operations of domestic companies).

Another management story explaining M&As is the notion that it is the managers of the acquiring firm (rather than of the acquired firm) who are inefficient, using their power to acquire assets. These acquisition bound managers receive enjoyment from driving their firms larger even when such acquisitions are not to the benefit of the owner shareholders. Many observers suggest that the conglomerate merger wave of the 1970s, a wave that eventually saw most such mergers redivided, was driven by ambitions of acquiring firms' managers. Other explanations for M&As exist. One plausible story is that acquirers take advantage of underpriced assets in the acquired firm. This story could explain merger waves, since assets could become undervalued across a broad spectrum of companies. A more recent hypothesis is that some M&As occur in order for management to break contracts (explicit or implicit) with labour, this ability being unavailable to incumbent managers. Numerous specific reasons such as the benefit of tax losses which decrease income taxes to the acquiring firm exist for M&As as well. Other explanations that have been advanced for trans-border M&As utilize differential tax regimes in the two countries that make it profitable to cross the border, differential costs of capital, differential movements in exchange rates (making assets in one country relatively cheap), and differential movements in stock market prices.

As the reader can see, the list of potential explanations is long and with each explanation lies a potentially different public policy story. For example, the notion that some M&As can serve to break implicit contracts with workers suggests that M&As may create winners and losers and the losers may have to depend on the government for assistance. If M&As are driven by management whims that are not coincident with the maximization of shareholder value, that is another public policy story. If cross-border M&As are generated by differential taxation, implications for tax policy are evident.

The papers in this volume do not examine all these issues, nor do they provide many answers. They do, however, provide significant new information and analyses which shed light on the process of corporate globalization through mergers and acquisitions. The first two papers (Khemani; Knubley, Krause and Sadeque) examine recent history to provide data on inward and outward FDI (in Canada) in a global context. These papers add to our knowledge of the extent of M&As in Canada, the growth of Canadian multinational activity abroad, and how these developments relate to M&A activity in other industrialized nations. Rugman and Waverman analyze the cases examined by FIRA and Investment Canada according to some recent general corporate strategy theories of MNEs. Baldwin and Caves examine foreign and domestic Canadian M&As to determine if and how they differ in their effects on important issues such as productivity. Patry and Poitevin analyze ten recent hostile takeovers in Canada and examine the sources of gains — is value created for shareholders and if so, at whose expense? Halpern and Mintz examine whether tax issues can explain Canada-U.S. cross-border M&As. Daniels analyzes the public policy issues of the various motivations for M&As and discusses whether a new M&A specific policy is required. Safarian, as noted, summarizes the studies and provides his policy guide.

Together these eight papers provide significant new research on the important topics of the extent of M&A activity in Canada, its similarity across countries, and the determinants and impacts of mergers and acquisitions. This research will whet the appetite of the reader to consider new questions and engage in more research on the topic.

LEONARD WAVERMAN
AUGUST, 1991

R.S. Khemani
Faculty of Commerce and Business Administration
University of British Columbia

1

Recent Trends in Merger and Acquisition Activity in Canada and Selected Countries

INTRODUCTION

DURING THE 1980s, the Canadian financial press, business analysts, economists and others often focussed attention on the amount of merger and acquisition (M&A) activity taking place in Canada. According to some observers, the pace of this activity rivals that of the "merger waves" around the turn of the century and during the late 1920s when the foundations of many present-day large corporations were first being laid. Many also claim that what is now taking place in Canada parallels that which is occurring in other industrialized nations. The proceedings of forums, such as the Competition Law and Policy Committee of the OECD, certainly provide some basis for this view as country after country submits reports on the high level of M&A activity in their respective jurisdictions. Moreover, the continued expansion of international trade, foreign direct investment, joint ventures and the changing nature of corporate economic activity in terms of input sourcing, product manufacturing, R&D and marketing, have led some to suggest that M&A activity in different countries is part of a larger phenomenon of globalization of markets. In order to compete more effectively in an increasingly competitive and integrated world economy, corporations merge, acquire, divest and restructure various business activities as part of the re-configuration of their competitive advantage. Many of these generalizations are, however, supported only by anecdotal facts, and so the need for further research and analysis is widely recognized.

Against this backdrop, the purpose of this paper is modest: to describe the recent trends and patterns of merger and acquisition activity in Canada and draw comparisons with developments in other industrialized countries. The questions relating to this activity include the following:

- What has been the level, pace and composition of M&A activity in Canada during the past decade?
- Has there been an increase in foreign vs. domestic transactions? Horizontal vs. vertical/conglomerate mergers? In large transactions?

- What types of industries has M&A activity centred on? Are there any sectoral shifts?

As comparisons with other countries, the questions of particular interest are:

- Are the trends and patterns in M&A activity across countries similar?
- Does Canada have a relatively high level of M&A activity?

The remaining part of this paper is divided into four sections. The section following briefly discusses the broad range of factors which may influence M&A activity. The next section describes this activity in Canada over the period from 1979 to 1989. This is followed by some international comparisons. The final section presents the conclusions.

Caveat   While M&A activity has been widely acknowledged as an important economic phenomenon, the quality and content of the data currently available in Canada and in other countries is seriously lacking. Much of the data consists of a simple count of acquiring and acquired firms. Information in terms of sales, assets, transaction value, assets vs. share purchases, negotiated vs. tender offers, partial vs. complete control, product class and range, financial performance ratios, domestic vs. foreign operations is not uniformly available for any given country or across different countries for any given year. Details on different data sources and various constraints confronted are described in the Appendix. Because of the scarcity of publicly available data, the discussion contained in this paper should be viewed as being impressionistic and preliminary in nature.

Factors Influencing Merger and Acquisition Activity

THE CAUSES AS WELL as the consequences of merger and acquisition activity is one of the unsettled areas in industrial organization economics (see papers in Browne and Rosengren, 1987; Scherer and Ross, 1990, pp. 159-67). The paucity of research and contradictory or inconclusive evidence aside, differences in views among members of different disciplines in the field of economics are persistent.

Finance economists contend that mergers and acquisitions are part of a market driven mechanism by which resources are reallocated from lower to alternative and higher valued uses. The process supplements the prevailing competitive forces in markets, in which firms purchase inputs and sell outputs, and stimulates these firms to adapt to changing demands, to respond rapidly to evolving technologies, and to adjust to fluctuating capital market conditions. Most importantly, the market for corporate control of publicly traded corporations unsettles comfortable managerial lives, minimizes the principal-agent problem between shareholders and inefficient or shirking management and eliminates obsolete and less productive processes and organizational structures.

Industrial organization economists concede that mergers and acquisitions may result in increased efficiency. But other possibilities, such as speculative motives and the desire to acquire market control or monopoly power, are not discounted. Moreover, many mergers are identified as unproductive and, in some instances, even socially wasteful.

A myriad of reasons, motives, economic forces and institutional factors may, separately or in combination, influence corporate decisions to engage in M&A activity. In recent years the pressures of international competition, financial innovation, economic growth and expansion, increased political and economic integration, and technological change have all contributed to the increased pace of merger and acquisition activity. Also, traditional business and economic rationales, such as related product line and geographic market extension, diversification, risk and benefits of vertical integration, continue to remain as possible explanations. In addition, changing or new tax regimes, cost of capital, government policy on matters such as foreign ownership, economic regulation and privatization also have an impact on the magnitude and inter-industry/country variation in merger and acquisition activity. For example, among the countries examined for this paper, Australia, Canada and Sweden have legislation in place to review (and if necessary disallow) foreign takeovers of domestic firms, while Germany, the United Kingdom and the United States do not. Restrictions on foreign ownership also vary across industry sectors such as transportation, finance, energy and communications. The universal banking system in Germany facilitates, if not promotes, high levels of integration and various institutional ownership links between financial and real sector firms (see Marfels, 1988). The percentage of German corporate assets capitalized on the Frankfurt stock exchange is significantly lower than on the New York, London or Toronto stock exchanges. Tender offers and contested takeovers are consequently more difficult to mount in such an environment. In Japan, inter-corporate ownership links, and a system of "corporate collectivism or Keiretsu" (see Pettway, 1991) also has similar implications, and when mergers and acquisitions occur, they tend to be among the group of associated firms. In Canada, the high level of ownership concentration of companies listed on the Toronto Stock Exchange (see Khemani, 1988) helps to explain the observed large number of negotiated takeovers. Without extensive resources, time, and in-depth research, it is not possible to delineate clearly the firm-, industry- and country-specific factors that are constantly at play and which underlie merger and acquisition activity.

CANADA

AN INDICATION OF THE PACE AND TRENDS in merger and acquisition activity in Canada over the past decade can be seen in Table 1, which is based on data derived from the Merger Register maintained by the Bureau of

TABLE 1

THE NUMBER OF MERGERS AND ACQUISITIONS IN CANADA 1979-1989

YEAR	FOREIGN*	DOMESTIC	TOTAL
1979	307	204	511
1980	234	180	414
1981	200	291	491
1982	371	205	576
1983	395	233	628
1984	410	231	641
1985	466	246	712
1986	641	297	938
1987	622	460	1082
1988	593	460	1053
1989	691	400	1091

NOTES: * Acquisitions involving foreign-owned or foreign-controlled acquiring company.

SOURCE: Merger Register, Bureau of Competition Policy, Ottawa-Hull

Competition Policy (see Appendix). Examining first the total number of mergers and acquisitions, the earlier period (up to 1982) shows some variation in the level of activity. The years 1980 and 1981 coincide with a period of volatile and generally slow economic growth in Canada with the recession setting in during the fourth quarter of 1981. From 1982 to 1987, the total number of mergers and acquisitions persistently increased. The highest point of this activity was reached in 1987, with the later years (to 1989) essentially showing a plateau in the number of mergers and acquisitions.

A similar trend can be seen with respect to the number of foreign mergers and acquisitions while that of domestic firm activity shows some (albeit minor) variation. The long-term pattern of M&A activity is frequently described by economists as occurring in "waves"; it would therefore appear that the period between 1979 and 1990 is characterized *primarily* as being that of an *upswing*.

Previous research (see Tarasofsky, 1990) and the discussion contained in the last section of this paper suggests that the overall trend in M&A activity in Canada shadows that of the United States.[1] The underlying statistics indicate that the majority of the foreign acquisitions in Canada are generally made by U.S.-based or -controlled firms. The United States has historically accounted for the largest proportion of foreign direct investment, including both greenfield and mergers and acquisitions, into Canada (70 percent of $110.3 billion in 1988 alone; see Nymark, 1990). Since 1982, the number of foreign mergers and acquisitions exceeds that undertaken by domestic firms. Statistics on M&A activity since the end of World War II, which are not explicitly presented here, indicate that this is a reversal of a trend that existed in Canada until 1977.[2]

FIGURE 1

MERGER AND ACQUISITION ACTIVITY IN CANADA NORMALIZED BY REAL GDP, 1979–1989

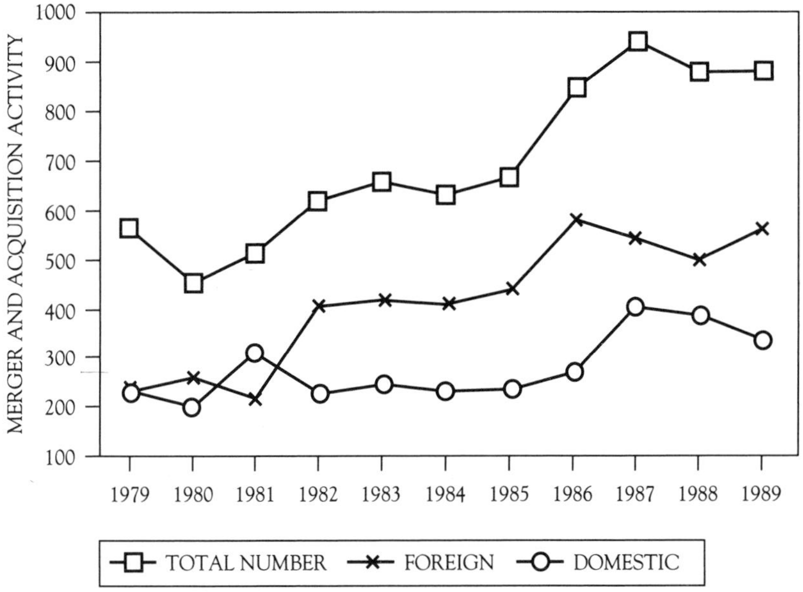

SOURCE: Merger Register, Bureau of Competition Policy, Ottawa-Hull

The similar trends in M&A activity in Canada and the United States, and the high degree of American ownership and direct investment in Canadian industry generally, is indicative of the extent of economic integration between the two countries. This is further reflected in the high volume of bilateral trade flows. Each country is the other's single largest trading partner. Approximately 30 percent of Canadian GDP is accounted for by exports, the bulk of which are destined for the United States. Moreover, effective January 1, 1989, Canada and the U.S. entered into a Free Trade Agreement (FTA). While the full impact of the FTA will only be felt over the subsequent 10-year period as various tariff and non-tariff barriers are staged for reduction, the pace of mergers and acquisitions in Canada may be due in part to the process of structural rationalization. Firms divest and realign different production facilities in order to exploit potential economies of scale and scope, and to position themselves strategically to operate in a larger, more competitive market environment. In examining M&A activity in the context of EC 1992 economic integration, Caves (1990b) hypothesized that the increased magnitude of trans-border transactions possibly reflects firms seizing new business opportunities, to expand geographically, specialize product lines and/or to avert or limit diversion of profits to rival firms. Surveys of large firms in Europe identified expectations or plans for increased productivity and re-organization of corporate economic activities so as to operate competitively in the larger unified post-1992 market. For example, Geroski and Vlassopoulos (1990) and Jacquemin et al (1988) have observed an increase in trans-border M&A activity during the late 1980s in Europe.

The *number* of mergers and acquisitions as an indicator of this type of corporate activity is admittedly a crude measure — a more preferable one being the dollar value of these transactions. Moreover, the value ought to be normalized or deflated by an appropriate measure such as total corporate sector assets. Data on the value of these transactions is not available, however. Since the level of M&A activity may vary directly with economic growth,[3] Figure 1 presents a graph of the trend in M&A activity normalized by real (1979) GDP. The overall pattern remains the same as that derived from the preceding discussion pertaining to Table 1.

Some figures on the number and value of mergers and acquisitions for the post-1985 period can be derived from data published by Venture Economics Inc. According to this data source, the total number and transaction values of mergers and acquisitions in Canada between 1984 and 1990 increased as follows:

TABLE 2

NUMBER AND TRANSACTION VALUES OF M&A ACTIVITY IN CANADA

	TOTAL NUMBER M&A ANNOUNCEMENTS	NUMBER AND (%) OF CASES WITH TRANSACTION VALUES AVAILABLE	TOTAL TRANSACTION VALUE ($ BIL)	PERCENTAGE ACCOUNTED BY TRANSACTION VALUES OVER $100 MILLION
1985	1177	135 (11.5)	14.4	n.a.
1986	1196	238 (20.0)	19.4	n.a.
1987	1364	244 (18.0)	16.9	80.0
1988	1300	524 (40.0)	23.7	73.0
1989	1285	348 (27.0)	30.0	78.0

SOURCE: Venture Economics Inc., Toronto, Annual Reports

It appears that where data are available, the transactions that exceed $100 million account for a large percentage of the total value. It should be noted that not all of these transactions entail change in management or ownership control of the acquired firm and that the data includes partial acquisitions as well. In addition, the total number of transactions include deals that have been publicly announced but which have not necessarily been completed in the reported year. Also, some of these transactions may have been abandoned. For

TABLE 3

THE NUMBER AND TRANSACTION VALUE OF LARGE (IN EXCESS OF $100 MILLION) MERGERS AND ACQUISITIONS IN CANADA

YEAR	NUMBER	TOTAL VALUE ($ MILLIONS)	AVERAGE VALUE ($ MILLIONS)
1979	9	3 411	379
1980	13	4 825	371
1981	23	14 231	619
1982	2	466	233
1983	3	1 274	425
1984	4	778	195
1985	38	8 716	229
1986	51	18 347	360
1987	69	31 195	452
1988	49	16 561	338
1989	42	18 127	432

SOURCE: Stanbury, W.T., Appendix 1 in Khemani et al. *op. cit.* with updates by the author; Venture Economics, Toronto. Merger Register and file data, Bureau of Competition Policy

these reasons the total number of mergers and acquisitions reported here differs from those presented in Table 1.

A complete series of *large* (in excess of $100 million in value) mergers and acquisitions can be compiled using the Venture Economics Inc. data base along with the data collected by W.T. Stanbury (1988). Such a series is presented in Table 3. I have adjusted the two data bases to include missing observations obtained from the Bureau of Competition Policy files and to account for only completed deals where changes in ownership control occurred. These statistics, therefore, do not directly correspond to those presented in Table 2. The data suggest that the number of large mergers and acquisitions, particularly, increased after 1985 and reached a peak in 1987. The average transaction value in that year reached $452 million but, during the period under review, there were variations ranging between $195 million and $619 million (nominal dollar values).

These trends in the number of mergers and acquisitions by foreign firms and the number and value of large transactions portends increased levels of foreign ownership and aggregate concentration within the Canadian economy. Although data are not available for the most recent years of the period under review, Statistics Canada (1990, pp. 19-21, 24-26) indicates that the overall percentage of total industrial assets (both financial and non-financial corporations) under foreign control increased from 16.9 percent in 1983 to 18.2 percent in 1987. A number of factors influence the level of foreign control. These include the relative growth rates of corporations, formation of new corporations, and mergers and acquisitions. Statistics Canada estimates that the effect

FIGURE 2

MERGERS AND ACQUISITIONS BY FOREIGN & DOMESTIC CONTROLLED FIRMS, CONSOLIDATED YEARS 1978 & 1979

Acquired Firm Industry Category

Acquiring Firm Industry Category	1	2	3	4	5	6	7	8	9	10	11	12	13	14	15	16	17	18	19	20	21	22	23	24	25	26	27	28	29 (Total)
1	4																								1	2		5	12
2												1																	1
3			1																										1
4				67		1										1					1	2						14	86
5	2				40																			1				5	48
6																													
7							5	2																					7
8																		2											2
9									9														1			1		1	12
10																													
11											3						1			1		1	1						9
12											1	23								1	1	1	2	2		1	5		36
13												10		5	3														15
14		1										2	5	5															11
15					1										16	2	1							1		2	1	5	25
16															2	2	1									1		1	5
17													4	3	1	1	27	3	2	1		2	2	1		5	1	8	57
18																	1	17	5	2						6		6	36
19																	3	1	14									6	26
20																				19		1		2		1		6	32
21																					7	1			2		1	9	22
22																					4	2				1			6
23					2				1		1									1		2	29	12	2		1	10	50
24				2	2			1			1	1		1			2			1		12	1			1	1	11	30
25																									12				14
26	1	1		1	3	1				1			1	1	1	1	1				1					55	1	8	73
27			1	4	5										4	1	8	18	5	10	1	4	14	13		1	80	41	216
28				2											1		1	5	2	1	1			2			1	54	65
29				1	4										2		1	3	2	1		2	2	2		2	2	41	128
	6	1	2	84	57	2	5	5	10	5	27	14	10	27	5	45	47	32	37	10	16	50	36	16	66	94	246	70	1025

Diagonal Total: 582

SOURCE: Merger Register, Bureau of Competition Policy, 1978 and 1979

FIGURE 3

MERGERS AND ACQUISITIONS BY FOREIGN & DOMESTIC CONTROLLED FIRMS, CONSOLIDATED YEARS 1983 & 1984

Acquired Firm Industry Category

Acquiring Firm Industry Category	1	2	3	4	5	6	7	8	9	10	11	12	13	14	15	16	17	18	19	20	21	22	23	24	25	26	27	28	29	(Total)
1	3																													3
2		3																												3
3																														4
4			4	28	1													3		2			2					1		42
5					27														1				1				5	1	3	37
6					1	2																								3
7							1																				1			2
8																														
9									11	1											1		1				1			14
10											6																		1	1
11												8																	8	8
12												1	3										1						8	8
13							1		1			1	3	21			1										3			11
14					2							1		7	28			2		1			2	2			3		3	30
15															28			2		1			2	2			3		3	37
16																														56
17					1								1				41	2	1	1	1		1	1			7	1	1	50
18																1	1	32	1	2			2				10	1	1	35
19																1		1	20		1		1	2			8		1	83
20							1										2	3		43	15		3	2			25	7	7	23
21																		1			15				1		2	1	1	9
22																						1					7		1	73
23			1	1	1												3	2	2	2	2		46	14			12	8	8	42
24																	3			2	2		1				16	3	3	15
25							1	1									1	1		1	1			14	12			1	1	62
26					2																			1		53	4	1		92
27					1					1	1						1	2	2	1	1		1	2		9	74		4	336
28	1		1	7	7	2	2	1	1		3	4	1	7	2	2	20	8	8	12	9	1	18	13	2	6	57	59	84	167
29															1		1	2		1	1								155	
	3	3	5	36	43	2	4	1	14	2	10	14	5	29	31	4	74	57	32	63	34	2	77	38	15	62	247	62	277	1246

SOURCE: Merger Register, Bureau of Competition Policy, 1983 and 1984

Diagonal Total: 710 (excludes unclassified)

FIGURE 4

MERGERS AND ACQUISITIONS BY FOREIGN & DOMESTIC CONTROLLED FIRMS, CONSOLIDATED YEARS 1988 & 1989

Acquiring Firm Industry Category (rows) × Acquired Firm Industry Category (columns)

Acq.→	1	2	3	4	5	6	7	8	9	10	11	12	13	14	15	16	17	18	19	20	21	22	23	24	25	26	27	28	29	(Total)
1	5																													5
2																														
3			2																											2
4				152	1		2				1	1			2	1	1	2		1			2	2		2	3	1	1	175
5				1	95	1																				1	7		4	109
6									1																					1
7							2	1																			6			9
8								1																			1			2
9									1	1	1																1			4
10																														
11											8																1			9
12												14	1																	15
13													8														2		1	11
14														14	1											1	2		2	20
15															72	4	1	1					1	1		1	1		2	84
16																1	4	1											1	7
17																	32	19												51
18																		19									5	1	3	28
19																			19								2	1	8	30
20																		1	2	33			1			11	2	9	5	89
21				4																	26						4			34
22																						1	1			2	12	2	1	19
23																	1	1		1	1		30	1		1	19	1	1	57
24															1		1	1						19			7		2	31
25				1																					7			1	4	13
26																							1			103	3		17	124
27				4	2																					3	116	2	6	133
28			1	10	10	2	2	1	1		1	2	2	5	10	1	14	9	13	9	5		9	14	3	17	48	149	65	402
29																				5			1			2	6	6	159	179
Total	7	2	3	175	109	6	2	3	1	1	11	20	10	19	92	7	61	39	43	48	32	1	51	42	12	137	269	164	276	**1643**

Diagonal Total: 1091

Industry Codes

1 Agriculture	8 Leather	16 Primary Metal	24 Miscellaneous Manufacturing
2 Forestry	9 Textiles	17 Metal Fabricating	25 Construction
3 Fishing and Trapping	10 Knitting mills	18 Machinery	26 Transportation, Communication, Utilities
4 Mines, Quarrying, Oil Wells	11 Clothing	19 Transportation Equipment	27 Trade
5 Food and Beverage	12 Wood	20 Electrical Products	28 Finance, Insurance, Real Estate
6 Tobacco Products	13 Furniture and Fixtures	21 Non-metallic Mineral Products	29 Community, Business or Personal Services
7 Rubber	14 Paper	22 Petroleum and Coal Products	
	15 Printing, Publishing	23 Chemicals and Chemical Products	

SOURCE: Merger Register, Bureau of Competition Policy, 1988 and 1989

of mergers and acquisitions in 1988 and 1989 alone should increase the 1987 value of total industrial assets under foreign control to 19.2 percent. Data on aggregate concentration also show an increase. In 1983 the 25 leading enterprises accounted for 39.1 percent of total industrial assets, whereas in 1987 the share was 40.9 percent.

To obtain a more detailed profile of the merger and acquisition activity in Canada over the past decade, particularly in terms of the broad industry characteristics of the acquiring and acquired firms, I refer the reader to Figures 2, 3 and 4. For the consolidated years of 1978/79, 1983/84 and 1988/89, these figures classify the merging parties into 29 industrial categories. Within manufacturing, the categories correspond generally to the two-digit Standard Industrial Classification (major group) codes, whereas outside manufacturing they represent one or more industrial divisions, (i.e., several major groups). The 29 industry categories are too broad to coincide with any particular concept of a market or industry in the usual business economics sense. A more detailed breakdown — at the three- or four-digit SIC level, for example — would probably yield fewer observations within each of the categories. While this would more accurately reflect the inter- and intra-industry aspects of M&A transactions, the broad patterns of this activity which are of interest in the present context, would not be easily discernible.

The totals along the diagonal in these figures represent the number of acquiring and acquired firms that fall into the same broad industrial category. The transactions may be viewed as "broadly horizontal" in nature (i.e., where the firms have operations in the same or similar products). The industry categories are sufficiently broad, however, that these numbers probably include related product diversification mergers as well. The totals at the base of the columns indicate the industry categories in which the target (acquired) firms operate. Similarly, the totals at the end of the rows indicate the total number of firms in each industry category in which the acquiring firms are based. The number of mergers and acquisitions *not* located on the diagonal suggest the extent of non-horizontal activity; these include transactions that are conglomerate and vertical (forward-backward) in nature.

Comparing these figures, it is notable that the majority of mergers and acquisitions tend to be broadly horizontal — approximately 57 percent of total activity in the years 1978/79 and 1983/84, respectively, and at a significantly higher level of 66 percent in 1988/89. There is, however, considerable variation in horizontal merger activity within different industry categories during the three time periods.[4] While the overall extent of conglomeration appears to have declined over the years, it still remains a notable phenomenon judging by both the number and proportion of such mergers and acquisitions and by the span of these transactions across different industry categories.

Also of interest is the variation in total merger activity in different industry categories. Generally, the level of activity tends to be high in the following categories: 26 - Transportation, Communications and Utilities; 27 - Trade; 28 -

Finance, Insurance and Real Estate; and 29 - Community, Business and Personal Services. The number of mergers and acquisitions is also high in category 4 - Mines, Quarrying and Oil Wells, particularly in the years 1978/79 and 1988/89. Toward the end of the decade, M&A activity was also pronounced in category 5 - the Food and Beverage sector, most of which tended to be horizontal.

Another striking fact that emerges from the data is the proportion of firms in category 27 - Trade, which were acquired by firms outside that category. Acquisitions in this category increased from 14 percent in 1978/79 to 70 percent in 1983/84 and were at 57 percent in 1988/89. This probably reflects the forward integration of economic activity by firms located in different industries. The underlying statistics also suggest that many foreign firms located outside the Trade category have made these acquisitions in order to gain access or control of the Canadian importers and/or distributors of their products. Also striking is the number of acquisitions made by firms in category 28 - Finance, Insurance and Real Estate spanning the broad spectrum of the non-financial sector. The magnitude of these mergers and acquisitions increased from 17 percent to 82 percent and then dropped to 62 percent over the three time periods. This trend in part reflects the changing regulatory environment which governs the operation of financial companies and the removal of certain barriers between different segments of financial markets. For example, for all the years considered, banks continued their acquisitions in the investment brokerage community; there were also various restructurings and ownership changes in the operation of trust and financial holding companies. The numbers also reflect the classification of holding companies which have extensive conglomerate-type investments in different sectors.

COMPARISONS WITH OTHER COUNTRIES

AS INDICATED EARLIER (see also Appendix), there is a scarcity of M&A data for different countries. However, some relevant statistics and information is available for selected countries, notably, Australia, France, Germany, Japan, Sweden, United Kingdom and the United States. The quality and content of this data varies significantly across countries and, with the exception of Australia and France, the discussion presented here is based entirely on the number of M&A transactions or announcements in the countries mentioned. In the case of Australia, the data are for the number of countries de-listed on the stock exchange. For France, the data relate only to tender offerings and negotiated takeovers of companies listed on the stock exchange. The level of M&A activity may be, therefore, somewhat understated in these two countries but the direction of trends is probably more accurate, assuming the proportion of tender offerings and negotiated takeovers (of companies listed on the stock exchange), relative to the total number of mergers and acquisitions, is stable over time.

Table 4 presents data on the total number of mergers and acquisitions in the named countries over the period from 1979 to 1989, although relevant

TABLE 4

THE NUMBER OF MERGERS AND ACQUISITIONS IN SELECTED COUNTRIES, 1979-89

COUNTRY	1979	1980	1981	1982	1983	1984	1985	1986	1987	1988	1989
Australia	67	77	75	60	70	85	87	103			
Canada	511	414	491	576	628	641	712	938	1082	1053	1091
France	161	155	234	249	719	825					
Germany	602	635	618	603	506	575	709	802	887		
Japan	871	961	1044	1040	1020	1096	1113	1147	1215	1336	
Sweden	590	674	681	851	1037	805	765	637	631	694	
United Kingdom	534	469	452	463	447	568	474	696	1125	1224	1001
United States	1526	1558	2328	2298	2393	3175	3486	4448	4015	4001	3412

SOURCE: See Appendix

statistics for this period are not available for all countries. The number of mergers and acquisitions varies across countries in any given year and over time. The highest number reported is consistently for the United States and the differences observed between countries no doubt reflect the differences in the relative size of the economies among these countries. Adjustments to the data to accommodate these differences are discussed below. It is first worth noting, however, that correlation coefficients computed for M&A activity (normalized by real GDP) between various countries reveal some interesting patterns.

Merger and acquisition activity in Canada and the United States tends to be highly correlated (0.84). A high correlation was also found between M&A activity in Canada and the United Kingdom (0.81). Among other countries, a high correlation exists between France and Germany (0.90). The number of years for which observations are available is too small to provide any causal links or interpretation to these results. However, investment and trade links between the pairs of countries mentioned do tend to be close. This is particularly the case for Canada and the United States, where the overall trend in mergers and acquisitions tends to be parallel. In many instances, mergers and acquisitions in Canada arise as a result of restructuring transactions initiated by parent corporations south of the border. For all other countries the computed correlation coefficients were found to be low,[5] generally below 0.50.

A more appropriate method for comparing inter-country M&A activity is to adjust for differences in the relative size of the different economies. In a large economy there is likely to be a large number of corporations engaged in economic activity, and consequently there is likely to be an equally large (absolute) number of mergers and acquisitions. If it is assumed that M&A activity varies systematically with the size of the economy across different countries, then the relative incidence of this activity should be in proportion to that of the GDP between different countries. For example, an often-cited statistic is that the ratio of Canadian to American GDP (as well as other eco-

FIGURE 5

**MERGERS AND ACQUISITIONS IN SELECTED COUNTRIES
RELATIVE TO U.S. M&A ACTIVITY**

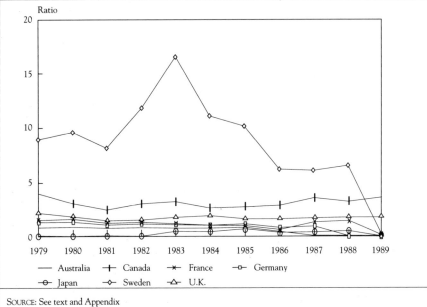

SOURCE: See text and Appendix

FIGURE 6

**MERGERS AND ACQUISITIONS IN SELECTED COUNTRIES
RELATIVE TO U.S. M&A ACTIVITY**

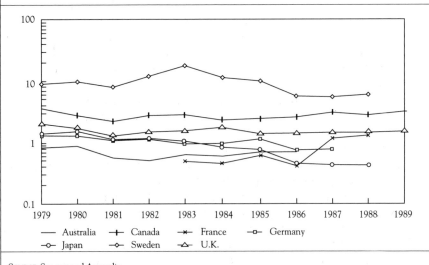

SOURCE: See text and Appendix

nomic variables such as population, industry and market size, etc.) is generally in the order of 1:10. It might therefore be expected that the ratio of Canadian to American M&A activity would be approximately the same. Assuming this relationship applies across other industrialized countries as well, Figures 2 and 3 graph the ratio of foreign to American mergers divided by the ratio of foreign to (real) American GDP for the period from 1979 to 1989. A value of one suggests that the incidence of M&A activity is no higher than the relative difference in the size of the two economies in terms of GDP.

An examination of Figures 5 and 6 shows that there is a difference in the incidence of mergers and acquisitions between countries. It is highest in Sweden, followed by Canada and then the United Kingdom. With the exception of Australia and France until 1986, and Japan after 1984, the relative level of M&A activity in all other countries has been higher than the prevailing level in the United States. Of particular interest is Japan, where the relative level of activity decreased during the later part of the 1980s. A similar but less pronounced trend is also evident for Germany.

To what extent are there similarities or differences in the incidence of horizontal merger activity across different countries? Economic theory suggests that if specific industries are experiencing increased pressures because of global competition, one form of corporate response may be to engage in horizontal mergers to exploit potential economies and/or to rationalize industry capacity. Figure 4 plots the relative proportion of horizontal mergers in five countries for which data are readily available. It is apparent from this figure that this type of activity varies dramatically across the named countries and over time. There is less variation in the case of Germany, but in all countries the proportion of horizontal mergers tends to be high, generally exceeding 45 percent of the total number of mergers and acquisitions.

An examination of mergers and acquisitions by industry category in different countries was also conducted in order to identify any systematic patterns. Data constraints made this analysis possible only for Canada, Japan, Sweden, United Kingdom and the United States. The analysis was also restricted to the ten leading industries in terms of mergers and acquisitions. Results show a fair degree of variation in the levels of merger and acquisition activity by industry category, within and between these countries, and over time. The probable reasons for these variations are country-, industry- and firm-specific and institutional factors prevailing in the different jurisdictions. Although the exact rank order of the M&A activity across industries differs, some salient patterns can nevertheless be discerned.

In all the countries examined, the number of mergers and acquisitions in the distribution (retail and wholesale) sectors was high. In Canada, Japan, Sweden and the U.K. this activity ranked among the top three industry categories for most years. Mergers and acquisitions were also at a high level in financial-sector-related industries in Canada, the United States and the United Kingdom. The chemical industry and the energy products industry also

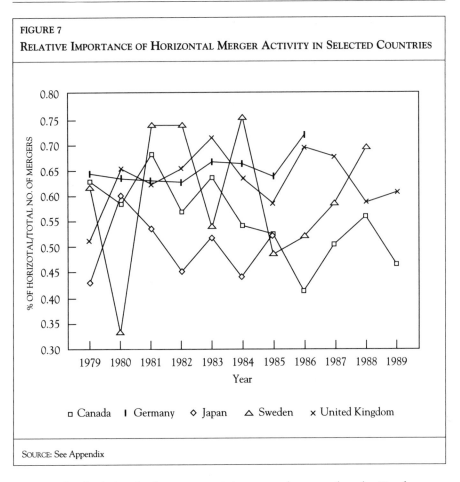

FIGURE 7

RELATIVE IMPORTANCE OF HORIZONTAL MERGER ACTIVITY IN SELECTED COUNTRIES

□ Canada | Germany ◇ Japan △ Sweden × United Kingdom

SOURCE: See Appendix

registered a high level of merger activity over the past decade. Food sector mergers and acquisitions ranked high in Canada, the U.K. and the United States and, to a lesser extent, in Japan. Further research is required as to whether there are some common technological and market driven forces which give rise to these developments.

CONCLUSION

The descriptive statistical analysis contained herein leads to the following principal conclusions:

- The trend in Canada over the past decade has shown a consistent increase in merger and acquisition activity.
- There has also been an increase in the number of large (in excess of $100 million) merger and acquisition transactions.

- The number of foreign acquisitions in Canada exceeds the number transacted by domestic firms through most of the period, but particularly since 1981.
- There has been an increase in the number of horizontal mergers since 1978/79.
- The level of merger and acquisition activity, generally, tends to be high in the following sectors: Business and Personal Services, Finance, Insurance and Real Estate, and Trade. The number of firms acquired in the Mining, Quarrying and Oil Wells, and Food and Beverage sectors was also high; moreover, the numbers increased during the latter part of the decade.
- Inter-country comparisons suggest trends in merger and acquisition activity in Canada and the United States and the United Kingdom appear to be parallel. However, no systematic pattern emerges between Canada and other countries.
- The incidence of merger and acquisition activity relative to activity in the United States is highest in Sweden followed by Canada and then the United Kingdom.
- The relative importance of horizontal merger activity varies dramatically across countries and over time but generally accounts for a large proportion of the total number of mergers.

Within the overall patterns of M&A activity observed during the past decade, there are likely firm-, industry-, and country-specific forces at play. As indicated earlier in this paper, many factors underly the levels and trends in M&A activity within and across countries and over time. Further research is required to separate these different, and at times disparate, factors.

ENDNOTES

1. Simple correlation between Canadian and American M&A activity normalized by GDP in the respective countries is 0.84.
2. See Figure 1-4 in Tarasofsky, 1990.
3. A simple regression between the number of mergers and acquisitions and real GDP in Canada is estimated as:

$$\text{M\&A} = -1451.74 + 0.007 \, \text{GDP} \quad R^2 = 0.91$$
$$\quad\quad\quad (18.50) \quad (9.82) \quad\quad n = 11$$

t-values are indicated in parentheses. Similar statistically significant regression coefficients and R^2 values are obtained for other countries as well. However, because of the small size of the sample caution must be exercised in interpreting the results. A cross-section pooled regression of M&A activity across all countries examined in this paper is estimated as:

$$\text{M\&A} = 374.0 + 0.0007 \quad\quad R^2 = 0.78$$
$$\quad\quad\quad (0.82) \quad (15.22)$$

The positive and statistically significant relationship between M&A activity and real GDP probably occurs through the effect of total number of firms. With higher GDP, we can expect a larger number of firms and higher levels of M&A activity. Since the total number of firms in different countries is not consistently available, deflating M&A activity by using real GDP as a proxy appears to be appropriate in light of these estimated relationships.

4. Spearman rank correlation between the level of horizontal merger activity in 1978/79 and 1983/84 and between 1983/84 and 1988/89 across 29 industry categories is 0.37 and 0.43 respectively. The low correlation coefficient is indicative of the variation in M&A activity over these years.

5. In the case of Japan, the correlation coefficient was negative across countries, registering –0.92 with respect to Canada. It may be speculated that the relationship (if any) is influenced by differential performance of the two economies plus other institutional factors. From 1979 to 1989 Japan consistently and significantly out-performed most western industrialized economies, including Canada. Also the *relative* incidence of merger and acquisition activity was low.

APPENDIX

VARIOUS SOURCES were used in assembling the statistical information on merger and acquisition (M&A) activity presented in this paper. Because of different coverage, definitions, reporting periods and other related issues, a number of constraints were imposed. The analysis conducted across different countries and over time should therefore be viewed primarily as a general indicator of the levels and trends in merger and acquisition activity.

CANADA

Merger Register, Bureau of Competition Policy
The Merger Register is limited to collating a simple count of foreign and domestic mergers and acquisitions reported in the business press. Since the register is based on published sources, it is an incomplete count of the overall number of mergers and acquisitions that occur in Canada each year. Moreover, since press coverage tends to focus on large or significant transactions, there is a likely bias in this direction in the data. This is particularly true for domestic acquisitions for which, until 1987, there were no notification requirements. Also, these requirements apply only to large transactions under the Competition Act. The coverage of foreign acquisitions, however, is more accurate due to the provisions of the *Investment Canada Act* (and the previous legislation, *Foreign Investment Review Act*). Further, information pertaining to characteristics of the firms involved in mergers, (e.g., assets, sales, employment, profits), or the characteristics of the transactions (e.g., methods of financing) are not systematically available. The register does, however, attempt to

distinguish between completed transactions and announcements. In addition, only those mergers and acquisitions are reported in the Register where effective (ownership of more than 51 percent of common voting stock) or acknowledged control of the acquired corporation has been attained. Thus the coverage and statistical count is different from the data published by Venture Economics Inc. which are discussed below.

Venture Economics Inc., Toronto (previously Harris-Bentley Ltd.) This data series has been available since 1985 and it provides greater details on transaction terms and merging parties (particularly target firms). However, transaction values and other pertinent statistics are not comprehensively or systematically available for all the years or for the companies surveyed. Moreover, the data relate to merger and acquisition *announcements* and as such not all deals may actually be consummated. In addition, the reported statistics cover both total and partial acquisitions and no distinction or threshold levels for effective or acknowledged control is indicated. The statistics presented in Table 3 relating to large transaction values have been adjusted to take into account change in control of the acquired firm using the ownership of more than 51 percent of common voting stock or acknowledged control as the criteria.

AUSTRALIA

Data on M&A activity in this country is particularly scant. The information used in this paper is derived from the Bureau of Industry Economics (1990) study which presents data on the number of companies *delisted* on the Australian stock exchanges. The use of other measures, e.g., the number of takeover bids which were not available for a longer time period, do not appear to affect the overall trends.

FRANCE

Data for this country were obtained from Franks and Mayer (1989) and are restricted to the number of domestic transactions of companies listed on the stock exchange.

GERMANY

Fairly comprehensive series of data on merger and acquisition activity are available from the Federal Cartel Office, Berlin. Information from this source and Marfels (1988) was used in this paper.

JAPAN

Data were obtained from the Japan Enterprise Institute and the Fair Trade Commission. It should be noted, however, that the reporting period is based on a financial year rather than a calendar year. This is not likely to alter the comparative results.

SWEDEN

A fairly detailed and comprehensive set of merger statistics is published by the National Price and Competition Board (SPK). The series is organized in terms of employment thresholds and related sales and other information. Details on transaction values and other financial measures are not published.

UNITED KINGDOM

Data published by the Office of Fair Trading and Mergers and Acquisitions (U.K.) were used. Information on asset values is available.

The data for Germany, Japan, Sweden and the United Kingdom pertain to acquired firms where change in effective or acknowledged control has taken place. However, the criteria employed was not indicated in the data sources used.

UNITED STATES

Mergers and Acquisitions, MLR Publishing Co., Philadelphia was the primary source of data. An extensive array of information including industry, target firm, transaction value and nationality is available. The aggregate data however do not distinguish between complete or partial control or acquisitions and are in this respect similar to statistics published by Venture Economics Inc.

The common denominator of the data extracted for these countries is the number of mergers and acquisitions and, in some cases, size and industry classifications.

ACKNOWLEDGEMENT

I WANT TO ACKNOWLEDGE WITH THANKS the diligent research assistance provided by Marco Aondio and excellent word processing preparation of this paper by Sandra Carter. Helpful comments and suggestions on the contents of an earlier version of this paper were provided by Zulfie Sadeque, Leonard Waverman and various participants at the Conference on Corporate Globalization Through Mergers and Acquisitions, University of Toronto, November 29-30, 1990. Any errors or omissions are exclusively mine.

BIBLIOGRAPHY

Brander, J.A. "Mergers, Competition Policy, and the International Environment" in Khemani et al, 1988.

Browne, L.E. and E.S. Rosengren (eds). "The Merger Boom", Proceedings of a Conference sponsored by the Federal Reserve Bank of Boston, October 1987.

Bureau of Industry Economics. *Mergers and Acquisitions*, Research Report #36, Australian Government Publishing Service, Canberra, 1990.

Caves, R.E. *Adjustment to International Competition*, Economic Council of Canada, Ottawa, 1990(a).

————. "Corporate Mergers in International Integration" prepared for CEPR/Instituto Mobiliare Italiano Conference on European Financial Integration, Rome, January 1990(b).

Emerson, M. et al. "The Economics of 1992", *European Economy*, March 1988.

Franks, J. and C. Mayer. "Capital Markets and Corporate Control: A Study of France, Germany and the U.K.", mimeo, London Business School, December 1989.

Geroski, P.A. and A. Vlassopoulos. "Recent Patterns of European Merger Activity", *Business Strategy Review*, Summer 1990, pp. 17-27.

Investment Canada. *The Business Implications of Globalization*, Working Paper, Ottawa, May 1990.

Jacquemin, A. et al. "Horizontal Mergers and Competition Policy in the European Community", *European Economy*, May 1989.

Johnston, C.G. *Globalization: Canadian Companies Compete*, International Business Research Centre, The Conference Board of Canada, Ottawa, February 1990.

Khemani, R.S., D.M. Shapiro and W.T. Stanbury (eds). *Mergers, Corporate Concentration and Power in Canada*, The Institute for Research on Public Policy, Halifax, 1988.

Marfels, C. "Aggregate Concentration in International Perspective: Canada, Federal Republic of Germany, Japan and the United States" in Khemani et al, 1988.

Mergers and Acquisitions (Journal of Corporate Venture). MLR Publishing Co., Philadelphia, 1979-90.

Nymark, A. *Globalization and Canadian Investment Abroad*, Notes for an Address, Division of International Business Studies and Executive Programmes, University of British Columbia, March 19, 1990.

OECD Competition Law and Policy Committee. Country Reports on Australia, Canada, France, Germany, Japan, Sweden, United Kingdom and United States, Paris, 1979-89.

Pettway, R. "Japanese Mergers and Direct Investment in the U.S." in W. Ziemba, W. Bailey and Y. Hamao (eds) *Japanese Financial Research*, North Holland, forthcoming, 1991.

Ravenscraft, D.J. and F.M. Scherer. *Mergers, Sell-Offs and Economic Efficiency*, The Brookings Institution, Washington, DC, 1987.

Rueber, G. and F. Roseman. *The Takeover of Canadian Firms, 1945-61*, Economic Council of Canada, Ottawa, 1969.

Scherer, F.M. and D. Ross. *Industrial Market Structure and Economic Performance*, Houghton Mifflin Co., Boston, 1990.

Schott, J.J. and M.G. Smith (eds). *The Canada-United States Free Trade Agreement: The Global Impact*, The Institute for Research on Public Policy, Halifax, 1988.

SPK Större Förestags-Förvärv, 1970-1988, Raportserie, Stockholm, Sweden, 1989 with updates.

Stanbury, W.T. Appendix 1 in Khemani, et al, 1988.

Statistics Canada. *Corporations and Labour Unions Return Act, Annual Report*, Part I, Supply and Services Canada, 1990.

Steiner, P.O. *Mergers: Motives, Effects and Policies*, Ann Arbor, University of Michigan, 1975.

Tarasofsky, A. "Corporate Mergers and Acquisitions: Evidence on Profitability", mimeo, Economic Council of Canada, February 1990.

John Knubley, William Krause and Zulfi Sadeque
Investment Canada

2

Canadian Acquisitions Abroad: Patterns and Motivations

INTRODUCTION

DURING THE 1980s, Canadian firms participated actively in global markets by employing direct investment abroad. The value of the stock of outward direct investment tripled over the decade and there was a marked rise in the relative importance of outward to inward bound direct investment.

A particularly important dimension of Canadian direct investment abroad (CDIA) during this period was mergers and acquisitions (M&A) activity. Consistent with the high level of domestic and international M&A activity discussed in the Khemani paper, the cross-border M&A activity of Canadian firms increased throughout the 1980s, showing a pronounced upswing in the last half of the decade. There were high profile acquisitions abroad by such Canadian firms as Bombardier, Northern Telecom, Dominion Textile and Campeau, among others (see Appendix A).

In an attempt to better understand these developments, this paper describes the patterns and motivations behind Canadian direct investment abroad, with a special focus on cross-border M&A activity. We begin with a section setting out the main international and domestic developments relating to CDIA and foreign direct investment (FDI) in Canada. The second section describes aspects of Canadian mergers and acquisitions abroad with reference to a database procured from Automatic Data Processing (ADP) of Ann Arbor, Michigan (see Appendix B). We then turn to the question of motivations behind Canadian acquisitions abroad, briefly reviewing the traditional economic rationale and examining the results of a questionnaire-based survey conducted by Investment Canada in the spring of 1989. Twenty-three Canadian corporations were interviewed to determine the managerial motives for direct investment abroad (DIA). We conclude with a summary of the principal findings and some suggestions for future areas of research.

At the outset, it is important to stress three points:

First, cross-border M&A activity by Canadian firms is but one component of CDIA, the others being new or so-called greenfield investments and expansions of existing direct investments. Second, this cross-border outward M&A activity is distinct from the purely domestic or "within border" M&A activity, as discussed by Khemani in this volume. Third, the data on this cross-border M&A activity are subject to a number of shortcomings.

There are several explanations for the weaknesses in the data. For those firms whose shares are publicly traded, the principal sources of data are limited to public information material such as Annual Reports, *Financial Post* corporate information and newspapers. In addition, many acquisitions are carried out by private companies which are often reluctant to disclose details of their transactions. As a result, data on private mergers and acquisitions abroad are often incomplete, if known at all. Moreover, there is no single authority that systematically collects information on acquisitions abroad by Canadian corporations.

Despite these difficulties, we reached a number of conclusions pertinent to the patterns and motivations behind Canadian acquisitions abroad. The paper identifies various patterns of CDIA and cross-border M&A activity with reference to such characteristics as number, value, the firms most active and their attributes, concentration, types of acquisition, and geographic and industry distribution. In general, the data show that along with a pronounced upswing in Canadian acquisitions abroad in the 1980s, Canada as a small country exhibited a greater tendency towards cross-border M&A activity than many large countries. In addition, there was some concentration with large Canadian-controlled firms most active. However, almost two-thirds of the total number of firms making acquisitions were small- to medium-sized. Three quarters of the acquisitions were made in the United States, and half were horizontal in type. Canadian cross-border M&A activity was dominated by manufacturing firms, followed by financial services and resources.

With respect to motivations, the economic rationale could not be tested because of data limitations, but a number of findings relevant to the theory are discussed. The Investment Canada survey findings show five main factors driving managers to undertake direct investment abroad, including the need for outward expansion, geographic/product line diversification, trade barriers and transportation cost, availability of skilled labour, and favourable regulations abroad. These factors are analyzed in terms of what Rugman (1987) calls "pulls" from abroad and "pushes" from within Canada. The results show that the top two factors are internal to firms and are part of unique corporate strategies and values. Five of the top seven factors are related to perceptions of advantageous conditions in the country abroad, although these perceptions are inevitably related to conditions in the home country.

CANADIAN DIRECT INVESTMENT ABROAD

TABLE 1 SHOWS the growth in the stocks of foreign direct investment (FDI) in Canada and Canadian direct investment abroad (CDIA) during the period from 1950 to 1989, as well as the ratio of CDIA to FDI. The growth in

TABLE 1
STOCK OF FDI & CDIA, SELECTED YEARS

YEAR	FDI ($B)	CDIA ($B)	CDIA/FDI (%)
1950	4.0	1.0	25.0
1960	12.9	2.5	9.4
1970	26.4	6.2	23.5
1979	54.3	20.5	37.8
1980	61.7	27.0	43.8
1981	66.6	33.8	50.8
1982	68.9	35.6	51.7
1983	77.4	29.9	51.6
1984	84.1	47.4	56.4
1985	87.2	54.1	62.0
1986	92.4	58.6	63.4
1987	101.5	66.1	65.1
1988	109.1	70.4	64.5
1989	119.2	74.0	62.1

NOTE: Data for the 1983-89 period just revised and 1989 figure preliminary.
SOURCE: Statistics Canada, 67-202

this ratio over time demonstrates the significant rise in the relative importance of outward to inward investment. In other words, Canada has a much more balanced relationship today between outward and inward investment.

Table 1 indicates that the stock of FDI increased from $4 billion in 1950 to $119.2 billion in 1989. In contrast the stock of CDIA rose from only $1 billion in 1950 to $74.4 billion at the end of 1989. In the 1980s, outward investment increased steadily relative to inward, with CDIA tripling as FDI doubled. The ratio of the stock of CDIA to FDI grew from 25 percent in 1950 to 43.8 percent in 1980, peaking at just over 65 percent in 1987.[1]

The change in the relative importance of Canada's inward and outward investment flows can only be fully understood with reference to other industrialized countries. Table 2 shows the changing relative importance of inward and outward direct investment flows for OECD countries. In the 1960s, Canada was the main recipient of inward investment among OECD countries, accounting for 23 percent of the flow of OECD inward FDI, and 5.3 percent of OECD outward FDI. This changed considerably in the 1970s and 1980s, as Canada's share of inward flows dropped significantly. Throughout the thirty-year period, the level of Canada's share of OECD outward flows has remained relatively constant. In dollar value terms, however, the level of Canadian outflows in the 1980s was about double that of the 1970s.

Table 2 also shows that the change in the relative importance of Canada's outward investment flows over the past two decades is not unique, but rather consistent with global trends. There is a more balanced relationship between

TABLE 2

INWARD AND OUTWARD DIRECT INVESTMENT FLOWS
OECD COUNTRIES, SELECTED PERIODS, 1961 - 1983

COUNTRY	INWARD FLOWS (%)			OUTWARD FLOWS (%)		
	1961-70	1971-80	1981-88	1961-70	1971-80	1981-88
Canada	23.0	15.7	7.4	5.3	6.1	6.0
France	5.8	7.8	5.7	3.6	4.5	7.2
Germany	13.1	6.5	2.1	5.6	7.5	8.4
Japan	1.3	0.6	0.6	2.0	5.8	16.6
Netherlands	4.8	5.0	4.2	3.7	9.0	6.5
United Kingdom	9.0	18.7	12.7	10.1	17.8	21.3
United States	13.1	26.0	50.3	64.2	43.4	21.4
Others	29.9	19.7	17.0	5.5	5.9	12.6
Total	100.0	100.0	100.0	100.0	100.0	100.0

1. Measured in current U.S. dollars including reinvestment earnings.
2. For Canada, from 1983 onward, inward flows include reinvested earnings and other factors as well as inward flows into the financial sectors. Also, after 1961, outward flows include reinvested earnings and other factors, and, after 1983, outward flows to the financial sector.

SOURCE: adapted from OECD "International Direct Investment and the New Economic Environment", (1989, Table A1, p.60, Table A2 p. 61-62) and Statistics Canada

outward and inward investment among most western industrialized countries, related in large part to the fact that the dominance of the United States as the home country to world FDI has declined markedly. Japan, which has very little inward direct investment, is the exception to this balanced relationship.

The shares of OECD outward flows have risen for OECD countries, except the United States and the Netherlands. In the case of the U.S., its share of OECD outward flows decreased by 50 percent between the 1970s and the 1980s. As the United States has declined as a source of outward investment, other industrialized economies such as France, Germany, Japan and the United Kingdom have emerged as major home countries. In the 1980s, the U.K. was almost an equal player with the United States. In terms of inward flows, the most remarkable change is the doubling of the American share of OECD inward direct investment flows during the 1980s, thus emphasizing the extent to which the U.S. is becoming a major host country to FDI.

When making international comparisons of outward investment among industrialized countries it is important to take into account the relative sizes of economies. Table 3 presents DIA as a percentage of GDP for ten industrialized countries for selected years during the period from 1960 to 1985. Two small countries, Switzerland and the Netherlands, consistently had the highest rankings with double digit percentages, significantly higher than the other countries. The United Kingdom ranked third in all of the selected years, also with double

TABLE 3

STOCKS OF DIA FOR TEN INDUSTRIALIZED COUNTRIES AS PERCENTAGE OF GDP, SELECTED YEARS

COUNTRY	1960 (RANK)	1975 (RANK)	1980 (RANK)	1985 (RANK)
United States	6.2 (6)	8.1 (4)	8.2 (4)	6.4 (7)
United Kingdom	17.4 (3)	15.8 (3)	15.2 (3)	23.3 (3)
Japan	1.1 (8)	3.2 (8)	3.4 (7)	6.3 (8)
Germany	1.1 (8)	4.4 (7)	5.3 (6)	9.6 (5)
France	7.0 (4)	3.1 (9)	3.2 (8)	4.2 (9)
Italy	2.9 (7)	1.7(10)	1.8 (9)	3.4(10)
Canada	6.3 (5)	6.3 (6)	8.2 (4)	10.5 (4)
Switzerland	26.9 (2)	41.3 (1)	37.9 (1)	48.9 (1)
Netherlands	60.6 (1)	22.9 (2)	24.7 (2)	35.1 (2)
Sweden	2.9 (7)	6.4 (5)	5.8 (5)	9.0 (6)

SOURCE: UNCTC, Transnational Corporations in World Development, New York, 1988

digit percentages. While Canada ranked fifth and sixth respectively in 1960 and 1975, it was fourth in 1980 and 1985, attaining a double digit percentage in the last year. This data further confirms the rising relative importance of DIA for Canada, particularly in the 1980s.

In addition and perhaps more importantly, Table 3 shows that four small countries — Switzerland, the Netherlands, Canada and Sweden — consistently ranked high in DIA measurement relative to their size. This suggests that smaller industrialized nations tend to undertake proportionately more DIA than larger economies.[2]

In the literature on CDIA, there have been a number of small country theses which are relevant for later discussion of Canadian cross-border M&A activity.

- According to Swedenborg[3], other things being equal, in order to exploit economies of scale and scope, a firm based in a smaller country may undertake DIA at a much smaller size than a firm based in a large country. (This implies, too, that two countries with the same firm and country comparative advantages are unlikely to have comparable levels of foreign production if the countries differ in size).
- The role of small- and medium-sized Canadian firms in this respect is consistent with the findings of the United Nations Centre on Transnational Corporations (UNCTC). It found that over 58 percent of Canadian transnationals fall in the small category.[4] The UNCTC argues that when first undertaking DIA, small firms make only one or two foreign acquisitions in their own field of specialization and typically move into neighbouring countries where there are long-standing links (in Canada's case, the United States). Only later do these firms spread to other locations.

TABLE 4

NUMBER OF FIRMS WITH CDIA, BY COUNTRY OF CONTROL

YEAR	CANADIAN	FOREIGN	TOTAL	% CANADIAN
1979	640	395	1 035	61.84
1980	729	386	1 115	65.38
1981	880	370	1 250	70.40
1982	956	368	1 324	72.21
1983	1 081	379	1 460	74.04
1984	1 129	389	1 518	74.37
1985	1 142	409	1 551	73.63
1986	1 113	366	1 479	75.25

SOURCE: Statistics Canada, Canada's International Investment Position, Cat 67-202

Table 4 shows the total number of Canadian resident firms with direct investment abroad from 1979 to 1986, and the number that are Canadian- and foreign-controlled. While DIA has been increasing in relative importance for
Canada, the total number of Canadian resident firms with investment abroad
is relatively small, with only 1479 firms in 1986. Among these corporations,
those that are Canadian-controlled have become increasingly dominant.
While less than 62 percent of firms with CDIA were Canadian-controlled in
1979, by 1986 the proportion had increased to more than 75 percent.
Underlying this shift was a significant increase in the number of Canadian-
controlled firms with direct investment abroad and a decline of more than
seven percent in the number of foreign-controlled firms with such investment
activity. Still, the fact that foreign-controlled firms undertook CDIA should
not be overlooked. This suggests some subsidiary autonomy or strategic use of
the Canadian subsidiary by its foreign parent.

In Table 5, the total value of CDIA is shown with its Canadian- and foreign-controlled shares for the period 1979 to 1986. As in Table 4, the share represented by Canadian-controlled firms increased over the period. In value terms,
the share rose from nearly 81 percent in 1979 to almost 87 percent in 1986.

To provide further meaning to the data already described and to serve
as background for later discussion of Canadian cross-border M&A data, it is
useful to summarize the main results of a recent Statistics Canada Research
Paper by Paul Gorecki titled "Patterns of Canadian Direct Investment
Abroad" (1990). This paper identifies various characteristics of CDIA with
reference to Statistics Canada, Balance of Payments data, including the
following:

- There is a high degree of concentration of CDIA. In 1986, for example,
  the four largest parent firms accounted for 23 percent of all CDIA, and
  the leading eight for 33 percent.

TABLE 5

VALUE OF CDIA ($ MILLIONS) BY COUNTRY OF CONTROL

YEAR	CANADIAN	FOREIGN	TOTAL	% CANADIAN
1979	16 595	3 901	20 496	80.97
1980	22 033	4 934	26 967	81.70
1981	28 138	5 709	33 847	83.13
1982	29 157	6 401	35 558	82.00
1983	31 716	6 077	37 793	83.92
1984	36 720	7 399	44 119	83.23
1985	42 595	7 601	50 196	84.86
1986	46 209	6 964	53 173	86.90

SOURCE: Statistics Canada, Canada's International Investment Position, Cat 67-202

- Over time the degree of concentration has been falling as more Canadian firms invest abroad. For example, the leading eleven parent firms accounted for 65 percent of all CDIA in 1970, but only 38 percent in 1986.
- CDIA is typically in the form of majority or wholly owned affiliates, rather than joint ventures (as measured by minority ownership). However, joint ventures increased in importance in terms of value from 1983 to 1986.
- Of the total number of parent firms with CDIA in 1986, 859 or 65.2 percent had only one affiliate. Those with five or fewer affiliates accounted for 93 percent of the total number of firms with CDIA. So the bulk of parent firms undertaking CDIA have a few, relatively small affiliates.
- Nine firms had 30 or more affiliates abroad. In light of the high degree of concentration of CDIA, the implication is that these nine firms with many affiliates would account for a large part of the total value of CDIA.
- CDIA is heavily concentrated in the U.S. It accounted for 53 percent of all CDIA in 1970 and 71 percent in 1986. The second-ranked destination was the European Community (EC) at 12.6 percent in 1986, with the United Kingdom alone receiving 7.9 percent of CDIA destined for Europe.
- Most CDIA is located in the manufacturing sector, followed by the resource and financial sectors. Parents usually invest abroad in the same industry in which they are active in Canada. In other words, CDIA is mainly horizontal in nature.

CANADIAN ACQUISITIONS ABROAD

THE FOLLOWING SECTION PRESENTS DATA on Canadian acquisitions abroad. These M&A data obtained from ADP Data Services of Ann Arbor, Michigan[5] are qualitatively different from the CDIA data. The M&A data are

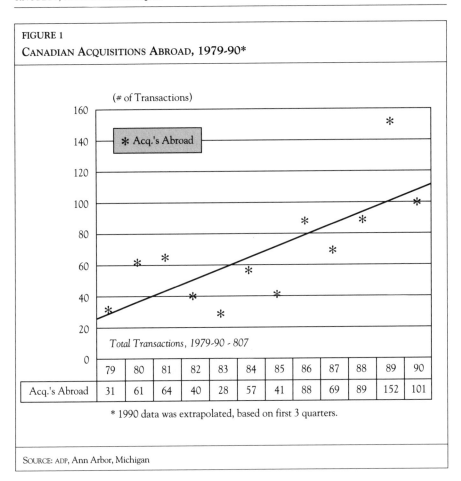

FIGURE 1

CANADIAN ACQUISITIONS ABROAD, 1979-90*

(# of Transactions)

* Acq.'s Abroad

Total Transactions, 1979-90 - 807

	79	80	81	82	83	84	85	86	87	88	89	90
Acq.'s Abroad	31	61	64	40	28	57	41	88	69	89	152	101

* 1990 data was extrapolated, based on first 3 quarters.

SOURCE: ADP, Ann Arbor, Michigan

event oriented, identifying individual transactions at one point in time. As a result, firms can have multiple transactions in the M&A data set. Moreover, most analysis on M&A data is conducted in terms of the number of transactions, rather than of the value. This is because only a relatively small portion of the total stock value of cross-border M&A is known. In contrast, analysis of CDIA data is mainly in terms of value as in Tables 1, 3 and 5 which refer to the cumulative stock value of CDIA.[6]

Figure 1 shows a scatter diagram of Canadian acquisitions abroad by year as well as a trend line fitting the data. The number of acquisitions from 1979 to 1990 are listed below the x-axis. The total number of acquisitions in the data base is relatively small at 807. Figure 1 leads to a number of observations about Canadian M&A activity abroad:

- The trend line shows a pronounced upward movement in Canadian cross-border M&A activity from 1979 to 1990.

TABLE 6

VALUE OF CANADIAN ACQUISITIONS ABROAD, 1979-90

YEAR	NUMBER OF CASES	CASES WITH TRANSACTION VALUES REPORTED		
		NUMBER	VALUE ($ MILLIONS)	
			TOTAL	AVERAGE
1979	31	0	0.0	0.0
1980	61	1	1.2	1.2
1981	64	5	166.5	33.3
1982	40	25	811.0	32.4
1983	28	14	1 178.5	84.2
1984	57	33	2 475.2	75.0
1985	41	19	997.4	52.5
1986	88	50	6 880.0	137.6
1987	69	35	11 551.0	330.0
1988	89	43	10 052.8	233.8
1989	152	62	4 527.3	73.0
1990	87	28	5 186.0	185.2
Total	807	315	43 826.8	139.1

SOURCE: ADP, Ann Arbor, Michigan

- The scatter diagram reveals two distinct phases of M&A activity —from 1979 to 1985 and from 1986 to 1990. (The higher level of Canadian cross-border M&A activity in the second phase is consistent with higher levels of M&A activity worldwide.)
- There was considerable year-to-year variation in cross-border acquisition activity. (Such variation is also typical of domestic M&A activity and the M&A literature suggests this variation is explained by the fact that corporations tend to consolidate operations following an expansionary phase.)

Table 6 reports by year the total number of transactions in the ADP database, the number of cases where the value is known, the value for these cases, and the average value. Of the 807 total number of acquisitions, only 315 or 39 percent include transaction values. As discussed above, this under-reporting of values is typical and, for this reason, the subsequent analysis is confined to number of transactions.

Nevertheless, Table 6 appears consistent with Figure 1. The value data also show two distinct phases of M&A activity —with the 1986 to 1990 phase at a significantly higher level than the 1979 to 1985 phase. However, these results may have unknown biases as nearly two thirds of transaction values were missing from the earlier period and significant gaps in reporting existed in selected years in the later period.

The total value of these 315 transactions for the 12-year period was $US 43.8 billion. While the data show the activity peaking in 1987 and 1988, this

TABLE 7
ACQUISITIONS ABROAD BY MAJOR OECD COUNTRIES*

COUNTRY	1985		1986		1987	
	ACTUAL	WEIGHTED	ACTUAL	WEIGHTED	ACTUAL	WEIGHTED
Canada	42	42	89	89	70	70
United States	175	18	180	18	142	15
United Kingdom	64	40	89	55	223	139
France	70	41	134	78	194	113
Italy	31	20	43	28	70	45

* Comparable data for Japan and Germany could not be found.

NOTE: Weighted numbers are actual number of transactions normalized for differences in the size of GDP between Canada and the respective countries (i.e., deflated by GDP).

SOURCES: ADP; OECD, "Country Surveys", various issues; UNCTC, 1988

should be interpreted with caution. Given the small number of transactions, the total value in any one year can be significantly influenced by one or two large transactions. This was the case in 1987 and 1988 when Campeau Corporation acquired Federated Department Stores for $US 6.7 billion and Seagram bought Tropicana for $US 1.2 billion.

Table 7 compares the number of Canada's acquisitions abroad with that of four other major industrial countries in the years 1985, 1986 and 1987. For each year, the number of acquisitions has been weighted to take into account the relative economic size of each country. The data for the years 1985 and 1986 show Canada with the highest weighted number of acquisitions. This is consistent with the small country theses referred to earlier. In 1987, however, Canada ranked third and the United Kingdom and France had a greater weighted number of acquisitions. This development likely reflects a surge in outward cross-border activity in these two countries as part of the integration of the European market. Overall, there is some evidence that relative to its economic size, Canada exhibited a greater trend towards outbound cross-border acquisitions than the larger countries.

ACTIVE ACQUIRERS

THE INDIVIDUAL TRANSACTIONS in the ADP M&A data were grouped by firm, and 347 firms had transactions.[7] This is a considerably smaller number than the cumulative total number of 1479 firms with CDIA in 1986 (see Table 4). Of these 347 firms, Table 8 lists the 39 Canadian resident firms that were most active (four or more transactions) in terms of cross-border acquisitions over the 1979-1990 period. However, these frequent acquirers represent 38 percent of the 807 transactions in the data set. A relatively high level of concentration is thus implied with 11 percent of the firms accounting for 38

TABLE 8

CANADIAN FIRMS MOST ACTIVE IN FOREIGN ACQUISITIONS 1979-90

FIRM	NO. OF ACQUISITIONS	FIRM	NO. OF ACQUISITIONS
Alcan Aluminum Ltd.	7	Ivaco Inc.	7
Arc International	4	Jannock Ltd.	13
Bank of Montreal	4	John Labbatt Ltd.	6
Bombardier Inc.	6	Laidlaw Transportation	7
Campeau Corp.	4	Lawson Mardon	4
Canadian Pacific	10	MacLean-Hunter Ltd.	12
CCL Industries	6	McCain Foods Ltd.	5
Cineplex Odeon	6	Memotec Data Inc.	5
Crownx Inc.	4	Mutual Life Assurance Co.	5
Derlan Industries	6	National Business Systems Inc.	6
Dominion Textiles	5	Noranda Inc.	5
Domtar Inc.	7	Olympia & York Development Ltd.	6
First City Financial Corp.	20	Royal Trustco Ltd.	7
First Toronto Capital Corp.	6	Seagram Company Ltd.	7
Genstar Ltd.	7	SHL Systemhouse Inc.	4
George Weston Ltd.	4	Thompson Newspapers Ltd.	17
Hollinger Inc.	12	Trimac Ltd.	4
Imasco Ltd.	6	Trizec Ltd.	4
International Thompson Organization	38	Unicorp Canada Corp.	14
		Unicorp Financial Corp.	9

SOURCE: ADP, Ann Arbor, MI

percent of the transactions. The high level of concentration is consistent with Gorecki (1990), although his findings showed an even higher level, with the top 50 firms accounting for 70 percent of the book value of long-term CDIA. The difference in level of concentration may be explained in part by the use of value in the case of CDIA and number in the case of Canadian acquisitions abroad.[8]

Table 8 indicates that large, Canadian-controlled firms dominate Canadian acquisitions abroad. Thirty seven of the 39 firms listed had revenues greater than $100 million. The two small- to medium-sized firms were Arc International and Memotec.[9] The vast majority of firms listed are Canadian-controlled and the so-called "Crown Jewel" companies. The names of many firms in this Table are well known to Canadians, and they have a long history in Canada and abroad. These firms include Canadian Pacific, Alcan Aluminum, Seagram and Noranda. The two foreign-controlled companies with four acquisitions or more during the period were Imasco and Genstar, both from the United Kingdom.

In terms of sectors, among those firms with four or more acquisitions abroad, printing and publishing and financial services were the most active.

International Thompson Organization and its sister-firm, Thompson Newspapers, had the highest number of transactions.[10] Other publishing and communications firms such as Maclean-Hunter and Hollinger were also major foreign M&A players. In finance, First City Financial Corporation, Unicorp Financial and Royal Trustco were particularly active.[11]

While the bulk of firms with four or more acquisitions were large, examination of the ADP database reveals that a number of small- and medium-sized Canadian firms were also active. Of the 347 Canadian acquirers, 220 or over 63 percent can be classified as small- or medium-sized firms.[12] These firms included Glenayre Electronics (3 acquisitions), Lumonics (3 acquisitions), Fleet Aerospace (3 acquisitions) and FuturTek Communications (2 acquisitions). Many of these acquisitions took place in R&D-intensive industries in the areas of information technology, microelectronics, laser technology, and avionics. The fact that over 63 percent of the Canadian firms with cross-border acquisitions were small- and medium-sized is consistent with the small country theses discussed earlier (Swedenborg and U.N.C.T.C.).

Examination of the ADP database shows a low level of participation by foreign-controlled firms in Canadian acquisitions abroad. Of the total 807 transactions from 1979 to 1990, only 5.6 percent (45 acquisitions) were undertaken by some 28 Canadian subsidiaries of foreign-controlled firms. The majority were U.S.-controlled, typically with one or two acquisitions in the United States. This foreign-controlled share of cross-border M&A activity is smaller than the foreign-controlled share of CDIA, where they accounted in 1986 for almost 25 percent of activity abroad (see Table 4).

However, the foreign-controlled Canadian firms with the highest number of acquisitions were mostly non-U.S.-owned subsidiaries. Apart from Imasco and Genstar (BAT Industries, U.K.), they included: Redpath Industries (Tate & Lyle, U.K.), Rio Algom (RTZ Corporation, U.K.), Total Petroleum of Canada (Total Petroleum, France), and Bonar (Bonar PLC, U.K.). These non-U.S.-controlled Canadian companies were likely considered the vehicles for expansion across North America, with the parent in effect treating Canada and the United States as one integrated market.

NATURE OF ACQUISITIONS

TABLE 9 BREAKS DOWN THE CANADIAN CROSS-BORDER acquisitions into horizontal, vertical and conglomerate types by number and percentage, using four broad categories of industries.[13]

Horizontal acquisitions dominated overall at 50 percent of the total number of classified transactions, and in every individual sector but the financial sector. Note, the dominance of horizontal transactions is also seen in Canadian domestic M&A activity (see Khemani in this volume). Among the sectors, manufacturing and resources had the highest percentages of horizontal activity — 60 percent and 56 percent respectively. The overall shares of vertical

TABLE 9

TYPE OF ACQUISITION BY INDUSTRY, 1979 - 1990

TYPE INDUSTRY	HORIZONTAL NO.	%	VERTICAL NO.	%	CONGLOMERATE NO.	%	TOTAL
Resourses	64	56	27	23	24	21	115
Services	75	47	43	27	42	26	160
Manufacturing	194	60	98	30	33	10	325
Financial	44	29	50	33	57	38	151
Totals	377	50	218	29	156	21	751*

* 56 transactions could not be classified
SOURCE: ADP, Ann Arbor, MI

and conglomerate acquisitions were 29 percent and 21 percent respectively. The pattern in the financial sector can be explained by the fact that many of these firms are effectively holding companies undertaking conglomerate acquisitions.

Gorecki (1990) also found that in 1986 CDIA was mainly horizontal (75 percent of the book value of CDIA in any industry). The proportion of horizontal transactions is considerably smaller in the case of the cross-border M&A activity. Again, the different type of analysis is at play — value versus number. Nevertheless, a main reason for this different pattern is that M&A activity involves relatively more conglomerate activity. The implication is that the drive to diversification is more prevalent in acquisitions. Conversely, it can be expected that with new greenfield investments, a component of CDIA, a diversification strategy is far less common. The difference in the degree of horizontal activity may therefore not be surprising.

Campeau Corporation, discussed in Appendix A, illustrates a case where a Canadian firm undertook conglomerate acquisitions abroad in an attempt to diversify, albeit without success. In fact, in the early 1980s, a number of Canadian corporations including Imasco, Dylex, Canadian Tire and Consumers Distributing followed a similar diversification strategy.

As reflected in Table 10, Canadian manufacturing corporations accounted for more than 40 percent of the number of acquisitions abroad, followed by the financial industries (18.7 percent) and resources (14.2 percent). In total, these three industrial sectors accounted for 73.2 percent of all Canadian acquisitions abroad. The concentration of acquisition activity in the manufacturing, financial and resource sectors parallels the findings of Gorecki (1990), who noted that 78.4 percent of the book value of long-term investment originated from the manufacturing, financial and petroleum sectors.

Also note that firms active in construction, merchandise trade and utilities had relatively low levels of acquisition activity. In total, firms in these three industries made only 13.3 percent of acquisitions abroad. Here again, the relatively low levels of acquisition activity for these industries mirror the results

TABLE 10

DISTRIBUTION OF CANADIAN ACQUISITIONS ABROAD BY THE INDUSTRIAL
CLASSIFICATION OF THE ACQIRING FIRM, 1979 - 1990

INDUSTRY	ACQUISITIONS	
	NUMBER	%
Resources	113	14.0
Manufacturing	313	38.8
Construction	24	3.0
Utilities	43	5.3
Merchandise Trade	40	5.0
Services	67	8.3
Financial	151	18.7
Non-classified	56	6.9
All Industries	807	100.0

determined by Gorecki (1990), who found 15.6 percent of CDIA originated from firms in the utilities, merchandise and other (includes construction) industries.

Table 11 shows the geographic distribution of the acquisitions in the ADP database from 1987 to 1990. This period is used because ADP only began recording Canadian acquisitions in countries other than the U.S. in 1987. The bulk of Canadian acquisitions abroad, approximately 70 percent, were in the U.S., while the United Kingdom was second at 8.7 percent, followed in rank by Australia and France. As in Gorecki (1990), however, when the EC countries are grouped together, they are by far the second largest destination with 80 transactions, or over 18 percent of the activity. Japan is conspicuous by its absence from the Table.

This is partly explained by the Japanese corporate culture that has tended to discourage potential foreign buyers of its firms, except in the form of strategic alliances with Japanese partners.[14]

MOTIVATIONS FOR CANADIAN ACQUISITIONS ABROAD

ECONOMIC RATIONALE

THERE IS A LARGE ECONOMIC LITERATURE on what causes individual firms to invest in production facilities in other countries. One rationale is provided by the "internalization theory",[15] which is described in detail in the introduction to this volume. The theory postulates that firm-specific characteristics create competitive advantages. The theory usually applies to horizontal activity where the firm is involved in the same activity at home and abroad. The characteristics can be intangible assets such as technical expertise, marketing ability or superior management.

TABLE 11 ACQUISITIONS ABROAD BY CANADIAN FIRMS, 1987 - 1990	
COUNTRY	NO. OF ACQUISITIONS
United States	307
United Kingdom	38
France	11
Germany	8
Other EC	23
Other Europe	3
Australia	15
Other Pacific Rim	11
Other	22
Total	438

NOTE: "Other" consists of Bermuda, Cayman Islands, Chile, Guyana, Israel, Liberia and Mexico.

SOURCE: ADP, Ann Arbor, Michigan and Investment Canada

These assets have public good properties and this implies that being a public good within the firm, the asset can be used at zero marginal cost to the firm. These public goods are also subject to market failures. In the case of innovation, appropriability problems may exist. Or, the asset may be such that it is not easily separated or disembodied from the operations (for example, a reputation for reliable, quality products). Thus, direct investment "... allows such assets to be applied to a very large scale of operations, yet keeps them internalized within the firm".[16]

Transaction cost theory is another economic rationale for FDI. The transaction cost theory is often used to explain vertical FDI where the investment abroad supplies a tangible asset to the parent's operations (for example, a raw material that serves as an intermediate input in the firm's production process). Under this rationale, the parent requires predictability with respect to price, delivery and quality of product, and chooses direct investment abroad to limit transaction costs.

For both theories, the central issue is: why do parent companies choose to undertake direct investment abroad, rather than to use other organizational methods? These alternative methods might include, for example, contracts or licenses with local firms and exporting. The logic for direct investment abroad can be summarized as follows:

- a firm owns a set of tangible and intangible assets and seeks to maximize their net present value;
- the calculus of net present value may entail geographic diversification of those assets; and
- such geographic diversification is best undertaken by transferring assets from one affiliate to another.

Accordingly, the firm considers the various benefits and costs of direct investment. The main benefits include: exploitation of intangibles such as special knowledge regarding production, distribution and marketing; possible gains from discriminatory pricing; the avoidance of the costs of bilateral bargaining; the elimination of buyer uncertainty; and the use of transfer pricing to minimize the firm's tax burden. Possible costs of DIA are: communication and administrative expenses; and the political/exchange rate risks of overseas investment.

Internalization and/or the minimization of transaction costs are therefore undertaken to the point where benefits equal costs to the firm. Thus, John Dunning states that firms choose DIA as a mode of entry mainly on the perception that it enables the firm to:

"capture a fuller economic rent or better protect their property rights, and/or that the control exerted over the resources transferred could recoup the gains to the parent company external to those accruing to the foreign subsidiary."[17]

SURVEY OF MANAGERIAL MOTIVATIONS: INVESTMENT CANADA SURVEY OF CANADIAN DIRECT INVESTMENT ABROAD

IN THE SPRING OF 1989, Investment Canada surveyed a cross section of 23 Canadian resident firms with direct investment abroad. Personal interviews with senior management were conducted, using a questionnaire prepared for this purpose.[18] The firms surveyed were all Canadian-controlled, private enterprises.

The survey was another in a series conducted on Canadian firms undertaking DIA. The motivational questions and their rating scheme covered similar ground to:

- Litvak and Maule, 1981 (this survey, conducted in 1978, concentrated exclusively on 25 small- and medium-sized technology-based secondary manufacturing firms);
- Matheson, 1985 (this survey included a high proportion of very small companies, with 8 of 18 firms having 1984 revenues of less than $1 million); and
- Forget and Denis, 1985 (this questionnaire survey was mailed to Canadian firms with branch plants in the United States on behalf of the then federal Department of Regional Industrial Expansion).[19]

Relative to these other surveys, the Investment Canada survey has some unique characteristics. It has a higher concentration of relatively large firms, with only five firms having 1988 revenues of less than $100 million.[20] Moreover, unlike the above surveys, it focusses on selected companies with CDIA regardless of destination. Although most of the CDIA in the survey was destined for the United States, more than two-thirds of the sampled companies also undertook

TABLE 12
REVENUE DISTRIBUTION OF FIRMS WITH DIA, 1988

REVENUE* ($ MILLIONS)	NO. OF FIRMS
less than 100	5
101 - 500	4
501 - 1,000	2
1,001 - 5,000	8
greater than 5,000	4
Total	23

* Sources of revenue include worldwide operations

investment in other parts of the world. In addition to assessment of the motivational factors underlying the firms' investment strategies, the Investment Canada survey also collected a range of economic information.

This was done to provide some quantitative insights regarding the firms and the representative nature of the sample.

CHARACTERISTICS OF SURVEYED FIRMS

Revenue: As shown in Table 12, the 23 surveyed firms had considerable revenue variability. Their worldwide revenues ranged from less than $100 million to more than $5 billion. This reflects the survey selection criteria of broad representative sample without bias towards any specific size range.

Value of Direct Investment Abroad: The 1988 value of direct investment abroad for the 23 firms was $22.6 billion. This represents approximately 32 percent of the total stock of CDIA, but more than 37 percent of the CDIA for Canadian-controlled firms. Note, as three of the surveyed firms accounted for almost 80 percent of the total value, the sample reflects a high degree of concentration. This concentration is consistent with Gorecki (1990) and the ADP M&A data.

Location of Investment Activity: While the surveyed firms had investment activity in 45 countries, the greatest presence was in the United States. In fact all surveyed firms had at least one investment there. The second favoured destination for investment was the European Community. The remaining investments were scattered among countries including Australia, Japan, Indonesia, China, Singapore, Hong Kong, Malaysia, Brazil and Mexico. This finding is consistent with Gorecki (1990) and the ADP M&A data.

Sources of Financing Investment Activity: As reflected in Table 13, the single largest source for financing foreign investment activity was borrowing abroad, which accounted for more than 57 percent of the financing

TABLE 13

SOURCES OF DIA FINANCING FOR SURVEYED FIRMS

SOURCE	PERCENTAGE OF DIA
Retained Earnings	31.9
Borrowed in Canada	9.0
Borrowed Abroad	57.5
New Equity (Canada)	1.5
New Equity (Abroad)	*.*
All	99.9

. data value too small to be expressed

of CDIA for the surveyed firms. Given the historical interest rate spreads between the United States and Canada, and between the Eurodollar market and Canada, there is an indication of interest rate sensitivity among the firms. The next most utilized financing methods were retained earnings (31.9 percent) and borrowing in Canada (9 percent). The data demonstrate a significant preference for both capital markets and retained earnings over the use of equity markets. Only 1.5 per cent of financing was through the issuance of new equity in Canada, while virtually no equity was raised abroad.

Sample Reliability: Given the finite population of Canadian-controlled firms with CDIA (1113) and the relatively small sample (23), it is not possible to develop precise statistical estimates from the survey. However, the conformity of the survey data on CDIA values and location with published statistical aggregates is sufficient to find the sample representative of the population in those respects and adequate as a pilot sample.

Survey of Investment Motivations

EACH OF THE 23 CORPORATIONS SURVEYED was asked to rate the importance of 17 factors in motivating their investment strategy abroad. Each factor was rated on a scale of 1 (unimportant) to 4 (very important). For the purpose of providing some industrial comparison, the respondents were divided into four mutually exclusive groups. These consisted of resources (5 firms), R&D-intensive manufacturing (5 firms), low R&D manufacturing (8 firms) and processing (4 firms). Results were averaged within each industrial group. Aggregate results were obtained by summing the group means so that there would be no bias toward any specific industry. Survey results are presented in ranked order of importance in Table 14.

The three factors identified as the most significant in influencing investment motivations were: the perceived need for outward expansion, geographic/

TABLE 14
SURVEY RESPONSE* BY INDUSTRY RANKING OF MOTIVATIONAL
FACTORS AFFECTING CDIA

| | | INDUSTRY | | | |
| | | MANUFACTURING | | | |
FACTOR	RESOURCE	R&D INTENSE	LOW-TECH	PROCESSING	ALL
Perceived need for outward expansion	3.25	3.8	3.9	4.0	14.95
Geo/product line diversification	2.75	3.4	3.5	2.5	12.15
Trade barriers & transport costs	3.5	2.5	3.5	2.5	12.00
Availability of skilled labour	3.0	3.0	3.0	2.5	11.50
Favourable regulations abroad	3.5	2.4	2.6	3.0	11.50
Tax treatment & subsidy abroad	3.4	2.2	2.5	3.0	11.10
Ability to finance abroad	3.25	2.5	2.9	2.0	10.65
Ease of financing	2.4	2.0	2.5	3.5	10.40
Resource availability	4.0	1.7	2.4	2.0	10.10
Availability of managerial skills	2.2	2.4	3.0	2.5	10.10
Maintain/increase market share	1.0	3.8	3.9	1.3	10.00
Availability of technology	2.0	3.5	2.0	2.0	9.50
Supplement exports	1.3	3.5	2.5	1.25	8.55
Enhanced product recognition	1.0	2.8	2.6	2.25	8.65
Integration	1.25	2.0	2.0	2.0	7.25
Canadian taxes & regulations	1.4	1.4	1.4	1.4	5.60

* survey response (4 = very important; 3 = important; 2 = somewhat important; 1 = unimportant). Cell contents are average values.
"All" column contains sum of averages across industries. The individual factors of "Canadian taxes" and "Canadian regulations" were combined due to identical scoring and last place ranking.

product line diversification, and trade barriers and transportation costs. The next two factors in importance were: availability of skilled labour, and favourable regulations abroad.

These factors are self-explanatory, with the exception of the perceived need for outward expansion. In this case, those surveyed were asked whether their firm's outward investments were driven by the perceived need to "globalize". This was defined by such factors as the rapid growth in world trade and investment, the emergence of mega-trading blocs, the standardization of markets, the growth of strategic alliances, and the emergence of "global" firms.

When considering the significance of these factors, it is useful to refer to what Rugman has termed "pull" and "push" factors.[21] Pull factors are those elements that attract or encourage Canadian firms to make direct investments in another country. In general, they are external to the firm and primarily concerned with the market and policy factors originating in the host country. In contrast, push factors, which are also external to the firm, come from Canadian markets and policies. They are perceived as negative factors (government policy changes, high rates of taxation, less favourable market conditions, etc.) which encourage domestic firms to invest abroad in order to enhance their competitive position.

As Rugman stresses, the distinction between pull and push factors is merely a device to highlight the potential determinants of CDIA. In reality, the two are interdependent and relative in nature. Investment decisions are ultimately made by managers taking into account all the factors in combination.

While the top two factors are internal to the firms as part of unique corporate strategies, it is interesting to note that the next three highest ranking factors in the survey all fall in the category of pull factors. Trade barriers and transportation costs associated with exporting to third markets influenced managers to invest abroad. The significance of the availability of skilled labour emphasizes that technological innovation and its skilled labour requirements influences investment decisions. The importance of favourable regulations abroad is indicative of a global market perception for these firms. In summary, these factors demonstrate that Canadian managers were motivated by perceptions of markets and policies in the host country.

These top five factors are followed in importance by favourable taxes and subsidies abroad, and the ability to finance abroad.

These are again additional pull factors of slightly less significance. When considering these particular factors, the distinction between pull and push is not sharp, since relative perceptions of foreign and domestic conditions are clearly at play.

Also of note, financing factors ranked seventh and eighth overall. Given the fact that survey respondents reported that more than 57 percent of CDIA was financed through borrowing abroad, a higher ranking might have been expected for these factors. The implication here is that "how" an investment opportunity will be realized is much less important than the selection of the opportunity itself and its associated market factors.

TABLE 15

COMPARISON OF STUDIES ON THE MOTIVATIONAL DETERMINANTS OF CDIA

STUDY	INVESTMENT CANADA	MATHESON	LITVAK & MAULE
Year	1989	1985	1978
Sample Size	23	18	25
Factors	Need for outward expansion	Trade barriers	Market share
	Geographic/product line diversification	Serve foreign markets	Faster growth abroad
	Trade barriers and transportation costs	Access to raw materials	Trade barriers and transportation costs
	Avaiability of skilled labour	Strengthen existing business	Geographic/product line diversification
	Favourable regulations abroad	Business diversification	Responsiveness to customer demands

SOURCE: Matheson, "Canadian Investment Abroad", in Rugman (1987) and Litvak and Maule, "The Canadian Multinationals", (1981)

Furthermore, it is interesting to note that those factors ranking particularly low in the survey included supplementing exports (14th), forward/backward integration (15th), and Canadian taxes and Canadian regulations which tied for last place in the survey. In view of the importance attached to vertical integration in industrial organization literature, the low rating given to integration was unexpected.

The two "push" factors of Canadian taxation and Canadian regulatory environment were assigned the lowest rating by Canadian managers. Given recent business and press commentary about the negative impact of Canadian policies and programs on the nation's competitive position, it might be expected that these factors would have ranked much higher, even back in the spring of 1989.

It is difficult, however, to conclude from the survey that push factors are not significant. Once again, the interdependent and relative aspects of pull and push mitigate against a definitive conclusion. There is no doubt that certain Canadian firms have made acquisitions abroad due to poor domestic markets. The case of Dominion Textile, discussed in Appendix A, is one example.

To a large extent, the findings of the Investment Canada survey are similar to those identified by Matheson, and Litvak and Maule. Table 15 presents a summary comparison of the three studies. The table confirms that "geographic/product line diversification" and "trade barriers and transportation cost" were identified as significant in all three surveys. The most significant factor in the Investment Canada survey — "perceived need for outward expansion"

— was not specifically included in any of the previous studies. The low rank-ing of the push factors is also generally consistent with the findings of Litvak and Maule, Matheson, and Forget and Denis.[22]

The Investment Canada survey results are also in line with other inter-national surveys. For example, in a survey of European companies undertaking cross-border acquisitions, "entry to new market" and "geographic and product diversification" were assigned the highest ratings.[23] An earlier survey of American and European firms by the Group of Thirty also indicated the rela-tive importance of such pull factors as "access to market", "trade barriers" and "integration of foreign operations with existing investment".[24]

CONCLUSIONS

HAVING DESCRIBED AND IDENTIFIED various patterns and motivations relating to Canadian acquisitions abroad with reference to data, theory and survey results, we now address issues relating to the economic rationale and suggest areas of future research.

ECONOMIC RATIONALE

Earlier in this paper we briefly reviewed the economic rationale — internalization and transaction cost theories — for firms undertaking direct investment abroad. The purpose was to explain the basic rationale. No attempt was made to link these theories to the actual behaviour of firms. The data limitations outlined in the paper made this impossible in any rigorous form (for example, regression analysis).

There are, nevertheless, some findings relevant to the theories.

- The internalization theory suggests that horizontal investment, where the industry of origin and destination are the same, is typically based on some kind of intangible asset. If the internalization theory holds, a distinct preference for horizontal expansions would be expected. Thus, the fact that horizontal acquisitions dominate in cross-border M&A activity and CDIA is significant in this respect (see Table 9).
- Under the internalization theory, a firm keeps its assets within the firm when there are significant costs or impediments to moving them out-side the operation. An example would be the service sector, where typi-cally the assets of a firm cannot be exported or, in other words, disem-bodied. The M&A data supports this theory since the service sector (including financial services) accounted for 41 percent of industrially classified Canadian acquisitions abroad (see Table 9).
- The transactions costs theory suggests that in order to keep these costs to a minimum, the firm's preferred form of investment is in a wholly owned affiliate. In this respect, the Investment Canada survey showed

that almost one half of the surveyed firms held all their investments in the form of wholly owned subsidiaries.

AREAS OF FUTURE RESEARCH

There is much more work required to understand fully the patterns and motivations behind Canadian acquisitions abroad. The preceding suggests a number of fruitful areas for future research.

First, we have noted a number of shortcomings with the M&A data. As explained, these problems are not unique, but unfortunately are characteristic of work in the M&A field, especially relating to cross-border acquisitions. Given the recent increase in the pace and value of cross-border acquisitions by Canadian firms, it is all the more imperative that concrete steps be taken to create a more comprehensive M&A database. To this end, it will no doubt be necessary for public and private organizations interested in M&A to work together and to pool resources.

Second, we identified some theses relating to the small country case and to Canada having a relatively high proportion of smaller firms investing abroad. There was some evidence supporting these theses. However, more rigorous work is necessary of the kind that Swedenborg and Dunning have undertaken for Sweden and the United Kingdom respectively. This work is contingent on the improvement of the database.

Third, we showed that among the firms with four or more acquisitions abroad, the printing and publishing sector was most active abroad. This industry has been identified by others as an area where Canada has a comparative disadvantage. More work needs to be done to apply rigorous tests to the related proposition that firms invest abroad in those sectors where the home country has a comparative disadvantage.

Fourth, the data on Canadian cross-border M&A activity are particularly deficient with respect to non-U.S. destinations. More work is required on the geographic distribution of Canadian acquisitions. This is imperative since Canadian policy makers often view geographic diversification of investment as desirable, particularly in order to address the implications of the emergence of the so-called mega-trading blocs in the Triad (EC, North America and Pacific Rim). In this context, the Investment Canada survey revealed that some companies limit acquisitions to the United States and Europe in large part because of common cultural values and corporate goals. This fact is particularly highlighted by the Bombardier case (see Appendix A). Further survey work might seek to determine how widespread this view is among Canadian corporations investing abroad and whether this occurs as a result of perceived market failures associated with information gaps.

Finally, the Investment Canada survey, and indeed earlier surveys, did not directly link the internalization and transaction cost theories to managerial motivations. Future work might better attempt to address these linkages. In any case, a survey of the sort undertaken by Investment Canada, if repeated at appropriate intervals, could be designed to yield a time series and cross-sectional data that might allow for more rigorous testing.

APPENDIX A

CASE STUDIES

Appendix A describes the experience of four selected Canadian corporations active in acquisitions abroad. These case studies are illustrative. To the degree possible, the motivations and goals behind each firm's direct investment abroad are discussed.

Two cases, Bombardier and Northern Telecom, are in the forefront of advanced technology in their respective fields. Furthermore, they are in industries — rail/air transport and telecommunications — which are considered "global" industries. By and large, they are Canadian success stories, pursuing a strategy of outward expansion by selected acquisitions in their respective niche markets.

The other two cases, Dominion Textile and Campeau Corporation, are in more mature industries — textiles and retail trade/real estate. Their direct investment activity has had more mixed results. To offset slack in its domestic markets, Dominion Textile has successfully increased foreign production and market share abroad. Campeau's forays into the retail trade business in the United States have proved to be its undoing, at least in the medium-term.

For each case, there is a brief summary of the firm and its history, followed by a list of foreign investments and acquisitions. The case studies conclude with some discussion of corporate motivations and goals. For Bombardier, Northern Telecom and Dominion Textile, the discussions of corporate strategy are based on interviews with senior officials (as part of the Investment Canada survey in 1989).

Case 1: Bombardier

Bombardier is engaged in the design, development, manufacture and distribution of four main products —mass transit equipment, civil aerospace products, military aerospace products and motorized consumer products. The company's head office is in Montreal, and it operates plants in Canada, the United States, Austria, Belgium, Finland, France, Sweden and the United Kingdom. In 1902, the company was incorporated under the name of The Locomotive and Machine Company of Montreal Limited; since June 1978, the company has been called Bombardier Inc. Les Entreprises de J. Armand Bombardier Ltd is the majority shareholder, with 67 percent of the voting interest. In fiscal year 1990 the company had revenues of over $2 billion, up sharply from $1.4 billion in 1989. As of May 1990 the company had 22,500 employees worldwide.

Foreign Investments and Acquisitions

- The company's first venture abroad was Bombardier-Rotax GmbH, undertaken in the 1960s in Austria.
- In February 1984 the company acquired Alco Power Inc. of Auburn, New York (now Auburn Technology Inc.), for just under $31 million. Alco makes diesel engine components.
- In April 1986 the company took a 45 percent equity stake in BN Constructions Ferroviares et Métalliques, a Belgian manufacturer of railway rolling stock and mass transit equipment. In 1988 this equity stake was raised to over 90 percent.
- In February 1989 the company's acquisition of the tract vehicle operations of Universal Go-Tract Ltd of Pointe Claire, Quebec led to the indirect acquisition of the latter's American subsidiary, Universal Go-Tract of Georgia.
- Bombardier maintains a 50 percent interest in Scanhold Oy Co. of Finland.
- In October 1989 Bombardier acquired Short Brothers PLC of Belfast, Northern Ireland for $58.2 million.
- In December 1989 Bombardier purchased ANF-Industrie, France's second largest manufacturer of railway equipment, for about $22 million.
- In April 1990 the company purchased the assets and operations of the Learjet Corporation of Wichita, Kansas for $US 86.4 million.
- In October 1990 Bombardier completed a deal to buy Procor Engineering Ltd., a British firm that manufactures body shells for railway passenger cars and locomotives.
- Bombardier has also forged strategic alliances through its acquired subsidiaries in recognition of its limited resources and its small size by international standards. For example: in the production of surveillance systems, Bombardier has a strategic partnership with Dornier GmbH of Germany; and in the area of mass transportation, it has formed strategic relationships with General Electric Company of Canada Inc. and the Franco-British group GEC Alsthom.

Corporate Motivations and Goals In recent years, the company has pursued twin goals: expansion and internationalization of operations, and consolidation and broadening of its industrial and technological base.

Bombardier officials believe that the company must attain a critical mass in order to maintain an effective market presence in its chosen niches. Through such a critical mass, it can achieve the requisite economies of scale and scope. Acquisitions of existing companies are preferred to greenfield investments. This allows Bombardier to establish a significant immediate presence in the chosen niche through the acquired firm's recognized name and distribution network. In addition, the acquisition of an existing facility avoids adding excess capacity to the industry.

In choosing acquisition targets, Bombardier concentrates on industries where there are few players and effective barriers to entry. Company officials also typically seek complementarity in terms of technology, and production and distribution expertise. As a result, all acquisitions abroad have been horizontal. Mixing and matching products is, of course, critical from this perspective. A useful illustration of this strategy was the acquisition of Short Brothers. Bombardier had been engaged in the design and development of a regional jet; Short Brothers was working in the same area. The acquisition allowed Bombardier to exploit synergies resulting from joint expertise in regional jets and to eliminate a potential competitor.

As confirmed by company officials, the choice of the United States and Europe as investment targets was deliberate. Bombardier officials apparently place a high value on common cultural values and corporate goals, which exist in the United States and Western Europe. The company made a conscious decision to stay out of Third World markets in terms of direct investment for reasons of financial and exchange rate security. Canada, the United States and Europe will likely continue as the major markets for its products. In particular, North America is perceived as the main market for business jets, military aircraft, aerospace-related defense products, snowmobiles and sea-jets. Western Europe is expected to remain as the fastest growing market for railway transportation products.

CASE 2: NORTHERN TELECOM

Northern Telecom (NorTel) is the world's leading supplier of fully digital telecommunications systems. It has been in operation since 1882. In 1914, the company was chartered as Northern Electric Co. with the company owned 50 percent by Bell Canada and 44 percent by Western Electric Co. In 1964, through the acquisition of Western Electric Co., the company became a wholly-owned subsidiary of Bell Canada. Today, NorTel is headquartered in Mississauga, with Bell Canada Enterprises as the majority shareholder (a 53 percent stake). NorTel itself holds a 70 percent interest in its subsidiary, Bell Northern Research Ltd. For the year ending 1990, Northern Telecom had worldwide assets of $US 6.8 billion, revenues of $US 6.8 billion, and a net income of $US 376 million. The number of employees approached 48,000 worldwide. It has operations in over 70 countries, with 40 manufacturing plants in Canada, Australia, China, Ireland, Malaysia and the United States.

Foreign Investments and Acquisitions

- In 1967 NorTel undertook its first major investment abroad. NETAS-Northern Electric TeleKomunikayson A.S. was established in Turkey with NorTel as an equal joint partner with the country's Post, Telephone & Telegraph Department.

- In 1971 it set up Northern Telecom Inc. in the United States.
- In 1973 Northern Telecom (Ireland) was created to manufacture telephone sets and equipment for the EC.
- In 1976 the company acquired Cook Electric Co. and Telecommunication System of America Inc. in the United States.
- Since 1976 a number of American acquisitions have been made including: Intersil Inc. (a manufacturer of semiconductors in California); Data 100 Corp. (a manufacturer of computer terminal systems in Minnesota); Danray Inc. (a Texas-based manufacturer of telecommunication switching equipment); Syncor Inc. (Michigan); Eastern Data Industries; and Spectron Inc.
- In 1983 Northern Telecom Japan and Northern Telecom PLC (U.K.) were created, along with Bell Northern Research's laboratory in the U.K.
- In 1987 NorTel increased its interest in STC PLC of U.K. (a diversified electronics firm, manufacturing telecommunication and information technology equipment) from 3 percent to 27.5 per cent at a cost of $US 730 million. In November 1990, NorTel announced its intention to buy the remaining 73 percent interest for $US 2.6 billion.
- In 1989 Northern Telecom Meridian S.A. was established in Paris, France.
- In addition, NorTel is engaged in a number of strategic alliances including those with major information technology such as Wang, Digital Equipment, NCR, Apple and Hewlett Packard.

Corporate Motivations and Goals NorTel officials consider the company a world player in the telecommunications industry. Substantial restructuring of this industry is currently ongoing. While industry giants like AT&T, Alcatel, Siemens, NEC, Fujitsu, Ericsson and NorTel dominate the industry today, it is expected that there will be no more than four of five dominant firms by the end of the decade. NorTel's principal goal is to be one of those four or five successful global firms at the turn of the century. From this perspective, it has targeted revenues of $US 30 billion by the end of the decade.

Company officials feel that NorTel's strengths are in telecommunications equipment and wish to develop this expertise through their constant commitment to R&D. NorTel did try, unsuccessfully, to diversify into computer networking during the 1980s. However strategic investments in this area continue to be an option for consideration (see above).

To enhance the firm's global competitiveness, officials think that the company might profit from moving away from its current concentration on the North American market, and seeking instead production and distribution facilities in other key parts of the world, particularly Europe and the Pacific Rim.

CASE 3: DOMINION TEXTILE

Dominion Textile (DomTex) is a major manufacturer and distributor of textile and related products. The present company was incorporated in 1922. With headquarters in Montreal, the corporation controls about 70 subsidiaries and associated companies. It is a widely held public company with approximately 30,000 shareholders. The company specializes in yarns, denim fabrics, apparel fabrics, consumer products, industrial products and technical fabrics. DomTex operates 42 manufacturing facilities in Canada, the U.S., Europe, South America, North Africa and the Far East. In fiscal year 1990 the company recorded sales of $1.44 billion. As of June 1990, the company had a workforce of 10,500.

Foreign Investments and Acquisitions

- Until 1975 DomTex was a domestic Canadian firm with no manufacturing facilities abroad. In 1975 it successfully staged a hostile takeover of DHJ Industries in the United States for $US 9.2 million. DHJ has been subsequently consolidated with Facemate Corporation under control of DomTex.
- The company's other acquisitions in the United States include: Erwin Mills Inc. ($US 208 million), Wayn-Tex Inc. ($US 136 million), Mirafi Inc., Howard Cotton Company, and the industrial textile division of Uniroyal Goodrich Tire ($US 80 million in a joint venture).
- In Europe DomTex has subsidiaries in France, Ireland, Germany, Britain, Italy, Spain and Switzerland. In 1988 the company acquired a 51 percent stake in Nordlys S.A. of France, and in 1990 it raised its controlling interest to 100 percent. In 1989 it also bought Compagnie du Faing S.A., France.
- In the Far East DomTex has a manufacturing plant in Hong Kong, operated by its fully owned subsidiary, DHJ (Hong Kong) limited. The company also runs a distribution facility in Singapore —DHJ Industries Distribution (Singapore) Ltd.
- Other operations include production and distribution companies in Morocco (DHJ Industries Maroc S.A.), Columbia, (Entrellas DHJ LTDA) and Brazil (Entrellas DHJ S.A.).

Corporate Motivations and Goals   DomTex has demonstrated a strong outward orientation in its corporate strategy. Officials confirm that, since the company is in a mature industry, there is not a great deal of scope for further expansion in Canada. DomTex officials also stressed that the company is open to the negative effects of further liberalization through changes to the Multi-Fibre Agreement and the ongoing Uruguay Round of GATT negotiations. The company has stated its intention to respond effectively to the pressures emanating from the globalization of markets, products and consumers, as well as from the emergence of trading blocs. Being in a mature industry the company must demonstrate flexibility and innovation in terms of corporate growth and restructuring.

To stay competitive and to gain the benefits of economies of scale and scope, senior officials said the company has sought expansion along geographic and product lines. The working philosophy has been to seek ways to position the company for sustained future growth. According to officials, the company's acquisitions in the United States have provided a solid base upon which the corporation can plan its future directions. The facilities in Morocco were cited as the means to assure access into the lucrative EC market, since this North African country has special privileges for exporting textile products to the European Community under the Lome Agreement. The plant in Hong Kong was also noted as the mechanism to serve the burgeoning markets in the Pacific Rim.

CASE 4: CAMPEAU CORPORATION

Campeau Corporation owns and develops commercial real estate in Canada and the United States. It is also a holding company for interests in department store and supermarket retailing in the United States. The corporation's real estate assets, consisting of shopping centres, offices and mixed-use properties are mostly concentrated in the provinces of Ontario and Quebec, and in the states of Massachusetts, Washington and California. The retail operations are entirely in the United States. Robert Campeau and his family held 100 percent of the convertible subordinate preference shares and 54 percent of the ordinary shares at the end of 1990. Olympia & York Developments hold another 12 percent of the ordinary shares. In the year ending January 1990 the corporation had revenues of $US 10.44 billion, up from $US 8.67 billion in 1989. However, this increase in revenue was not adequate to cover operating expenses and debt service charges. On January 15, 1990 both Campeau's American affiliates, Allied and Federated Department Stores, filed for bankruptcy.

Foreign Investments and Acquisitions

- Campeau's first major acquisition abroad took place in the fall of 1986. It acquired Allied Stores Corporation in the United States for $US 3.6 billion. The debt financing and transaction fees raised the acquisition cost to $US 4.4 billion. It was a highly leveraged acquisition with financing through a consortium led by Citibank, bridge financing from First Boston and $US 300 million in equity with half from the Edward J. DeBartolo Corp. Prior to this retail acquisition, Campeau had not been very active in real estate outside of Canada.
- Over the course of 1987, Campeau sold off 16 of Allied's smaller divisions for $US 1 billion in order to pay down its short-term debt. Divisions

divested included such chains as Block's, Cain-Sloan, Dey's, Herpol-sheimer's, Miller & Rhoads, Pomeroy's, Bonwit Teller and Garfinckel's. Larger, well-known divisions were retained such as Brooks Brothers, Jordan Marsh, Stern's, Maas Brothers, The Bon and Ann Taylor's.

- In 1987 Campeau also sold off real estate assets in southern California for $US 110 million, again to meet debt obligations.

- In early 1988 Campeau initiated a lengthy and hostile takeover of Federated Department Stores Inc., the fifth largest retailer in the United States. The transaction was completed on April 1, 1988 for $US 6.7 billion. As with Allied, it was highly leveraged with many of the funds raised by using short-term debt instruments against Federated's assets.

- In 1988, as part of the restructuring plan for Federated, Campeau sold for a combined value of $US 2.6 billion four divisions —I. Magnin, Bullocks/Bullocks Wilshire, Foley's and Filene's. The company also sold Brooks Brothers of the Allied Stores chain to Marks & Spencer PLC of Britain for $US 750 million in this year.

- By the end of 1988, through further divestitures, Campeau had pared Federated down to following divisions: Bloomingdale's, Lazarus, Rich's, Goldsmith's, Abraham & Straus, Burdines and Ralph's.[25]

- On January 15, 1990, when the Allied and Federated Department Stores filed for bankruptcy, Campeau Corp. (U.S.) also changed its name to Federated Stores, Inc. and appointed a new chairman and Chief Executive Officer in place of Robert Campeau.

Corporate Motivations and Goals   Campeau's retail acquisitions were the archetypal debt-financed activity, so prevalent in the United States during the mid- to late-80s. Campeau relied on a leveraged buy out to move into the large retail activity in the United States. Taking on these large debt-loads, mostly in the form of "junk" bonds financed at very high interest rates, forced the company to over-stretch its financial resources and ultimately led to failure and bankruptcy.

There appears to have been two main motivations behind these acquisitions: a desire to diversify out of the cyclically vulnerable real estate business in Canada; and expectations that synergies would develop from combining well established retail chains with future real estate developments in the United States.

Campeau had tried unsuccessfully in the past to meet diversification objectives in Canada. For example, the company failed to acquire a controlling interest in Bushnell Communications Limited in 1974 when the Canadian Radio-Television and Telecommunications Commission denied the sale. Again in 1980, Campeau attempted, without success, to buy a controlling interest in Royal Trustco. It can be argued that Campeau turned to the United States because of the company's inability to diversify in Canada.

The expected synergies between Campeau's retail and real estate operations never fully materialized. Nevertheless, it was this objective that primarily led first to Campeau's alliances with the Edward J. DeBartolo Corporation, the largest shopping mall developer in the U.S., and second to agreements with Olympia & York, the Toronto-based real estate giant. For as long as it could in 1989 and early 1990, the company used these alliances to meet rising repayment charges and to acquire bridge financing.

APPENDIX B

CROSS-BORDER M&A DATABASES

ADP Database on Canadian Acquisitions Abroad

The database on Canadian acquisitions abroad, used as the primary source of information in this study, was obtained from Automatic Data Processing (ADP). ADP is a private consulting firm, based in New York City and Ann Arbor (Michigan), specializing in data on mergers and acquisitions. Other data sources considered were Micromedia Ltd., KPMG Peat Marwick Thorne, and Business Sales and Acquisitions Digest (see below). The ADP database was selected over other sources as it offered a more comprehensive set of data in terms of the number of transactions, length of time series, industrial classification of transactions, and scope of cross-border acquisition coverage.

ADP Data File

Time Series: 1979 to September 1990
Sources of Information: Public media sources, including *Mergers & Acquisitions*, *Wall Street Journal*, and various national and local newspapers and financial journals.
Data contents:
- name and industrial classification of the Canadian acquirer
- name and industrial classification of the acquired firm abroad
- date of the transaction
- location (country) of the acquired firm
- status of the transaction
    • completed
    • pending
    • unsuccessful
- transaction value
- characterization of transaction
    • acquisition of 100 percent interest
    • acquisition of majority interest
    • acquisition of minority interest exceeding at least 20 percent
    • acquisition of additional interest

Data Qualifiers:
- transaction values not known in all cases
- data for foreign countries other than the United States does not exist prior to 1987

OTHER M&A DATABASES

Micromedia Limited, Toronto

In the summer of 1990, Micromedia took over the publication of "Mergers & Acquisitions in Canada" (the monthly and the annual) from Venture Economics Canada and are currently a premier public information source on M&A activity in Canada. Through their access to Dialog, the U.S.-based information firm and review of public information sources, they provide information on acquisitions abroad — primarily in the United States — by Canadian-based firms.

KPMG Peat Marwick Thorne, Toronto

This firm (known in Montreal as KPMG Poissant Thibault Peat Marwick Thorne) is the Canadian branch of the Netherlands-based international M&A and accounting firm KPMG. Their publication, *Deal Watch*, first published in November 1988, focusses solely on cross-border acquisitions. It relies primarily on published sources as well as the firm's international network of M&A specialists.

Business Sales and Acquisitions Digest, Toronto

This digest is published by the Canadian Institute of Chartered Accountants and covers selected M&A transactions. The data is available beginning in 1988.

Merger Registry, Bureau of Competition Policy
Consumer and Corporate Affairs Canada, Ottawa

The register provides a count of foreign and domestic M&A activity reported in the business press. It attempts to distinguish between completed transactions and announcements. Only those transactions are reported where effective or acknowledged control of the acquired corporation is obtained.

ENDNOTES

1. Note that the stocks represent book value, not market or replacement value. Other things being equal, more recent investments will be more highly valued. Since a good part of FDI is older than CDIA, the difference between the value of FDI and CDIA is likely larger than indicated. Thus, the CDIA/FDI ratio shown in Table 1 is probably biased in favour of CDIA.

2. The successful foreign investments carried out by the large, trans-national firms of Sweden (SKF, Electrolux, Volvo, Alfa-Laval, ASEA, Atlas-Copco, Ericsson), the Netherlands (Phillips, Unilever, Royal Dutch Shell) and Switzerland (Ciba-Geigy, Sandoz, Nest) support this conclusion.

3. Swedenborg in Dunning (1985).

4. UNCTC (1988), p.37. Small is defined as sales up to $US 18.4 million (or alternatively, $CDN 25 million).

5. See Appendix B. Halpern and Mintz elsewhere in this volume use M&A data from KPMG.

6. The focus on the number of transactions means that each event is assigned equal weight. Analysis based on value allows the researcher to take into account the relative weight of individual transactions.

7. In fact, the ADP data show there are 379 "parties" that made foreign acquisitions. 347 firms are identified, along with 15 multiple investors with several firms involved, and 17 private, unnamed parties.

8. Comparing the ADP data to the Gorecki results is difficult for this reason. Nevertheless, lacking other comparisons, it was felt useful to refer to Gorecki in most cases.

9. At the time of its foreign acquisitions, Memotec still qualified as a small-to medium-sized firm. Following its domestic acquisition of Teleglobe Canada, its revenue base increased and the firm attained the rank of a large firm.

10. Many of the Thompson acquisitions were of small-town newspapers in the United States.

11. Note that in the late 1980s, many of Canada's largest banks which had earlier built up a presence in Europe divested much of their European operations. The Royal Bank, for example, divested its German, Belgian and French operations.

12. Defined as those with annual revenues of less than $100 million. This definition is not consistent with the U.N.C.T.C. and general practice at Statistics Canada. The selection of this revenue threshold is consistent with the Investment Canada survey and, in any case, it was judged that these thresholds tend to be arbitrary.

13. Horizontal means that the acquiring industry of origin and that of the affiliate are the same. Vertical is such that the affiliate is either prior or subsequent to the industry of origin of the acquiring firm. Conglomerate is where the affiliate activity has no relationship with the industry of origin of the acquiring firm.

14. Gorecki (1990) found that 39 percent of the stock value of CDIA in Japan was in the form of strategic partnerships, the highest among industrialized countries and a level four times higher than in the United States and Canada. He defined as minority ownership voting rights greater than 10 percent and less than 50 percent. In fact, many Canadian companies including Alcan, Cominco, and MacMillan Bloedel have for many years

maintained a presence in Japan in the form of joint ventures and minority equity positions.

15. See Gorecki (1990), pp. 7-13 for a more complete discussion of internalization, intangible assets and transaction costs related to FDI. The internalization theory can be traced among others to Coase (1937), Hymer (1960, 1976), Caves (1971), McManus (1972), Williamson (1975), Buckley and Casson (1976), Rugman (1981) and Caves (1982).

16. Morck and Young (1990).

17. Dunning (1985). Note that this calculus of net benefit does not always fully take into account social costs. These may include any loss of competitive advantage and the burden of structural alignment in the home country. Dunning suggests that the greatest divergence between private and social interests associated with DIA may be in knowledge-intensive "sunrise" industries.

18. The interviews were carried out by Zulfi Sadeque and Geoff Nimmo, Investment Canada.

19. These three surveys along with a study done on CDIA in the New York State by Prem Gandhi (1984) are summarized in Rugman (1987).

20. The survey included seven of the 20 large Canadian industrial multinationals that Rugman (1987) identified. In fact, no firms in the service sector were surveyed.

21. Rugman (1987), p. 11.

22. Forget and Denis did find that Canadian firms in the petroleum sector and financial services were motivated to go to the United States in part by Canada's tax policies, which represent a "push" factor. Rugman (1987) also observed that smaller Canadian firms tend to go to the U.S. because of trade union attitudes, labour legislation and unit labour costs in Canada.

23. Centre for Business Study, London Business School (1990).

24. Group of Thirty (1984).

25. At the time of the sale, Federated owned 669 department stores and other outlets, with 1987 revenues of $US 11 billion.

ACKNOWLEDGEMENT

THIS PAPER WAS PREPARED for the Centre for International Studies and Investment Canada Study on Corporate Globalization Through Mergers and Acquisitions. We wish to thank Randall Morck, Barry J. Olivella, Len Waverman and David Husband for their guidance.

BIBLIOGRAPHY

Auerbach, Alan J. (ed). *Mergers and Acquisitions*, National Bureau of Economic Research, Chicago, University of Chicago Press, 1987.

_____. (ed). *Corporate Takeovers: Causes and Consequences*, National Bureau of Economic Research, Chicago, University of Chicago Press, 1988.

Bartlett, Christopher. *Managing Across Borders: The Transnational Solution*, Cambridge, MA, Harvard Business School Press, 1989

Brozen, Yale. *Concentration, Mergers, and Public Policy*, London, Macmillan 1982.

Buckley, Peter J. & Mark Casson. *The Future of the Multinational Enterprise*, London, Macmillan, 1976.

Caves, Richard E. *Mergers, Takeovers, and Economic Efficiency: Foresight vs. Hindsight*, Harvard Institute of Economic Research Discussion Paper # 1405, 1988.

_____. *Multinational Enterprise and Economic Analysis*, Cambridge, Cambridge University Press, 1983.

_____. "International Corporations: The Industrial Economics of Foreign Investment", *Economica* 38, 1971, pp. 1-27.

Centre for Business Study. *Continental Mergers are Different*, London, London Business School, 1990.

Clark, John J. *Business Merger and Acquisition Strategies* Englewood Cliffs, NJ, Prentice-Hall Inc., 1985.

Coase, Ronald H. "The Nature of the Firm", *Economica*, 1937, pp. 386-405.

D'Cruz, Joseph R. & James D. Fleck. *Canada Can Compete*, Montreal, The Institute for Research on Public Policy, 1985.

Dunning, John H. (ed). *Multinational Enterprise, Economic Structure and International Competitiveness*, Chichester and New York, John Wiley & Sons, 1985.

Eden, Lorraine. "Multinational Responses to Trade and Technology Changes: Implications for Canada" in *Foreign Investment, Technology and Economic Growth*, Donald McFetridge (ed), Calgary, University of Calgary Press, 1991.

Eckbo, B. Espen. "The Market for Corporate Control: Policy Issues and Capital Market Evidence" in *Mergers, Corporate Concentration and Power in Canada*, R.S. Khemani, D.M. Shapiro and W.T. Stanbury (eds), Halifax, Institute for Research in Public Policy, 1988.

Forget, Claude A. & Daniel Denis. *Canadian Foreign Investment in the United States: Reasons and Consequences*, Department of Regional Economic Expansion, Ottawa, 1985.

Gandhi, Prem. "Foreign Direct Investment and Regional Development: The Case of Canadian Investment in New York State", State University of New York at Plattsburgh, mimeo, 1984.

Gorecki, Paul. "Patterns of Canadian Foreign Direct Investment Abroad" Statistics Canada, Analytical Studies Branch, # 33, 1990.

Graham, Edward M. & Paul R. Krugman. *Foreign Direct Investment into the United States*, Washington, DC, Institute for International Economics, 1989.

Group of Thirty. *Foreign Direct Investment 1973-87*, New York, 1984.

Hymer, Stephen. *The International Operations of National Firms: A Study of Direct Foreign Investment*, Cambridge, MA, MIT Press, 1976.

Investment Canada. "Business Implications of Globalization", Discussion Paper # 1990-V, 1990.

Litvak, Isaiah A. *Canadian Cases in International Business*, Toronto, McGraw-Hill Ryerson Ltd., 1984.

Litvak, Isaiah A. and C.J. Maule. *The Canadian Multinationals*, Toronto, Butterworths, 1981.

Matthews, Roy A. "Structural Change and Industrial Policy", Prepared for The Economic Council of Canada, Ottawa, Supply & Services Canada, 1985.

McManus, John. "The Theory of the International Firm" in *The Multinational Firm and the Nation State*, G. Pacquet (ed), Toronto, Collier-Macmillan, 1972.

Morck, Randall & Bernard Young. "Internalization and Managers' Interests: An Event Study Test", Edmonton, Institute for Financial Research, Faculty of Business, University of Alberta, 1990.

Niosi, Jorge. *Canadian Multinationals*, Toronto, Between the Lines, 1985.

Porter, Michael. "From Competitive Advantage to Corporate Strategy", in *Competition in Global Industries*, M. Porter (ed), Cambridge, MA, Harvard Business School Press, 1986.

Richards, C.F.J. "Canadian Direct Investment Position Abroad: Trends and Recent Developments", Statistics Canada, mimeo, 1985.

Rugman, Alan M. *International Diversification and Multinational Enterprise*, Lexington, 1979.

_____. "New Theories of the Multinational Enterprise: An Assessment of Internalization Theory", *Bulletin of Economic Research* 38:2, 1986.

_____. *Outward Bound: Canadian Direct Investments in the United States*, Toronto, McGraw-Hill Ryerson, 1987.

_____. "Internalization as a General Theory of Foreign Direct Investment: A Re-Appraisal of the Literature", *Literatur, Weltwirtschaftliches Archiv* Bd. CXIV, 1980.

Tarasofsky, A. "Corporate Mergers and Acquisitions: Evidence on Profitability", Ottawa, Economic Council of Canada, mimeo, 1990.

Tolchin, Martin & Susan. *Buying into America*, New York, Times Books, 1988.

United Nations Centre for Transnational Corporations. "The Process of Transnationalization and Transnational Mergers", Series A, No. 8, New York, 1989.

_____. *Transnational Corporations in World Development: Trends and Prospects*, New York, 1988.

Wallace, Cynthia Day. *Foreign Direct Investment and the Multinational Enterprise: A Bibliography*, Dordrecht, Martinus Nijhoff Publishers, 1988.

Williamson, Oliver E. *Markets and Hierarchies: Analysis and Antitrust Implications: A Study in the Economics of Internal Organizations*, New York, Free Press/Macmillan, 1975.

Alan M. Rugman   and   Leonard Waverman
Faculty of Management   Centre for International Studies
University of Toronto   University of Toronto

3

Foreign Ownership and Corporate Strategy

THIS PAPER EXAMINES THE FOREIGN MERGERS AND ACQUISITIONS, and new businesses established by foreigners in Canada over the 1974 - 1990 period. Data on these foreign acquisitions in Canada are interpreted from the viewpoint of corporate strategy and international competitiveness. We use as a basis for comparison, among other theories, the traditional "internalization" view of multinational acquisitions and the work of Porter (1990) on the competitiveness of nations as a basis for comparison. Another paper in this volume "Foreign Multinational Enterprises and Merger Activity in Canada", by Baldwin & Caves, examines the conduct of all foreign multinational enterprises (MNEs) in the 1970 - 1979 period.

Data on the number and nature of foreign acquisitions and new business ventures in Canada from 1974 to 1990, are used to detect changes in regulatory policy before and after Investment Canada was established in 1985. Data files supplied by the Foreign Investment Review Agency (FIRA) and its successor agency, Investment Canada, are used to distinguish between three groups of industries: resources, manufacturing, and services. We aggregate all foreign takeovers in Canada from 1974 to 1990 by the triad blocks, i.e. the United States, the European Community (EC), and Japan. We also consider "Other Europe" and all "Other Countries".

The modern theory of the MNE is used to interpret the data and policy implications of the first section and to re-interpret the model of international competitiveness developed by Porter (1990). The focus is on firm-level analysis of the corporate strategies of leading MNEs, both foreign-owned and Canadian-owned, as related to a standard conceptual model of triad power and global competition (see Rugman and Verbeke, 1990).

THEORETICAL PERSPECTIVES

THE INTERNALIZATION OR TRANSACTION COST model (see Rugman, 1980 and Caves, 1982) can be re-interpreted by bringing together in a matrix framework, the concepts of country-specific advantages (CSAs) and firm-specific

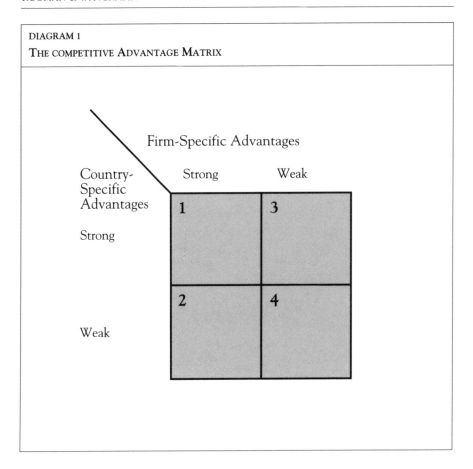

DIAGRAM 1

THE COMPETITIVE ADVANTAGE MATRIX

advantages (FSAs). CSAs consist of natural resources and other environmental factors, as well as "created" factor endowments, such as human capital and social infrastructure; these endowments are usually location-bound and specific to that nation. These CSAs can be considered the comparative advantage factors of the nation. FSAs are the proprietary knowledge attributes of the MNE, which may be based on company strengths in technology, management and/or marketing. The FSAs represent the firm's competitive advantages or disadvantages. In Diagram 1, the CSAs are represented on the vertical axis and the FSAs on the horizontal axis. Parts of this framework are similar to the Porter (1990) model, but parts are different, as discussed below.

It is assumed in this paper that the CSAs are exogenous parameters. Since CSAs capture the natural and created factor endowments of Canada, its market characteristics, and the nature of its government policy as well, the vertical axis also reflects aspects of international competitiveness, especially the extent to which governments can attempt to change the CSAs through industrial policy and strategic trade policy. In principle, we believe that it will be extremely difficult for government policy to implement a sustainable shift in Canada's underlying comparative advantage in resource-based manufactured products. Our theoretical analysis of resources differs from that of Porter (1990), since we include manufacturing and marketing value added as FSAs in resource-based industries, whereas Porter does not.

In what follows we relate the theoretical discussion of CSAs, actual and potential, with the FSAs of companies in three broad industrial sectors: resources, manufacturing and services. We then link this work on CSAs and FSAs to the data on foreign ownership of Canadian industries. We conduct simple tests to see whether there are any significant differences in the ownership patterns in industry sectors across the triad blocks, and between the two periods before and after Investment Canada was created in June 1985.

It has already been found that there are no discernible differences in the relative FSAs of foreign-owned as compared to Canadian-owned companies, see Rugman (1980, 1981 and 1990); building on Safarian (1968) who, using earlier data, discovered a similar performance on exports and research, but not on imports. Shapiro (1980) also has similar findings. The reason is that the ownership of capital is less important than its performance. Canadian-owned enterprises now have as much access to capital and technology as foreign-owned firms, so their participation in services, manufacturing and resources is approximately equal.

Largely consistent with the above approach, Baldwin and Caves (1990) (henceforth referred to as BC) use a traditional analytical framework to examine acquisitions (foreign and domestic). They begin by presenting the theory of the market for corporate control, where the acquirer is able to make better use of the specific assets under the control of the acquiree's managers. The internalization view of foreign direct investment (Caves, 1982) suggests that the foreign acquirer has certain lumpy (large-scale) overhead and intangible assets (brand-name [R&D] marketing ability) which can be spread over a number of nations, yielding capacity to outbid local entrepreneurs for the specific assets of the acquiree. BC suggest that this market for corporate control, however, can be welfare reducing if purchases are made to obtain market power or to feed the enlarged egos of the managers of the conglomerate raider. This internalization version of the theory of FDI leads to certain testable hypotheses. Do the patterns of acquisitions among acquiring groups reflect the asset specificity of the home region? Do acquisition and greenfield ventures differ? Are foreign acquisitions a function of the "lumpiness" of assets in an industry? And are they a function of the degree of multi-plant operation in the home country of the investor? (These latter two issues are not examined here.)

BC also develop a managerial implication of internalization theory, suggesting that the effectiveness of asset deployment is a function of the ability of managers to earn the rents. This ability is a type of FSA. It is "tied to [managers'] familiarity with the ambient language, culture, polity and traditions" (p. 92, this volume). This is to say that a home country CSA is internalized into an FSA. Thus another testable hypothesis emerges. Are foreign takeovers in various Canadian sectors (FSAs) consistent with this CSA "similarity"? If so, we should find acquirers based in non-English-speaking countries (such as home country-based Japanese firms) more concentrated in the resource field and less in the service field. To test this hypothesis we shall use our data on the interactive nature of CSAs and FSAs, and in particular our tests across the triad by major industry groups.

The relevance to this study of internalization theory and the FSA/CSA approach is their usefulness for explaining the controversy over foreign owner-ship of the Canadian economy. Economic nationalists such as Watkins (1978) argue that Canada is still an economic colony of the United States, since the perceived high degree of foreign ownership restricts Canada's political sovereignty and leads to an inefficient branch-plant economy. This view fails to recognize the decline in American ownership and control in Canada and the considerable evidence that Canadian-owned multinationals are now com-petitive internationally (Rugman and McIlveen, 1985). The Canadian econo-my, in general, has become more globalized and more highly integrated with that of the United States, in particular (see Crookell, 1990).

Many Canadians still believe that a high degree of economic integration has to be traded in exchange for a low degree of sovereignty. However, Canada can be economically efficient because of a high degree of globalization and inte-gration, and also independent, with political institutions exercising a high degree of sovereignty. For evidence, see D'Cruz and Fleck (1985) and Rugman and D'Cruz (1990).

PORTER'S MODEL OF INTERNATIONAL COMPETITIVENESS

MICHAEL PORTER'S BOOK, *The Competitive Advantage of Nations*, poses a "non-traditional" theory of FDI. Basically, Porter views outward FDI as a source of competitive advantage and widespread, non-passive, inward FDI as usually "not entirely healthy" (p. 671), since foreign subsidiaries are importers and thus a source of competitive disadvantage (p. 18). This theory is in stark contrast to Reich (1990), who recognizes that inward FDI is a source of nation-al competitive advantage for a host nation (such as the United States).

The Porter (1990) model is based on four endogenous determinants and two exogenous variables: chance and government. The four determinants and two outside forces interact in the diamond of competitive advantage, with the nature of a country's international competitiveness depending upon the type and quality of these interactions. The four determinants for a nation "shape the environment in which local firms compete and promote or impede the creation of competitive conditions" (p. 71). The four determinants of the diamond are:

1. Factor conditions - the nation's factors of production, including natural resources and created factors, such as infrastructure and skilled labour.

2. Demand conditions - the nature of home demand for products or services.
3. Related and supporting industries - the presence or absence of supplier and related industries that, themselves, are internationally competitive.
4. Firm strategy, structure and rivalry - the domestic rivalry of firms and the conditions governing how companies are created, organized and managed.

None of these determinants is new or unexpected, and all of them have already been discussed extensively in studies of international competitiveness in Canada. In particular, a rich tradition of work in Canada using industrial organization theory has attempted to model these determinants. Indeed, the nature of the tariff and industrial concentration in Canada has led to the development of such theories as the Eastman and Stykolt (1967) conditions for pricing and performance of foreign-owned and domestic manufacturing companies in Canada, under conditions of domestic tariffs and high concentration ratios. Further, studies of the nature of inter-firm competition in Canada probably better reflect the reality of foreign ownership than do those of most other economies, especially those of the United States (see Daly, 1989; Rugman, 1990; and Fuss and Waverman, 1991).

The two outside forces, chance and government, present interesting contrasts. Government is clearly of critical importance as an influence on a home nation's competitive advantage. For example, it can use tariffs as a direct entry barrier, penalizing foreign firms, or it can use subsidies as an indirect vehicle to penalize foreign-based firms; in both cases "domestic" firms benefit in terms of short-run competitive advantages. However, Rugman and Verbeke (1990) develop models in which these types of discriminatory government actions can lead to "shelter" for domestic firms, where shelter is defined to prevent the development of sustainable (long-run) competitive advantages. In contrast, little work has been done on "chance". What has been done is probably confined to those economists who inject "shocks", such as the OPEC oil crises, into a model system to forecast aggregative responses. Porter, himself, uses the term to refer to events such as wars.

To the extent that Porter brings together the firm-specific linkages between the four determinants and the two outside forces, his model is useful and potentially predictive. Also to be welcomed are Porter's policy recommendations to restrict the nature of government industrial and strategic trade policy, and instead to open markets and apply no arbitrary restrictions on foreign investment.

To make the model operational, Porter constructs 16 industry clusters and tests the model across eight countries. These countries include: West Germany, Italy, Japan, South Korea, Sweden, Switzerland, the United Kingdom, and the United States. In addition, Denmark and Singapore are listed, (p. 282) but are not discussed in the book. The 16 industry clusters include four "upstream" clusters, six clusters for industries and supporting sectors, and six clusters for final consumption of goods and services. The four "upstream"

clusters consist of materials and metals, forest products, petroleum and chemicals, and semiconductors and computers. The six "industry and supporting" sector clusters include multiple business, transportation, power generation and distribution, office, telecommunications, and defense. The six industry clusters for
"final consumption expenditure" include food and beverages, textiles and apparel, housing and household, health care, personal, and entertainment and leisure.

Finally, Porter describes four stages of "national competitive development": factor driven, investment driven, innovation driven, and wealth driven
(p. 546). The last stage is associated with a decline in international competitiveness. At several points in the book Porter states that Canada is stagnating
in Stage 1, because of its reliance on resource industries (p. 548).

PORTER'S VIEWS ON FOREIGN DIRECT INVESTMENT (FDI)

WE CONSIDER THAT PORTER'S ANALYSIS contains a flawed understanding
of the nature of two-way FDI. In the Canadian context, foreign capital
and technology have added enormously to Canada's assets. Fully 70 percent of
Canadian trade is done by 50 multinationals, and half of these are foreign-
owned (see Rugman, 1990). The methodology used by Porter permits only an
examination of the exports and outward FDI of Canada's "home" industries.
Yet there is as much inward FDI as outward, and the imports of the foreign-
owned subsidiaries are matched by their exports. Indeed, Canada runs a slight
surplus on the intra-firm trade of the sum of American firms in Canada plus
Canadian-owned firms in the United States (see Rugman, 1990). This finding
demonstrates that foreign-owned firms play as significant a role as do the
domestically owned Canadian corporations.

Foreign firms in Canada are not simply micro-replicas of their parents
and do not exist only because of unnatural entry barriers such as the tariff.
Porter states that "judgement" is used in examining the competitive performance and "managerial autonomy" of foreign-owned subsidiaries, yet he does
not specify how this is done; he then indicates that this judgement does not
apply to "production subsidiaries of foreign companies" (p. 25). This concept
then rules out the broader nature of the foreign-owned subsidiaries' contributions to the development of Canada's manufacturing base.

The main point of our criticism of Porter's methodology is that a clear
recognition of the need to model multinational activity correctly in a
Canadian context is necessary if policy prescriptions and activities are to be
properly defined and undertaken. This requires a deep and consistent understanding of the transaction cost theory of the multinational enterprise, cou-
pled with a rich empirical and practical understanding of the actual performance of multinationals in Canada.

In an attempt to incorporate the vital role of multinational activity and
overcome some of the flaws in Porter's framework, Dunning (1990) has adapted some of Porter's model. Dunning adds multinational activity as a third

exogenous variable to Porter's two exogenous variables of chance and government. This addition is an ingenious idea, but itself raises problems, especially in a Canadian context. Multinationals operate so widely in Canada that it is difficult to believe that the role of these firms has been designated as merely equal to that of chance. On the other hand, the role of government in Canada is not inconsequential.

If one were to accept Dunning's basic premise, namely that multinationality is missing from Porter, where else could this factor appear? Perhaps the most logical place is in the determinant called "firm strategies, structure and rivalry". To some extent Porter is already trying to include multinationality here, especially in his attempts to deal with "global" industries. Yet his diamond is also supposed to explain "multidomestic" industries. However, it does not make sense that the same rivalry determinant should include multinationality for global industries yet exclude it for multidomestic industries. This inconsistency may explain why Dunning wants multinationality to be laid across the four determinants in the diamond in a broad and even manner, like chance and government.

Dunning (1990) may be quite correct in his insight that:

> "... there is ample evidence to suggest that MNEs are influenced in their competitiveness by the configuration of the diamond in other than their home countries, and that this, in turn, may impinge upon the competitiveness of home countries." (p. 11)

Dunning cites the example of Nestlé making 95 percent of its sales outside Switzerland; the result is that the Swiss diamond of competitive advantage is less relevant than that of foreign countries in shaping the contribution of Nestlé to the home economy. If that is true for Switzerland, it is just as applicable in a Canadian context. Virtually all of Canada's large multinational firms rely on sales in the United States and other triad markets (see Rugman and McIlveen, 1985). Indeed, it could be argued that the U.S. diamond is likely to be more relevant for Canada's multinationals then is Canada's own diamond since, on average, over 70 percent of U.S. sales take place in Canada. The Canada-U.S. Free Trade Agreement reinforces this point. However, it rather devalues the approach of Porter's book when Canada's diamond is found not to be relevant.

Reich (1990) argues, in effect, that the host country diamond is a vital aspect of FDI. In a recent study Rugman and D'Cruz (1991) develop a model in which they demonstrated a "North American diamond" that is relevant for explaining Canada's international competitiveness.

We can examine several of Porter's hypotheses by examining FDI by region, aggregated into several of his industry clusters. In Porter's terms, inward FDI, associated with the resource sector, for example, is factor driven and increases dependence on natural resources (which, in Porter's terms, is inferior to upstream manufacturing). The data show that inward FDI in the resource sector is small. While most of this FDI was U.S.-based, it mainly represented acquisitions, not new ventures, (based on the number of transactions). Acquisitions do not necessarily increase "dependence", as they are asset transfers. While U.S. firms were the major source of inward FDI in resources, a surprisingly large amount came from the European Community. Japanese new business ventures were an important part of the larger transactions (i.e., valued above $5 million). Furthermore, as we see below, over 50 percent of the acquisitions and close to 70 percent of new greenfield ventures were in the service sector. There was a higher proportion of Japanese investment in the service sector than there was of investments for other acquirers. Does this mean that there is a Japanese "home country diamond" comparative advantage in services? We find that it does not, since the firms acquired were predominately smaller wholesale trade establishments. Thus, the pattern of inward FDI is complex and dependent on a number of factors, including the home country comparative advantage and many other influences. The acquisition patterns for each block of the triad are quite similar, pointing to the importance of Canada's diamond, not the home country diamond, in determining inward FDI in the Canadian case.

EMPIRICAL EVIDENCE ON ACQUISITIONS

WE BEGIN WITH AN OVERVIEW of Figures 1 and 2 which together report the data supplied by Investment Canada on all the foreign acquisitions of Canadian companies from 1974 to 1990. The data do not distinguish between direct and indirect acquisitions and are determined by case, not by value. Two caveats are important. First, any analysis of cases over this time period ignores the other factors which could affect acquisitions: macro economic factors generally and specific factors such as the National Energy Program of 1980. Second, we cannot account for acquisitions which were not brought forward because of the regulatory climate; the data contain only those transactions brought to the attention of the Canadian authority.

The total population of 6490 cases is reported. In both figures the data are arranged across three "sectors": resources, manufacturing and services. (Services being a simple aggregation of the three service categories of finance, real estate and other services recorded by the agency.) See Appendix A, which provides the aggregation of two-digit industries (1980 SIC Code) into these three categories. The data are also arranged according to the "triad", that is, investments from the United States, the EC, and Japan, as well as for "Other Europe" and "Other Countries". The data do not reflect the changes in the annual membership of the EC, as a result of the limited number of cases when Greece, and Spain and Portugal joined in 1981 and 1986 respectively. Figure 1 reports data for the 1974 - 1985 period, when FIRA existed. Figure 2 reports data from 1985 - 1990; the break point in the data is June 1985, when FIRA was abolished and replaced by Investment Canada.

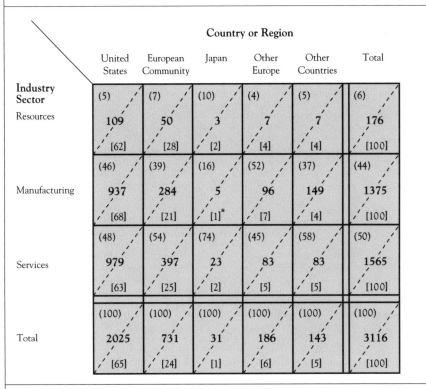

FIGURE 1

SUMMARY OF "ACQUISITIONS" SUBJECT TO THE FOREIGN INVESTMENT REVIEW ACT
(RESOLVED 1974 TO 1985, 1ST QUARTER)

Country or Region

Industry Sector	United States	European Community	Japan	Other Europe	Other Countries	Total
Resources	(5) 109 [62]	(7) 50 [28]	(10) 3 [2]	(4) 7 [4]	(5) 7 [4]	(6) 176 [100]
Manufacturing	(46) 937 [68]	(39) 284 [21]	(16) 5 [1]*	(52) 96 [7]	(37) 149 [4]	(44) 1375 [100]
Services	(48) 979 [63]	(54) 397 [25]	(74) 23 [2]	(45) 83 [5]	(58) 83 [5]	(50) 1565 [100]
Total	(100) 2025 [65]	(100) 731 [24]	(100) 31 [1]	(100) 186 [6]	(100) 143 [5]	(100) 3116 [100]

SOURCE: Investment Canada, 1990
*Less than 0.5 percent
( ) = Percent of Country, rounded to nearest one.
[ ] = Percent of Sector, rounded to nearest one.

A number of interesting general observations can be drawn from the data.

First, the total number of cases handled by the two agencies is nearly the same: 3116 over the eleven-year period of FIRA and 3374 over the six-year period of Investment Canada. This finding indicates that the number of cases for review by Investment Canada has doubled compared with the annual average during the period when FIRA was responsible for the reviews.

Second, the cases by sector are very similar under the two regimes: most acquisitions are in services, followed closely by manufacturing, and resources trail well behind. There is no evidence in these data, by number of cases, that Investment Canada has failed to control takeovers in manufacturing; there were proportionately more manufacturing acquisitions under FIRA than under Investment Canada (44 percent and 38 percent, respectively).

FIGURE 2

SUMMARY OF "ACQUISITIONS" SUBJECT TO THE INVESTMENT CANADA ACT
(RESOLVED JUNE 30, 1985 TO JUNE 30, 1990)

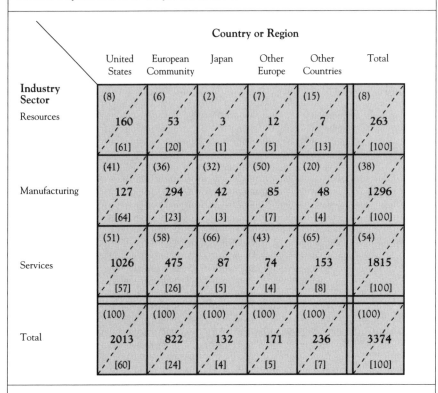

Industry Sector	Country or Region					
	United States	European Community	Japan	Other Europe	Other Countries	Total
Resources (8)	160	(6) 53	(2) 3	(7) 12	(15) 7	(8) 263
	[61]	[20]	[1]	[5]	[13]	[100]
Manufacturing (41)	127	(36) 294	(32) 42	(50) 85	(20) 48	(38) 1296
	[64]	[23]	[3]	[7]	[4]	[100]
Services (51)	1026	(58) 475	(66) 87	(43) 74	(65) 153	(54) 1815
	[57]	[26]	[5]	[4]	[8]	[100]
Total (100)	2013	(100) 822	(100) 132	(100) 171	(100) 236	(100) 3374
	[60]	[24]	[4]	[5]	[7]	[100]

SOURCE: Investment Canada, 1990
( ) Percent of Country, rounded to nearest one.
[ ] Percent of Sector, rounded to nearest one.

Third, there are over four times as many Japanese acquisitions under Investment Canada as there were under FIRA, but these still amount to a very small total compared to the two other triad powers (four percent of all acquisitions between June 30, 1985 and June 30, 1990).

A number of specific observations can be made in Figures 1 and 2. For example, while the Japanese share of all manufacturing acquisitions has increased from less than one percent to approximately three percent, in real terms it has increased from five cases to 42 cases: a 740 percent increase. Japanese FDI shows much larger gains than the American or European Community investment between the FIRA and the Investment Canada periods. This could result from the late-coming nature of Japan's foreign investment as compared to that of the United States and the EC, particularly with respect to

the United Kingdom, which easily represents the largest part of the EC's investment in the earlier period. The relative lack of Japanese acquisitions in
resources is also apparent, although this does not hold for larger new businesses.

The United States shows a gain in resource takeovers of 47 percent (160
as compared to 109), with a decrease of 12 percent in manufacturing and only
a marginal gain of five percent in services. Resource acquisitions represent a
smaller share of all acquisitions made during the Investment Canada period as
compared to the FIRA period. Even though the number of such acquisitions
was virtually the same (50 and 53), the EC's overall acquisitions increased at a
greater rate. Using June 1985 as the break point, EC and Japanese acquisition
interest in the Canadian resource sector has decreased, as indicated by the
number of cases, while the interest of the United States and especially of
"Others" (chiefly Hong Kong after 1985) has increased.

The relative decline of American investment acquisitions in manufacturing is also quite large in real terms (given that the period is only half as
long). The drop from 937 cases to 827 cases, represented a decrease of 110
cases, or nearly as many acquisitions as both Japan and the "Other" category
made during the Investment Canada period. The manufacturing share of total
American investment declined from 46 percent to 41 percent; the EC share of
its investment in manufacturing declined from 39 percent to 36 percent; and
"Other" countries' share of manufacturing investment declined from 37 percent to 20 percent of their total direct investment in Canada. The results
seem to indicate that the acquisition component of foreign direct investment
in Canada with respect to services is changing, but that there is some renewed
interest in resources, principally on the part of the United States. There is also
an increase in Japan's manufacturing interest: Japan has increased its share in
that sector from 16 percent to 32 percent.

Do Acquisition Patterns Differ Across the Triad?

A cursory examination of the patterns of acquisitions in each of the two time
periods shows similar patterns between the United States and the EC (and
"Other Europe"); by contrast, Japanese (and "Other Countries") acquisition
patterns are quite different. (The patterns of acquisition were examined on the
basis of the percentages of acquisitions in each of the three product categories
in each of the two time periods.) For example, from 1974 to 1985, 54 percent
of EC firms' acquisitions were in the service sector compared to 48 percent for
American firms and 74 percent for Japanese; 39 percent of EC acquisitions
were in manufacturing as compared to 46 percent for the United States and 16
percent for Japan; seven percent of EC acquisitions were in the resource sector
as compared to five percent for U.S. firms. Between 1985 and 1990, service
sector acquisitions by American and EC firms were 51 percent and 58 percent
respectively (66 percent for Japan); 41 percent and 36 percent respectively in
manufacturing (32 percent for Japan); and eight percent and six percent

respectively in resources (two percent for Japan). The Japanese acquisitions are proportionately greater in the service sector than are acquisitions by the United States and the EC, but the difference is smaller in the post-1985 period than in the earlier period.

Standard statistical analyses (based on Chi-square tests) show significant differences in the patterns of acquisition in these three broad product/service categories from 1974 to 1985 for: United States/Japan; EC/Japan; United States/EC; and EC/"Other Europe". It should be noted that these Chi-square tests are of limited value where the number of acquisitions is small. This applies particularly to Japan. From 1985 to 1990, except for United States/"Other Countries" and EC/Japan, all patterns of acquisition differ significantly.

These statistical tests, however, can be misleading. Clearly, the pattern of Japanese acquisitions differs from that of the United States and the EC. However, the patterns of acquisitions for the United States and the EC are so similar that it is difficult to imagine that some general theory could explain the greater inclination of EC firms at the margin than of American firms to invest in the Canadian service sector.

The entire difference between Japanese and EC/American acquisition patterns from 1974 to 1985 is explained by the far higher proportion of Japanese acquisitions in wholesale/retail trade: 58.1 percent of all acquisitions as compared to 25.3 percent for the United States and 27.5 percent for the EC. These data are not reported here. This Japanese acquisition pattern likely reflects the purchase of sales outlets to service Japanese exports to Canada. From 1985 to 1990, Japanese service-sector acquisitions in wholesale and retail trade were nearly identical to those of the United States and the EC (25.0 percent, 23.3 percent and 25.8 percent respectively). The greater proportion of Japanese acquisitions in the service sector in this later period reflects a far greater Japanese emphasis on real estate operations and "Other Services". Therefore, acquisition patterns in the triad are quite similar especially in view of the special nature of Japanese acquisitions in the wholesale trade sector in the early period and Japanese acquisitions in real estate in the later period.

The theories pertaining to foreign direct investment (FDI) of multinational enterprises (MNEs), particularly those of Porter (1990), would suggest substantial differences in acquisition patterns. Porter's model is embedded in an idiosyncratic mix of firm-specific advantages (FSAs) and country-specific advantages (CSAs) that depend on historical evolution. The home country diamonds in Porter (1990) are unique and so different from each other that the outward FDI resulting from these "diamonds" would also be unique. Examining FDI into Canada, we are impressed by its similarity across the country sources. This suggests that the Canadian diamond (or opportunities for investment in Canada) is an important determinant of inward FDI.

In addition, a Porter-type story that relied on the home country diamond of comparative advantage would argue that EC and Japanese firms had CSAs/FSAs superior to those of the United States in the service sector. (They invest more in Canada in this sector.) But the "cultural affinity" hypothesis of the Baldwin and Caves (1990) model suggests that American firms would have advantages over EC and Japanese firms. Even after netting out acquisitions in the trade sector, EC and Japanese firms acquire more Canadian firms in the service sector than do American firms. An explanation of these differences might rely more on relative latecomer arguments than on an emphasis on home country diamonds. A Porter-type story would also have to explain why "Other Europe" firms acquire relatively more in the manufacturing sector and less in the service sector than do their EC competitors. The fact that Japanese (and "Other Countries") acquisitions are proportionately far greater in the service sector than American or EC acquisitions casts some doubt on internalization theory, as the Japanese are unlikely to have had familiarity with Canadian language, culture or ways of doing business during this period.

Appendix B is a table of Chi-square statistics for the hypothesis that the pattern of investment (the percentage number of cases in each of resources, manufacturing, services) is the same for the FIRA and Investment Canada periods. (The earlier discussion examined differences between country groups, not differences over time for a region or group.) The first column provides the Chi-square values for the data on all acquisitions. These statistics show that the pattern of acquisitions was significantly different in the two periods for U.S., Japanese and "Other Countries" acquisitions, but statistically the same pattern existed for European (EC and "Other Europe") transactions. The reader will observe different patterns for larger acquisitions and new businesses. These differences are important, and we comment on these later.

Acquisitions Over $5 Million

Figures 3 and 4 repeat Figures 1 and 2 but now only for the subset of acquisitions over $5 million in value. The percentages of acquisitions by sector differ from those shown for all acquisitions in Figures 1 and 2. The United States accounts for a somewhat lower share of larger acquisitions (58 percent to 62 percent) than for all acquisitions (60 percent to 65 percent). Relative to all acquisitions, the larger U.S. and EC acquisitions are proportionately more in manufacturing and less in services in both periods. In Japanese acquisitions, larger purchases are proportionately more common in manufacturing than were all acquisitions, especially in the FIRA period. In this earlier period, all the larger Japanese service sector acquisitions were in the wholesale and retail trade subsector. A substantial shift is also apparent in manufacturing when the larger transactions for "Other Europe" are examined.

For the later Investment Canada period, we see a similar pattern for the United States, EC and "Other Europe" groups, larger acquisitions are more concentrated in manufacturing than in Figure 2 for total acquisitions.

After 1985 we can see a substantial shift in Japanese acquisitions valued at more than $5 million, from resources to manufacturing. One hypothesis to

FIGURE 3

SUMMARY OF "ACQUISITIONS" GREATER THAN $5 MILLION SUBJECT TO THE FOREIGN INVESTMENT REVIEW ACT (RESOLVED 1974 TO 1985, 1ST QUARTER)

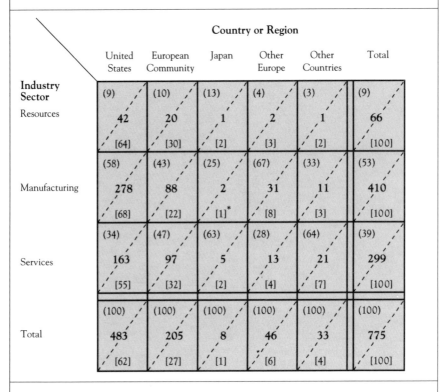

Industry Sector	United States	European Community	Japan	Other Europe	Other Countries	Total
Resources	(9)	(10)	(13)	(4)	(3)	(9)
	42	20	1	2	1	66
	[64]	[30]	[2]	[3]	[2]	[100]
Manufacturing	(58)	(43)	(25)	(67)	(33)	(53)
	278	88	2	31	11	410
	[68]	[22]	[1]*	[8]	[3]	[100]
Services	(34)	(47)	(63)	(28)	(64)	(39)
	163	97	5	13	21	299
	[55]	[32]	[2]	[4]	[7]	[100]
Total	(100)	(100)	(100)	(100)	(100)	(100)
	483	205	8	46	33	775
	[62]	[27]	[1]	[6]	[4]	[100]

SOURCE: Investment Canada, 1990
( ) Percent of Country, rounded to nearest one.
[ ] Percent of Sector, rounded to nearest one.
* = Less than 0.5 percent

explain this change is similar to the one presented earlier: the late entry of Japanese FDI into manufacturing, since Japan relied mainly on exporting in the 1970s, switching to FDI when trade barriers increased. EC acquisitions also shifted to manufacturing from services after June 1985. "Other Countries" larger acquisitions, however, shifted to resources in the later period, perhaps to provide inputs for manufacturing operations undertaken (set up) by the most recent entrants to world trade.

Tests of the significance of hypothetical acquisition patterns for the five groups forming the category with acquisitions valued at over $5 million suggest that U.S./Japan, U.S./EC, U.S./"Other Countries", EC/Japan, EC/"Other Countries" patterns are the same in the early period. Results of these tests could be misleading, however, due to the small number of observations for Japan and

FIGURE 4

SUMMARY OF "ACQUISITIONS" GREATER THAN $5 MILLION SUBJECT TO THE
INVESTMENT CANADA ACT (RESOLVED JUNE 30, 1985 TO JUNE 30, 1990)

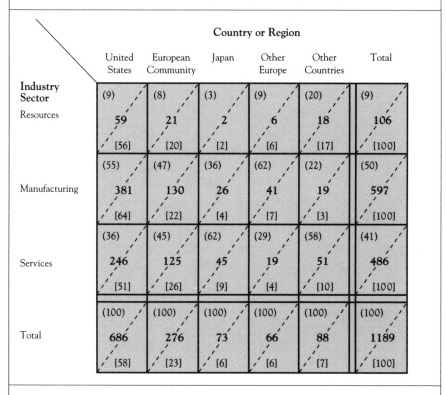

Industry Sector	Country or Region					
	United States	European Community	Japan	Other Europe	Other Countries	Total
Resources	(9) 59 [56]	(8) 21 [20]	(3) 2 [2]	(9) 6 [6]	(20) 18 [17]	(9) 106 [100]
Manufacturing	(55) 381 [64]	(47) 130 [22]	(36) 26 [4]	(62) 41 [7]	(22) 19 [3]	(50) 597 [100]
Services	(36) 246 [51]	(45) 125 [26]	(62) 45 [9]	(29) 19 [4]	(58) 51 [10]	(41) 486 [100]
Total	(100) 686 [58]	(100) 276 [23]	(100) 73 [6]	(100) 66 [6]	(100) 88 [7]	(100) 1189 [100]

SOURCE: Investment Canada, 1990
( ) Percent of Country, rounded to nearest one.
[ ] Percent of Sector, rounded to nearest one.

"Other Countries". Between 1985 and 1990 only the US/"Other Countries" acquisition patterns are significantly similar. When we examined all acquisitions, we argued that the patterns of acquisitions (although statistically different) were surprisingly similar, at least from the point of view that acquirer's FSAs/CSAs and "diamonds" should be dissimilar. Acquisitions valued at more than $5 million show that the EC and the United States do differ at the margin (and more than for all acquisitions), because of the relative emphasis on service acquisitions by the European Community.

In Appendix B, where we examine the hypothesis that acquisition patterns were the same over the entire period, it appears that there were no significant differences in large acquisition patterns before and after June 30, 1985 for U.S. and European (EC and "Other Europe") acquisitions. However, when all acquisitions were examined, only European purchases were the same. This result suggests that any change in acquisition patterns after Investment Canada took over from FIRA involved mainly smaller acquisitions by American firms. This pattern is consistent with the hypothesis that FIRA had a more stringent review process than Investment Canada for smaller (below $5 million) acquisitions by American firms, at least in terms of the pattern of acquisitions among broad categories, principally in the resource sector. (We note that the statistically significant difference in patterns for Japan is likely the result of Japanese change in behaviour, not Investment Canada's actions, and that the significant difference in patterns for "Other Countries" simply reflects the heterogeneous nature of the sample.)

A "story" which could explain the result can itself be based on internalization theory and transaction cost analysis. Dealing with FIRA involved higher transaction costs than dealing with Investment Canada because of the increased time and resources needed to apply for investment approval. Such transaction costs would have deterred marginal acquisitions. The deterred acquisitions would probably be those of smaller American firms. The larger acquisitions could bear the transaction costs. In addition, smaller acquisitions by European firms would already involve higher negotiating and transaction costs without the Canadian FDI regulation (because of distance, dissimilarity of culture, limited knowledge) and could bear the incremental transaction costs of FIRA. Other data contained in the tables, however, are not consistent with this story. For the five-year period after June 30, 1985, the rate of increase of acquisitions was greatest for Japan, "Other Countries", the EC and the United States, in that order. Thus if FIRA held back acquisitions at the margin in the United States, post-FIRA, there should have been an increase at the margin for smaller American acquisitions. That is evident in the resource sector only, not over all.

Evidence on New Business Investments

All New Business Transactions

Figure 5 presents a summary of all new business investments subject to FIRA from 1976 to the first quarter of 1985. (These data are only a subset of new businesses and our comparisons between acquisitions and new businesses is subject to this issue.) The United States is the predominant investor over this period, accounting for 1688 of 3048 investments; a 55 percent share of all new investments. The EC is next, with 28 percent of new business investments, while "Other Countries" and "Other Europe" follow with eight percent and six percent of new business investments respectively. Japan is a very minor player with only three percent of all new business investments during the FIRA period. In terms of the areas of investment by industry sector, the service sector is by far the largest area of investment, accounting for 1973 new business investments out of 3048, or 65 percent. The manufacturing sector accounts for less than half the number of service-sector new business investments and only 30 percent of total new business investments. Resources are a distinct third making up only five percent of all new business investments during the FIRA period.

Figure 6 summarizes all new business investments during the Investment Canada period. Once again, the United States is the predominant investing country, accounting for 58 percent of all new foreign businesses started over the period. The pattern of new businesses shows a distinct shift from manufacturing into services as compared to the FIRA period, when the number of total manufacturing investments declined from 929 to 260 (remember the difference in length of period), and by share from 30 percent to only 18 percent. Services rose by share from 65 percent to 86 percent of all new foreign business investments. These data differ from those shown in Figures 1 and 2, where total acquisitions between the FIRA and Investment Canada periods do not show as significant a change in pattern.

This change from manufacturing to service new business investments is predominantly due to two shifts in investment patterns. First, the United States has experienced a major decline in the number of new businesses established in manufacturing, falling from 517 investments over the FIRA period to 140 during the Investment Canada period. As a share of total U.S. new business start-ups in Canada by industry sector, manufacturing's share has fallen from 31 percent to 16 percent. While new service investments made by the United States also fell (from 1101 to 682), they increased from 65 percent of all new American business investments to a substantial 80 percent. Second, EC new business investments have fallen from 844 during the FIRA period to 298 during the Investment Canada period, decreasing the EC's area share from 28 percent to 20 percent of total new business investments in services. (That sector now accounts for 74 percent of all new business start-ups in Canada by the EC during the Investment Canada period, as compared to 62 percent during FIRA's period.) New EC manufacturing business investment has subsequently declined from 32 percent to 23 percent of the total number of start-ups.

While the EC has shown a real absolute decline of approximately 25 percent in the number of cases, Japan has apparently maintained the same number of new business investments from the FIRA period to the Investment Canada period — from 96 cases to 94 cases or from three percent of all new businesses begun during the FIRA period to six percent of all new businesses established during the Investment Canada period. In fact, Japan has increased its share of the triad's share of investment in all of the industry sectors. Japanese new business investment shows a slight preference for manufacturing, though more observations are needed. Both "Other Europe" and "Other Countries" show an increase in new business investments in services with a corresponding decline in manufacturing.

Appendix B shows that except for Japan, there has been a significant shift in the pattern of new business investments for each area since Investment Canada replaced FIRA. Since FIRA did not exercise much control over new businesses, this shift is probably not linked to the shift in government.

FIGURE 5

SUMMARY OF ALL NEW BUSINESS SUBJECT TO THE FOREIGN INVESTMENT REVIEW ACT
(RESOLVED 1976 TO 1985, 1ST QUARTER)

	Country or Region					
Industry Sector	United States	European Community	Japan	Other Europe	Other Countries	Total
Resources	(4)	(6)	(6)	(5)	(3)	(5)
	70	54	6	9	7	146
	[48]	[37]	[4]	[6]	[5]	[100]
Manufacturing	(31)	(32)	(17)	(37)	(24)	(30)
	517	270	16	70	56	929
	[56]	[29]	[2]	[8]	[6]	[100]
Services	(65)	(62)	(77)	(58)	(73)	(65)
	1101	520	74	110	168	1973
	[56]	[26]	[4]	[6]	[9]	[100]
Total	(100)	(100)	(100)	(100)	(100)	(100)
	1688	844	96	189	231	3048
	[55]	[28]	[3]	[6]	[8]	[100]

SOURCE: Investment Canada, 1990
( ) Percent of Country, rounded to nearest one.
[ ] Percent of Sector, rounded to nearest one.

NEW BUSINESSES OVER $5 MILLION

FIGURES 7 AND 8 PRESENT a summary of new business investments over $5 million during the FIRA and Investment Canada periods. These Figures emphasize the move toward investments in the service sector. Whereas manufacturing had a 43 percent share in the FIRA period with services accounting for 34 percent, this is reversed for the Investment Canada period with services now accounting for the larger share of 56 percent, and the manufacturing investments' share having declined to 32 percent, approximately the level where services were during the FIRA period.

In terms of the share of new business investments by the triad areas between the two periods, there is a definite reversal between the EC and the United States.

FIGURE 6

SUMMARY OF ALL NEW BUSINESS SUBJECT TO THE INVESTMENT CANADA ACT
(RESOLVED JUNE 30, 1985 TO JUNE 30, 1990)

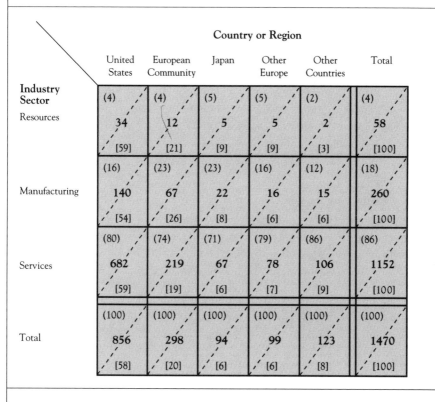

| Industry Sector | Country or Region | | | | | |
---	United States	European Community	Japan	Other Europe	Other Countries	Total
Resources	(4) 34 [59]	(4) 12 [21]	(5) 5 [9]	(5) 5 [9]	(2) 2 [3]	(4) 58 [100]
Manufacturing	(16) 140 [54]	(23) 67 [26]	(23) 22 [8]	(16) 16 [6]	(12) 15 [6]	(18) 260 [100]
Services	(80) 682 [59]	(74) 219 [19]	(71) 67 [6]	(79) 78 [7]	(86) 106 [9]	(86) 1152 [100]
Total	(100) 856 [58]	(100) 298 [20]	(100) 94 [6]	(100) 99 [6]	(100) 123 [8]	(100) 1470 [100]

SOURCE: Investment Canada, 1990
( ) Percent of Country, rounded to nearest one.
[ ] Percent of Sector, rounded to nearest one.

Figure 7 shows that the EC accounted for 42 percent of all larger new business investments during the FIRA period. Figure 8, however, shows that the EC's share of all new business start-ups over $5 million fell to only 23 percent, while the United States increased its share from 38 percent to 43 percent between the FIRA and the Investment Canada periods. The EC also had a major decrease in absolute terms in new business investments in manufacturing, falling from 30 cases to eight cases between the FIRA and Investment Canada periods. This decline, first in overall investment by the EC in Canada, and second in manufacturing, could be the result of a refocussed interest in the EC, as companies jockey for superior positions in that market before the full impact of 1992 takes effect.

While new business investments over $5 million by the United States in Canada, still show the trend toward the service sector, that trend is not as

FIGURE 7

SUMMARY OF NEW BUSINESS GREATER THAN $5 MILLION SUBJECT TO THE FOREIGN INVESTMENT REVIEW ACT (RESOLVED 1976 TO 1985, 1ST QUARTER)

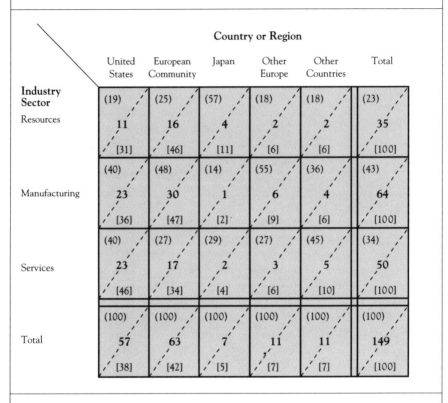

SOURCE: Investment Canada, 1990
( ) Percent of Country, rounded to nearest one.
[ ] Percent of Sector, rounded to nearest one.

marked as it was for all new business investments; it increased from 40 percent to 66 percent after June 30, 1985, as compared to 80 percent for all American new business investments as shown in Figure 6. American new business investment that occurred between the FIRA and Investment Canada period, particularly for smaller businesses, may simply be reflecting the overall move toward the service sector that occurred in the Canadian economy, including domestic investment. In new businesses over $5 million, the United States has definitely moved away from the resource sector during the Investment Canada period, falling from a 19 percent share of American new business investments to a four percent share.

Japanese interest in new investments in manufacturing is strong, showing an eightfold increase in the absolute number of investment cases.

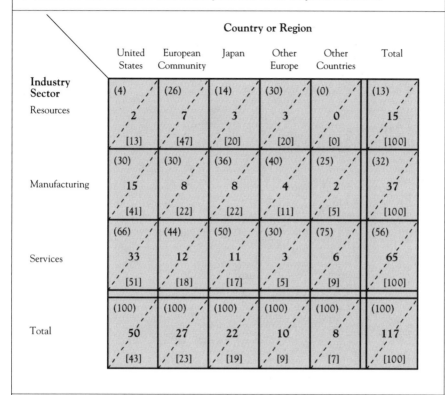

FIGURE 8

SUMMARY OF NEW BUSINESS GREATER THAN $5 MILLION SUBJECT TO THE
INVESTMENT CANADA ACT (RESOLVED JUNE 30, 1985 TO JUNE 30, 1990)

| Industry Sector | Country or Region | | | | | |
	United States	European Community	Japan	Other Europe	Other Countries	Total
Resources	(4)	(26)	(14)	(30)	(0)	(13)
	2	7	3	3	0	15
	[13]	[47]	[20]	[20]	[0]	[100]
Manufacturing	(30)	(30)	(36)	(40)	(25)	(32)
	15	8	8	4	2	37
	[41]	[22]	[22]	[11]	[5]	[100]
Services	(66)	(44)	(50)	(30)	(75)	(56)
	33	12	11	3	6	65
	[51]	[18]	[17]	[5]	[9]	[100]
Total	(100)	(100)	(100)	(100)	(100)	(100)
	50	27	22	10	8	117
	[43]	[23]	[19]	[9]	[7]	[100]

SOURCE: Investment Canada, 1990.
( ) Percent of Country, rounded to nearest one.
[ ] Percent of Sector, rounded to nearest one.

Similarly, as a share, Japanese new business investment in manufacturing has
grown from 14 percent to 36 percent. New Japanese business investments in
services have also increased from 29 percent of the Japanese total during the
FIRA period to 50 percent during the Investment Canada period. Again, some
caution may be necessary in interpreting the significance of Japanese investment patterns because of the small number of observations relative to the
United States and the EC.

Several other interesting points emerge in Figures 7 and 8. First, there is
a great decrease in the number of cases as compared with Figures 5 and 6. For
example, 99 "Other Europe" new businesses were started between 1985 and
1990, but only 10 of these were over $5 million in value. In the earlier period,
only 50 of a total of 1688 American new businesses were over $5 million in

value. Only 50 of the 856 American new businesses established in the later period were over $5 million in value. Second, as expected, new businesses over $5 million do not reach the same proportion in the service sector as do all new businesses, and the disparity draws attention to the small size of the new businesses in the service sector. Third, there is still a definite shift to the service sector after June 1985 for investments over $5 million. This trend is similarly pronounced over the triad. Significance tests on patterns among the five groups over the period from 1985 to 1990 show significant differences for all comparisons but EC/"Other Countries".

A Comparison of Acquisitions and New Business Investments

WE CAN COMPARE THE PATTERNS for new businesses with acquisitions for the FIRA period (Figures 1 and 5). In this period, the United States had a significantly smaller share of greenfield investments (55 percent) than acquisitions (65 percent). For all groups except Japan, the number of new businesses was proportionately greater in the service sector than were mergers and acquisitions. In the 1974 - 85 period, Japanese new businesses and mergers and acquisitions had nearly identical distributions over the three sectors. This relative emphasis on the service sector for new business investments reflects the lower cost of greenfield investments in the service sector than in manufacturing, as the former may not require a large plant. These data contain small wholesaling offices set up to service imports. Canadian regulations also affect the pattern. For example, American banks do not have retail branches in Canada, and this lack makes greenfield investments smaller. If we disaggregate new business investments in the service sector, we find the same pattern that applies to acquisitions. In the 1976 - 85 period, the entire difference between Japan, on the one hand, and the United States/EC on the other, in proportion to all new businesses in the service sector, lies in the far greater Japanese emphasis on the wholesale and retail trade sector. Yet, since 1985, Japanese new business investments in the trade sector represent a far lower proportion than do comparable investments of the United States and the EC.

In the 1985 - 90 period, the proportion of new businesses in the service sector was greater than that in mergers and acquisitions for all five area groups (see Figures 2 and 6). Comparing the two periods, we see a substantial shift in new businesses to the service sector in the later period for all areas but Japan. By contrast, since 1985 Japan, as noted, has shifted new business investments to the manufacturing sector.

A comparison of new businesses over $5 million (Figures 7 and 8) with mergers and acquisitions over $5 million (Figures 3 and 4) shows the following patterns (although generalizations are subject to small numbers problems). There are significant differences between the patterns for large acquisitions and those for large new business establishments. From 1976 to 1985, for all areas, the larger new businesses are proportionately greater in the resource sector than are acquisitions. For the United States and "Other Europe", this emphasis on the resource sector is primarily at the expense of manufacturing; for the EC and Japan (and "Other Countries"), this emphasis is at the expense of the service sector. From 1985 to 1990, larger American new businesses are proportionately far greater in services than are larger American acquisitions. This feature is unique to the United States. Larger new businesses in the EC and "Other Europe" occur more in the resource sector and less in manufacturing than their larger acquisitions. For Japan, larger new businesses as compared to larger acquisitions are more common in resources and less common in services.

Given these differences between mergers and acquisitions on one hand and new businesses on the other, and the differences between the larger (over $5 million) transactions and "all" transactions, it is clear that much more than the diamond of home country advantages is determining FDI.

SUMMARY OF EMPIRICAL WORK

IN EXAMINING ALL **6,490** FOREIGN ACQUISITIONS made in Canada between 1974 and 1985 and between 1985 and 1990, we observed that Japan, the EC and the United States had somewhat different acquisition patterns. Japan's emphasis on service-sector acquisitions is likely explained by the need to service burgeoning exports. In general, in the period from 1985 to 1990, American firms acquired relatively more Canadian manufacturing firms, EC firms acquired relatively more firms in services, while Japanese firms acquired many more service companies. The differences, in the 1985 - 90 period, between purchases by the triad are less than they were in the FIRA period, when the United States was the source of 60 percent of the acquisitions, and the EC was the source of 24 percent. The percentage share of total acquisitions by country bloc remained constant over the period, except for the expansion of Japanese acquisitions (but to only three percent of the total). This stability is surprising. Over the entire period, American acquisitions, and then EC acquisitions, shifted somewhat to services, the former somewhat at the expense of the resource sector. Japanese acquisitions shifted toward manufacturing. Larger acquisitions (over $5 million) show a somewhat different story: American, EC and Japanese acquisitions are proportionately greater in manufacturing and less in services. The Japanese shift to manufacturing accelerates over the period.

Examining the 4,518 new business investments provides some sharp contrasts with acquisitions. First, new business investments fall much more into the service category. Second, the United States was the source of 65 percent of all acquisitions but of only 55 percent of new business investments in the FIRA period. In the Investment Canada period, the United States was the source of 60 percent of all acquisitions and of 58 percent of all new foreign business startups. Third, most new businesses are small. New businesses of over $5 million represented just six percent of all new businesses; acquisitions over $5 million represented 31 percent of all foreign acquisitions. In the post-FIRA period, American and EC new business investments shifted to services; Japanese new business investments shifted to manufacturing (from a very high level of service concentration in the earlier period).

In terms of Porter's (1990) paradigm the following observations may be made. FDI in Canada by the United States, Japan and the EC has shifted away from the manufacturing sector, mainly towards the services sectors. This may be bad news, in Porter's terms, for three reasons.

First, the continued presence of FDI in manufacturing signals that the Canadian manufacturing sector has relied on inward FDI, which Porter says is a sign of competitive disadvantage. (However, FDI's relative shift to services might signal that Canadian manufacturing is becoming more competitive.)

Second, the slight shift to resource acquisitions (by the United States and "Other Countries") may, according to Porter, signal an increased dependency on a sector he considers of lesser value in establishing a nation's competitiveness. Given the relatively low percentage of FDI in the resource sector, however, the implication is taken too far. Resource companies made up seven percent of all acquisitions, nine percent of larger acquisitions and five percent of new business investments. Acquisitions are asset shifts to foreign owners (though some will be from existing foreign owners) and do not signal increased dependency. The tables show that FDI is not a major source of resource sector investment, as indicated by the number of cases. (This cannot be said for value, as this element was not tested.)

Third, Porter's model suggests that reliance on services may be a sign of a decaying economy; that is, one at the wealth-driven stage. There is limited support for this view, in both acquisitions and in new businesses, as there is a tremendous amount of FDI by the triad in Canada's service sector. We think, however, that the shift to services is to be expected in a wealthy, advanced economy like Canada's, as it largely represents the purchase and installation of trade outlets and financial intermediaries, and is not a sign of decay.

Within the manufacturing sector, foreign acquisitions have been mainly in secondary manufacturing, as have new businesses (or greenfield investments). While this situation can signal to Porter the lack of world competitiveness of Canadian business, it can also be explained by the traditional internalization story of FDI. The paper by Baldwin and Caves in this volume demonstrates that productivity improvements are correlated with FDI activity. This finding is consistent with a Reich — rather than a Porter — -type view of FDI. One result, as noted, is the proportion of service investments made by the Japanese: those with the least "cultural affinity" for Canada. At first glance, this appears to be inconsistent with internalization, but it is based on few observations; it is not yet possible to draw a strong conclusion. The observation is, however, consistent with the theory about the late entry of the Japanese as exporters into Canadian markets, their purchase of wholesale and retail trade outlets in the earlier period, and their shift to local manufacturing in the later period.

CONCLUSIONS

IN THIS PAPER we have examined the nature and performance of inward FDI in Canada between 1974 and 1990. This period encompasses, first, the regulatory framework of the FIRA from 1974 to 1985 and, second, that of Investment Canada, from 1985 to 1990. We have constructed a simplified theoretical framework and tested it by empirical methods.

The theoretical framework consists of a model in which CSAs are related to FSAs. The CSAs are considered from the viewpoint of the "triad": the United States, the EC and Japan. The FSAs are considered for three types of sectors in Canada: resources, manufacturing and services. This theoretical framework allows the theory of internalization (i.e., the manner in which the proprietary nature of the FSAs interact with the CSAs) to be compared with the work of Michael Porter (1990), in which the home country diamond is identified as the source of a nation's competitive advantage. Further, Porter states that substantial inbound FDI is not a source of competitive advantage.

In the empirical work, we find that analysis of FDI in Canada is not explained very well by the triad diamonds; it is, however, explained much better by Canada's "host country" diamond. We first study the pattern of acquisitions (among resources, manufacturing and services) for the United States as compared to the EC as compared to Japan. The differences between the EC and the United States that became apparent in these patterns was surprisingly small, too small, we think, to be explained by differences in the home country diamonds. The differences in acquisition patterns between Japan, on the one hand, and the United States or the EC, on the other hand, is better explained, we believe, by a simple hypothesis — Japan's late entry into exporting — than by complicated analyses of home country advantages (since the differences are largely the result of Japanese acquisitions of wholesale and retail trade offices, at least in the earlier period).

We believe that these results arise from elements of Canada's "host country" diamond as well as from the "home country" diamonds of the triad nations. Between 1974 and 1990 there were profound changes in the relative importance of the triad diamonds, especially with Japan's progress in globalization, yet these changes were not reflected in changing relative patterns of FDI in Canada. This finding implies that Porter's approach to international competitiveness (which focusses on the home country diamond alone) needs to be modified when applied in a Canadian context. To explain variation in inbound FDI, Canada's own diamond needs to be examined, as well as the diamonds of the triad nations. Indeed, rather than separate diamonds, it is entirely conceivable that a "North American" diamond needs to be constructed to explain U.S. FDI into Canada, since the economies of the two countries are highly interdependent, and the Free Trade Agreement reinforces their integration. (For an extension of this thesis, see Rugman and D'Cruz, 1991.)

Next we examined the pattern of acquisitions and greenfield investments by triad members during both the FIRA and Investment Canada periods. Several observations were made. First, in examining all acquisitions, we found no significant differences between the two periods for Europe (EC and "Other Europe") but we did find significant differences for the United States and Japan. We next examined acquisitions over $5 million, and here we found no significant differences for Europe or the United States. (We do find significant differences for new business FDI for the two time periods for the triad, but not for larger new business investments from Europe.) These observations are either a statistical artifact or else they suggest that FIRA's main effect was to diminish small-scale American acquisitions, principally in the resource sector.

We do not detect an increase in American FDI in Canada in the more recent period, at the expense of EC or Japanese FDI. In fact, in the Investment Canada period, the United States accounts for 60 percent of all acquisitions as compared to 65 percent under FIRA. There are clearly many determinants to consider, but we interpret these results as suggesting that public concern is misplaced over a perceived "sellout" of Canada resulting from weaker regulation of FDI under Investment Canada as compared to FIRA.

The nature of economic interdependence between Canada and the United States means that analysis of American FDI in Canada should always be set against an analysis of the matching Canadian FDI in the United States. While this paper, like others in this volume, was confined to one half of this relationship, it should always be remembered that Canada's regulation of FDI is a pointless exercise if it is conducted for nationalist reasons; the global reach of Canadian multinationals reinforces this conclusion. Although FIRA and Investment Canada have marched to different drummers, it is unlikely that either has succeeded in substantially disrupting patterns of FDI into Canada by the triad nations, or across the resource, manufacturing and service sectors. The interdependence of economies means that no nation is an island in a sea of global competition.

ACKNOWLEDGEMENT

THIS PAPER WAS COMMISSIONED by Investment Canada for an Author's Workshop at the University of Toronto, November 29, 1990. We thank Stephen Murphy for his assistance. Helpful comments were received from Ed Safarian, Grant Reuber and David Husband.

APPENDIX A

INDUSTRY DEFINITION	SIC CODE 1980
Resource Industries	
Agricultural and Related Service Industries	01, 02
Fishing and Trapping Industries	03
Logging and Forestry Industries	04, 05
Mining, Quarrying and Oil Well Industries	06 - 09
Manufacturing Industries	
Food Industries	10
Beverage Industries	11
Tobacco Products Industries	12
Rubber Products Industries	15
Plastic Products Industries	16
Leather & Allies Products Industries	17
Primary Textile Industries	18
Textile Products Industries	19
Clothing Industries	24
Wood Industries	25
Furniture & Fixtures Industries	26
Paper & Allied Products Industries	27
Printing, Publishing & Allied Industries	28
Primary Metals Industries	29
Fabricated Metal Products Industries (except Machinery & Transportation Equipment)	30
Machinery Industries (except Electrical Machinery)	31
Transportation Equipment Industries	32
Electrical & Electronic Equipment Industries	33
Non-Metallic Mineral Products Industries	35
Refined Petroleum & Coal Products Industries	36
Chemical & Chemical Products Industries	37
Other Manufacturing Industries	39
Service Industries	
Construction Industries	40 - 44
Transportation and Storage Industries	45 - 47
Communication and Other Utility Industries	48 - 49
Wholesale Trade Industries	50 - 59
Retail Trade Industries	60 - 69
Finance and Insurance Industries	70 - 74
Real Estate Operator & Insurance Agent Industries	75 - 76

APPENDIX B

CHI-SQUARED TEST OF COUNTRY OF ORIGIN PATTERN OF INVESTMENT

H_0: Pattern of Investment remains the same IC cf FIRA

	All Acquisitions X^2	Acquisitions over $5 Million X^2	All New Businesses X^2	All New Businesses Over $5 Million X^2
United States	39.1935	1.3996	84.392	15.543
EC	4.0274	2.6648	17.8636	4.888
Rest of Europe	5.0014	3.6935	18.8749	1.183
Japan	28.8447	8.8630	3.1018	18.330
Rest of World	67.2738	92.2535	11.2246	3.275
Critical Value X^2 2,.05	5.99	5.99	5.99	5.99

BIBLIOGRAPHY

Baldwin, John and Richard Caves. "Foreign Multinational Enterprises and Merger Activity in Canada", prepared for the Conference on Corporate Globalization Through Mergers and Acquisitions, Investment Canada, Toronto, November 29, 1990.

Caves, Richard E. *Multinational Enterprise and Economic Analysis*, New York, Cambridge University Press, 1982.

Crookell, Harold. *Canadian-American Trade and Investment Under the Free Trade Agreement*, Westport, CT, Quorum Books, 1990.

Daly, Donald. "Canada's International Competitiveness" in Alan M. Rugman *International Business in Canada*, Toronto, Prentice-Hall of Canada, 1989, pp. 37-54.

Dunning, John H. "Dunning on Porter: Reshaping the Diamond of Competitive Advantage", Paper prepared for the Academy of International Business, October 1990.

D'Cruz, Joseph and James Fleck. *Canada Can Compete! Strategic Management of the Canadian Industrial Portfolio*, Ottawa, Institute for Research on Public Policy, 1985.

Eastman, Harry C. and S. Stykolt. *The Tariff and Competition in Canada*, Toronto, Macmillan, 1967.

Fuss, Melvin and Leonard Waverman. *Costs and Productivity in the Automobile Industry: Japan, Germany, the U.S.A. and Canada*, New York, Cambridge University Press, 1991.

Porter, Michael G. *The Competitive Advantage of Nations*, New York, Free Press/Macmillan, 1990.

Reich, Robert B. "Who Is Us?" *Harvard Business Review*, 90:1 January/February 1990, pp. 53-64.

Rugman, Alan M. *Multinationals in Canada: Theory, Performance, and Economic Impact*, Boston, Martinus Nijhoff, 1980.

_____. "Research and Development by Multinational and Domestic Firms in Canada", *Canadian Public Policy* VII:4, Autumn 1981, pp. 604-16.

_____. *Multinationals and Canada-United States Free Trade*, Columbia, SC, University of South Carolina Press, 1990.

Rugman, Alan M. and Joseph R. D'Cruz. *Fast Forward: Strategies for Improving Canada's International Competitiveness*, Toronto, Kodak Canada, 1991.

Rugman, Alan M. and John McIlveen. *Megafirms: Strategies for Canada's Multinationals*, Toronto, Methuen/Nelson, 1985.

Rugman, Alan M. and Alain Verbeke. *Global Corporate Strategy and Trade Policy*, London and New York, Routledge, 1990.

Rugman, Alan M. and Joseph D'Cruz. *New Visions for Canadian Business: Strategies for Competing in the Global Economy*, Toronto, Kodak Canada, 1990.

Safarian, A. Edward. *Foreign Ownership of Canadian Industry*, Toronto and New York, McGraw Hill, 1968.

Shapiro, Daniel. *Foreign and Domestic Firms in Canada*, Toronto, Butterworths, 1980.

Watkins, Mel. "The Economics of Nationalism and the Nationality of Economics", *Canadian Journal of Economics*, Winter 1978.

John R. Baldwin   *and*   Richard E. Caves
The Economic Council of Canada   Harvard University   4

Foreign Multinational Enterprises and Merger Activity in Canada

I N THIS PAPER we show that the effects of mergers in Canada are associated with the presence of multinational enterprises and differ in the markets where those enterprises flourish from markets where their presence is less important. Mergers involving foreign multinationals have long received attention due to the offense given to preferences for national independence when control of Canadian business assets passes into foreign hands. Indeed, foreign acquisitions were made subject to review by the Foreign Investment Review Agency in 1974. The attention paid to these multinational transactions by policy-makers was not matched, however, by economic analysis of their determinants and consequences. How these transactions differ from merger transactions among domestic firms and what effects they have on the productivity of the transferred business assets are questions addressed in this paper. We use Statistics Canada data on individual establishments in the Canadian manufacturing sector to compare the contexts and consequences of international mergers and other control changes that occurred between 1970 and 1979.

ANALYTICAL BACKGROUND: MERGERS

E VEN IF THE ALIENATION OF CONTROL over business assets were not a matter of concern, mergers would remain controversial purely because of their economic effects. A favourable view of mergers arises from the theory of the market for corporate control, which holds that a market for corporate control exists and that as part of this, mergers and related transactions desirably shift control of business assets into the hands of managers who are more efficient or better situated to deploy them. Improvements in performance can arise from various sources. Changes in control can economize on the use of overhead and intangible resources in ways identified in the theory of corporate diversification. They can shift resources into the hands of managers who are simply more capable or better motivated to obtain the maximum value from them.

Although the basic value of an active market for corporate control is generally accepted, sceptics in the United States and Britain have claimed to detect significant inefficiencies in transactions that bring about changes in control. These inefficiencies occur not only in horizontal mergers that restrict competition — an issue not pursued here — but also in large corporate mergers in which the acquirer's motives and competence in deploying the assets more efficiently are open to doubt. Negative evidence about the productivity of large diversifying mergers in the United States was first fed by the "go-go conglomerates" of the 1960s. Analysis of data from the 1960s and 1970s indicated that acquisitions by large firms failed to raise — indeed lowered — the profitability of the transferred business units (Ravenscraft and Scherer, 1987). Mueller (1985) observed that market shares of business units transferred through large mergers during the period 1950 - 1972 experienced declines so large that they could hardly have resulted from the normal regression process. Indeed, until recently most of the *ex post* evidence on the effects of mergers in the United States has been negative, and the only specific benefit documented — increased reliance on tax-deductible debt — was private, not social.[1] These negative effects associated with mergers were blamed chiefly on the motives (or perhaps the *hubris*) of managers of large enterprises, who might be expected to derive from the mergers personal gains inconsistent (beyond some point) with maximum returns for the acquiring firms' owners.

The general drift of evidence in Canada, as exemplified in the report of the Royal Commission on Corporate Concentration (1978), was similar. The Commission (ch. 5) found evidence that unrelated diversification, usually pursued through mergers, had at best been neutral in its effects on a firm's profitability. In enumerating reasons for the occurrence of large mergers (pp. 150-54), the report acknowledged the play of managerial motives, as well as objectives that should increase efficiency. (Specific evidence is discussed below.)

In contrast to these negative *ex post* findings, there is much positive *ex ante* evidence about the efficiency in the market for corporate control. Ratios of market value to book value were found to be low for firms acquired in merger transactions, and stockmarket returns prior to their acquisition were subnormal. The substantial premiums paid to gain control of target firms — amounts beyond market values of those targets as free-standing firms — are evidence of anticipated increases in their value. These premiums certainly testify to the yawning gaps between buyers' and sellers' reservation prices. In contrast, the near-zero or negative values placed on the transactions by the acquirers' shareholders leave it doubtful whether the expected gains actually accrued to acquiring and acquired firms, taken together. Eckbo (1988) reported that studies of stockmarket valuations of mergers in Canada show that shareholders of both target and acquiring firms benefit. The Canadian findings of benefits to target firms correspond to findings from the United States; the Canadian findings for acquiring firms are more favourable than American findings. Eckbo attributed the difference to the fact that the sizes of Canadian acquiring and target firms differ less than do those of U.S. merger partners. The more nearly equal size of the Canadian merger partners makes it easier to separate the gains resulting from a merger from other influences.

Although this disparity between *ex ante* and *ex post* evidence on the efficiency of large mergers persists unresolved, recent developments have significantly changed the perspective. First, while large mergers continue at an irregular pace, other transactions have grown much more common. These include sell-offs, which transfer business units from one enterprise to another, and spin-offs and buy-outs that either simplify the managerial task or strengthen managerial incentives. Sell-offs seem to shift assets into managerial hands more competent to supervise them or able to produce synergistic gains in productivity. Spin-offs and buy-outs chiefly strengthen managers' incentives to maximize profits. Evidence from the United States (for example, Kaplan, 1989) has largely affirmed the value-creating potential of these transactions. Second, the *ex post* negative conclusions about the effects of large mergers on productivity do not seem to appear in more comprehensive data that display the consequence of mergers of all sizes and other types of changes in control as well (see Lichtenberg and Siegel, 1987, on the United States and evidence cited below on Canada). Although the American evidence suggests that some large mergers with questionable effects on productivity continue to occur, the mixture of transactions in corporate control apparently shifted for the better in the 1980s.

Most of these questions about the productivity of large mergers originate largely outside of Canada. They may be relevant to international mergers in Canada, however, simply because some control changes in Canada are made by just these large enterprises in their guise as multinational companies. We consider below whether research on changes of control in Canada supports the favourable normative view suggested by the theory of the market for corporate control.

ANALYTICAL BACKGROUND: MULTINATIONAL ENTERPRISES

THE ECONOMIC ANALYSIS OF MERGERS can be readily joined to that of multinational enterprises. The theory that identifies synergistic gains as a motive for (non-horizontal) mergers corresponds closely to the standard theory of the expansion of multinationals. Both lines of analysis assume that the production process requires lumpy[2] or intangible productive assets that a firm can employ simultaneously in more than one market. To the extent that the lumpy or intangible qualities of an asset prevent the owning firm from utilizing that asset fully in a single market, they induce the owning firm to enter another market by making the firm's incremental cost lower than that of an entrant who must pay for the lumpy asset's full cost. Entry by established firms, therefore, prevails over *de novo* entry. This same theory, based on lumpy and intangible assets, underlies the internalization hypothesis that foreign direct investment is a transaction linking markets across national boundaries. It also appears as a theory of diversification when mergers or other transactions unite business units in different product markets within the same nation. In both cases, the lumpy asset must serve multiple uses; its services must be portable between product markets in the case of diversification, and between geographic markets in the case of foreign investment.

A firm can accomplish both diversification and foreign direct investment by means of either the building of new plant (greenfield entry) or the acquisition of a going firm or plant (not to mention other transactions that involve sharing the lumpy or intangible asset or its services). However, the very characteristic (the lumpy asset that is too large to be fully exploited in the home market) that leads to international diversification also suggests that entry is more likely to be by acquisition than by greenfield construction. If the original home market was too small for full exploitation of the specialized asset, the Canadian market is likely to be small, relative to firm size. Markets that are small relative to the size of firms operating within them are concentrated markets, and entry into these markets occurs more frequently by acquisition than by greenfield entry.[3]

Empirical research on foreign investment in Canada (and elsewhere) has confirmed the predictions of this line of analysis, showing how the extent of the activities of multinational enterprises varies from industry to industry. The causal factors verified in Canada include not only the importance of lumpy and intangible assets but also an industry's affinity for multiplant operations within the United States (Caves, 1974). Analyses have confirmed the role of the multinational enterprise in Canada as an arbitrageur of its parent's innovations (DeMelto, McMullen, and Wills, 1980) and the importance of Canadian subsidiaries as marketing agents for their affiliates' differentiated goods (McFetridge, 1987). Baldwin and Gorecki (1986a, ch. 7) observed the implied positive net effect of the prevalence of foreign investment on total factor productivity in Canada. Another line of evidence affirming the parallel between diversification and foreign investment shows that these two modes of expansion are substitutes for the growing enterprise; within a limited period of time, its path of expansion tends to follow either the one vector or the other (Caves, 1975; Wolf, 1977).[4]

Although not devoid of normative issues, the internalization theory of multinational enterprise coincides with one line of the theory of the market for corporate control: mergers represent efficient redeployments of business assets, with the expected gains coming from better utilization of lumpy assets. However, the hypothesis that mergers increase productivity as a result of improved managerial competence or increased incentives for managers in its pure form fits the activities of the multinational poorly. A postulate that is highly plausible (if hard to test directly) holds that the effectiveness of managers is tied to their familiarity with the ambient language, culture, polity and traditions. Put simply, if a Canadian firm is ripe for takeover because of its managers' limitations or underperformance, a Japanese multinational (in the absence of other advantages it might possess) is probably not the most effective agent of upgrade.[5]

A final point about mergers and multinational enterprises relates to the negative assessment of large corporate mergers in the United States in the era of conglomerates. Multinational enterprises tend to be large, and large firms' managers tend to be less closely monitored than those of small public companies (not to mention privately held ones). Although the fixed costs associated with the multinational co-ordination of activity across the Canada-United States border are surely lower than those across most other national boundaries, bringing multinational status within the reach of smaller firms, it remains possible that some large multinational firms may undertake international mergers with poor value-creating potential. Some Canadian businesses may have suffered losses in productivity following trans-border transactions. Some changes in the control of Canadian business units from one foreign multinational to another may be incidental to such large mergers and have at best no favourable productivity effects in Canada. Of course, other foreign-to-foreign changes of control may be productive for later undoing just such mergers.

These considerations support several predictions about foreign mergers in Canada:

1. To the extent that mergers improve the use of lumpy and intangible assets, they should occur more often in industries with heavy foreign investment. Foreign firms should be active as both buyers and sellers, although not necessarily in disproportion to their combined share of a sector's activity. Mergers involving foreign enterprises should yield productivity gains for the transferred assets at least as large as those resulting from purely domestic mergers.[6]

2. To the extent that mergers serve to improve managerial capacity or motivation, multinational firms should be underrepresented as buyers, except as control changes in Canada are incidental to mergers between enterprises outside of Canada. The frequency of control changes involving foreign multinationals should be relatively independent of the percentage of activity in a sector accounted for by foreign-controlled business units. Purely domestic mergers should generate productivity gains at least has large as those involving foreign enterprises.

3. If international mergers in Canada should be infected by non-maximizing or "managerial" behaviour of large multinational firms, they would be concentrated in industries with extensive foreign ownership but be less productive than mergers involving domestic enterprises. The same prediction pertains to control changes in Canada resulting from mergers or other strategic changes occurring outside of Canada. Mergers should grow less productive as the sizes of the business increase.

PREVIOUS EVIDENCE ON MERGERS AND MULTINATIONALS IN CANADA

W E NOW SUMMARIZE the evidence available from prior research on mergers in Canada and the activities of foreign enterprises in control-change transactions. Baldwin and Gorecki (1986b) drew together evidence on merger patterns in the 1970s. Foreign and domestic enterprises made acquisitions roughly in proportion to their prevalence in Canadian manufacturing. Canadian firms acquired 56.3 percent of all unconsolidated firms that were absorbed; 42.8 percent of the acquired units were domestic, while 13.5 percent were foreign. The 43.8 percent acquired by foreign firms consisted of 22.6 percent domestic units and 21.2 percent other foreign units, with foreigners' acquisitions shifting from foreign toward domestic businesses over the decade.[7] Most acquired firms were small, and acquirers picked up units generally smaller and seldom larger than themselves.

Foreign firms tended to enter through the acquisition of plant rather than through the construction of new facilities. Domestic firms relied more heavily on greenfield entry. An analysis of the determinants of market entries through acquisition (Baldwin and Gorecki, 1987) showed that domestic acquirers are more sensitive than foreign acquirers to the inducements offered by the growth of both the domestic market and export sales, as well as to current profits.[8] As previous evidence suggested, neither domestic nor foreign established firms entering Canadian markets through acquisition are generally repelled by structural barriers to entry, and foreign entrants are actually attracted by scale economies and other factors that place small incumbent firms at a disadvantage.[9]

Baldwin and Gorecki found that changes in control during the 1970s were generally favourable to productivity (as measured by shipments per employee). Their findings indicated that plants that had undergone changes of control during that decade improved their positions relative to continuing plants that experienced no control changes. These results are consistent with the findings of Lichtenberg and Siegel (1987) for the United States in the 1970s: that when all types of changes in control and all sizes of units are taken into account, changes in control are typically favourable to productivity.

It is not clear whether Canada was spared the productivity losses associated with diversifying acquisitions by large firms in the United States, although the Canadian evidence suggests that firms which merged extensively or engaged in unrelated diversification did not particularly profit as a result.[10] Evidence on the motives of companies undertaking acquisitions in Canada was similar: generally favourable to the positive productivity of mergers but with qualifications for large-scale acquisitions by large enterprises.[11] Various other lines of analysis suggested that although productivity commonly faltered in assets acquired by large firms in the United States, this pattern was not evident in Canada.

EMPIRICAL EVIDENCE

THE HYPOTHESES developed in the first two sections of this paper offer competing predictions about the frequency of changes in control involving foreign enterprises and the effects of these changes on the performance of the transferred business units. We test these hypotheses using data from Statistics Canada that cover all establishments operating in Canadian manufacturing industries in the years 1970 and 1979. Each establishment is classified as being under domestic or foreign control. Furthermore, we observe the fate of each establishment existing in 1970: noting whether it continued in operation to 1979 under unchanged control, was closed down (if so, whether the owning firm continued or ceased operation), or continued in operation but underwent a change in control. When a change of control occurs, an establishment can pass from one incumbent (or established) firm in the industry to another, or it can pass from an incumbent to an entrant; similarly, transfers of control can occur between domestic controlling firms, between foreign controlling firms, or in either direction between domestic and foreign. Control changes include not only mergers and acquisitions but also sell-offs of businesses from one firm to another, spin-offs to shareholders, and buy-outs; all these types of transactions, of course, grew more popular in the 1980s than they were in the 1970s.

We eliminated changes in control involving all plants divested by continuing firms incumbent in the industry because they represented limited and special situations. That left the question of whether to separate the remaining sample of plants divested by exiting firms into two categories: those acquired by continuing incumbent firms (a horizontal merger) and those purchased by entrants (unrelated diversification). Some horizontal mergers increase the effective concentration of producers and cause price increases; in these instances any apparent gains in productivity could stem partly or wholly from increased monopoly rents. Despite this possibility, we retained the horizontal category in the analysis. Many of the mergers in this category, no doubt, represent closely related diversifications or transfers of control to managements experienced in the transferred plants' operations, and not mergers for monopoly gains. Since our hypotheses mark these mergers as likely sources of real productivity gains, we did not wish to disregard them; but neither did we want to confuse their effects with those of the main category of unrelated takeovers. We therefore present in tabular form the results of the divestitures that are associated with the unrelated takeovers. We repeat all calculations for the horizontal transactions, reporting the results where they substantially differ from those of the unrelated control changes.

We chose a simple strategy to highlight the frequency and effects of mergers involving foreign enterprises, while controlling for the structures of the industries in question. We ranked the four-digit industries in the standard industrial classification (SIC) in 1970 according to the proportions of their shipments accounted for by foreign-controlled establishments and divided them into thirds, ranked by high, medium, and low foreign shares. We then observed the turnover of establishments during 1970 - 79 for industries in each foreign-ownership group or tranche, using various weighting schemes when we calculated the average for each tranche. This simple procedure allows us to distinguish the incidence and consequences of changes in control involving foreign and domestic firms, while taking account of the structural characteristics of industries that govern their attraction for multinational enterprises. If mergers involving foreign firms differ from those of domestic companies, we can tell whether the difference stems from the opportunities inherent in their market structures or the intrinsic properties of the enterprises themselves by examining the extent to which the difference varies across the industry groupings. Because we observe the universe of Canadian manufacturing establishments to which the hypotheses pertain, we make only limited use of statistical inference.[12]

STRUCTURAL DIFFERENCES AMONG INDUSTRIES

PREVIOUS RESEARCH HAS SHOWN that the prevalence of multinational enterprises or their subsidiaries in an industry is closely associated with several underlying elements of the industry's market structure. Those elements of market structure also affect the scope for changes in control to bring about the various effects hypothesized above. Therefore, we start by reporting the averages of structural differences among industries in the three tranches grouped by foreign control. Table 1 shows the wide range and symmetrical distribution of mean shares of foreign ownership among the groups. The substantial decline in foreign shares that occurred during the 1970s is evident: the mean share fell 8.1 percent in the high-share industries and 10.2 percent in the medium-share industries, while it increased 5.0 percent in the low-share sector.

The internalization theory has successfully predicted the association of foreign ownership with several traits of market structure. Table 1 confirms that industries' ratios of advertising to sales, and of research and development employees to total employment increase sharply with foreign ownership. That does not prove true, however, for the extent of multi-plant operation in Canada of an industry's leading (four) firms.[13] Because these predictors of foreign ownership are also predictors of concentration (shipments accounted for by the largest four firms) among producers, we expect and observe that concentration increases with foreign ownership. In each group, small decreases in concentration occurred which might have been associated with the retreat of foreign ownership. Another substantial difference exists in the complexity and diversity of the product lines of industries in the various ownership tranches; the difference is shown by the average number of census-defined products classified to each industry. This number is more than twice as large in the sector with high foreign ownership than it is in the sector with low foreign ownership. Economies of scope in product-line distribution thus increase with foreign ownership, and the increase is consistent with the foreign subsidiary's role

TABLE 1

AVERAGE CHARACTERISTICS[1] OF INDUSTRIES AND CHANGES IN SELECTED
CHARACTERISTICS, BY FOREIGN-OWNERSHIP TRANCHE[2]

| CHARACTERISTIC | YEAR | FOREIGN-OWNERSHIP TRANCHE | | | ALL |
		LOW	MEDIUM	HIGH	INDUSTRIES
Foreign-ownership share[3]	1970	11.9	41.0	81.1	44.4
	1979	12.5	36.8	73.9	40.9
Advertising/sales	1975	0.8	1.1	1.7	1.2
R&D/employees (%)	1975	.12	.73	1.43	.76
Plants per firm[4], leading firms	1970	3.16	3.67	3.02	3.29
	1979	2.97	4.06	3.23	3.43
Plants per enterprise	1970	1.16	1.32	1.33	1.27
	1979	1.16	1.33	1.34	1.27
Four-firm concentration	1970	38.2	51.7	63.1	50.9
	1979	37.1	50.7	62.0	49.9
Number of products classified	1970	9.2	13.7	20.0	14.4
Nominal tariff rate	1970	15.3	10.3	9.2	11.6
	1978	13.3	9.0	7.9	10.1
Effective tariff rate[5]	1966	17.6	13.9	14.1	15.2
	1978	15.5	10.3	10.1	12.0
Domestic disappearance/ shipments	1970	1.06	1.10	1.27	1.14
	1979	1.11	1.15	1.31	1.19
Exports/shipments	1970	10.4	15.1	20.4	15.3
	1979	13.4	18.2	26.2	19.3

[1]Average characteristics are calculated across all four-digit industries within a foreign-ownership tranche. The three tranches are derived by dividing the four-digit population into three groups with an equal number of industries, based on foreign ownership.

[2]For details of definitions of variables, see Baldwin and Gorecki (1986, Appendix A, pp. 172-182).

[3]Foreign ownership is based on shipments under foreign control. A firm is defined as foreign-controlled if there is effective foreign control, although the percentage of stock owned by the foreign parent may be less than 50 percent.

[4]A firm is defined as all plants under common control.

[5]The effective tariff rate reported here is version 2 in Baldwin and Gorecki (1986, Appendix A).

SOURCE: Special tabulations, Business and Labour Market Analysis Group, Statistics Canada

as a distribution conduit for a product line assembled from both its own output and that of its foreign affiliates.

Tariff protection has served historically to promote foreign investment in Canada, but a strong relationship between tariffs and foreign investment was not apparent in the 1970s. Nominal tariffs decreased with foreign ownership, although effective tariffs did not differ between medium-share and high-share groups. All three tranches experienced moderate reductions in both nominal and effective tariffs. As Matthews (1985) showed, the expansion of intra-industry trade occurred in a surprisingly uniform fashion across the manufacturing industries. Import-intensity is shown by the ratio of domestic disappearance (domestic shipments minus exports plus imports) to domestic shipments. Each group of industries, on balance, is import-competing, especially the group with high foreign ownership. The ratio of net imports to production increased during the 1970s by about the same amount for each tranche. Export intensity increases with foreign ownership, and so industries with a high proportion of foreign ownership also exhibit high levels of intra-industry trade. Export intensity rose during the 1970s by about one-fourth, and its increase was independent of the extent of foreign ownership.

Because of our focus on mergers and acquisitions that occur across industry boundaries and result in a diversified enterprise, we also analyzed information on the diversification of companies classified to each industry (Table 2). The first section reports the average Herfindahl (inverse) index of diversification for consolidated enterprises that own plants in the industry, measured over all their plants in the Canadian manufacturing, mining and logging sectors. Foreign-controlled enterprises are more diversified than domestic enterprises in all groups (see Table 2, line 2). Diversification increases with foreign investment overall, partly because domestic companies are less diversified in industries with little foreign ownership, but mainly because of the increasing proportion of more diversified foreign-controlled companies.

In Table 2 line 3 repeats the mean number of products classified to the industry (from Table 1) and gives the mean of its inverse, which is approximately the lower bound for the Herfindahl index of diversification within the industry. Line 4 reports mean plant-level diversification at the four-digit product level.[14] Like enterprise diversification, mean plant-level diversification is lowest (for all establishments taken together) in industries with low foreign ownership, and highest for the tranche with high foreign ownership. Plant-level diversification increases across foreign-ownership tranches as one would expect, on the basis of the number of products classified to an industry (line 4). The increase is slightly greater for foreign plants, but the difference is small.[15]

Thus the industries with high foreign ownership also exhibit high levels of enterprise diversification. Potential diversification within the industry is also greater. The greater diversification stems from joint costs or complementarities in non-production activities and not from joint plant costs. Actual plant-level diversification increases correspondingly; the increase is slightly smaller in domestic plants than in foreign plants.

These structural differences imply differences in the processes of turnover of establishments and their control as shown in Table 3. The shares of shipments originated by each category of establishments were obtained for each industry in a group, and unweighted averages were then taken across industries.[16] Thus, in the average industry, establishments accounting for 19.1

TABLE 2

AVERAGE DIVERSITY CHARACTERISTICS OF CONSOLIDATED ENTERPRISES AND
PLANTS, INDUSTRIES CLASSIFIED BY FOREIGN-OWNERSHIP TRANCHE, 1979

CHARACTERISTIC	FOREIGN-OWNERSHIP TRANCHE			ALL INDUSTRIES
	LOW	MEDIUM	HIGH	
1. Herfindahl measure of interindustry diversification, enterprise level[1]				
All enterprises	0.89	0.77	0.72	0.80
Domestic	0.90	0.82	0.82	0.84
Foreign-controlled	0.74	0.64	0.64	0.67
2. Ratio of enterprise diversification for domestic divided by foreign enterprises	1.28	1.34	1.35	1.33
3. Average number of four-digit census products classified to industry[2]				
Number	9.21	13.66	20.02	14.41
Inverse	0.27	0.23	0.22	0.24
4. Average Herfindahl measure of plant-level diversification within industry[3]				
All establishments	0.80	0.79	0.76	0.79
Domestic	0.80	0.80	0.77	0.80
Foreign-controlled	0.81	0.78	0.75	0.78

[1]Enterprise level specialization is the parent's specialization calculated across all four-digit manufacturing, mining, and logging industries.
[2]"Number of products" is the number of four-digit Industrial Commodity Classification (ICC) commodities (2 326 in total) per industry.
[3]Plant specialization is the Herfindahl index of plant shipments at the four-digit ICC commodity level.

SOURCE: Special Tabulations, Business and Labour Market Analysis Group, Statistics Canada

percent of shipments in 1970 were closed down during the decade by firms that exited from the industry (Table 3, line 1), while establishments accounting for 18.9 percent of 1979 shipments were opened by firms entering the industry (line 2). Slightly smaller shares of shipments were accounted for in 1970 by plants subsequently divested by exiting firms (13.8 percent, line 5) and in 1979 by plants acquired by entering firms (11.7 percent, line 6). Mergers were thus important avenues for entry into (exit from) industries, although slightly more turnover of enterprises occurred through greenfield entry and exit via close down of plant. Openings and closures of plants by firms that continued in the industry accounted for about six percent of market share (lines 3 and 4). Plants subject to horizontal acquisition during the decade accounted for 5.4 percent of market share in 1979 (line 8), and plants to be divested by continuing firms, for 3.3 percent in 1970 (line 7).

The first three columns of Table 3 show that the relative frequency of turnover resulting from greenfield entry and close-down exit declines sharply

TABLE 3

AVERAGE MARKET SHARES[1] OF ESTABLISHMENTS STARTED, CLOSED, AND CHANGING CONTROL, BY STATUS OF FIRM AND EXTENT OF FOREIGN OWNERSHIP, 1970 AND 1979 (%)

| | FOREIGN-OWNERSHIP TRANCHE | | | ALL |
CHARACTERISTIC	LOW	MEDIUM	HIGH	INDUSTRIES
Establishments closed by exiting firms (1970)[2]	26.9	18.8	11.4	19.1
Establishments opened by entering firms (1979)[3]	25.0	18.7	13.0	18.9
Plants closed by continuing firms (1970)[4]	4.7	6.5	6.8	6.0
New plants opened by continuing firms (1979)[5]	4.5	7.4	7.3	6.5
Plants divested by exiting firms (1970)	11.3	15.7	14.0	13.8
Plants acquired by entering firms (1979)	9.3	13.6	12.1	11.7
Plants divested by continuing firms (1970)	3.9	2.2	3.9	3.3
Plants acquired by continuing firms (1979)	4.6	6.4	4.9	5.4

[1]These data are based on plant shipments and include all plants except head offices. For a discussion of the sample used, see Baldwin and Gorecki (1991a). The calculations in this table are unweighted averages at the four-digit industry level.

[2]Establishments closed are those plants in existence in 1970 in a particular four-digit industry that are no longer in that industry in 1979. Some will have been physically closed; others will have been switched to another industry. For the division between these, see Baldwin and Gorecki (1991a).

[3]Establishments opened are those plants in existence in 1979 in a particular four-digit industry which were not there in 1970. Some will be plant births; others will be switched from another four-digit industry.

[4]All divested plants are found in the same four-digit industry in 1970 and 1979.

[5]Entering firms are those which own a plant in a particular four-digit industry in 1979 but not in 1970. Exiting firms are the reverse. Continuing firms own plants in an industry in both 1970 and 1979.

SOURCE: Special tabulations, Business and Labour Market Analysis Group, Statistics Canada

with foreign ownership (lines 1 and 2), while turnover through the acquisition and divestiture of firms is less important in industries with low foreign ownership than in other industries. Turnover associated with plants opened and closed by continuing firms is also less important for industries with low foreign ownership (lines 3 and 4), while horizontal changes in control are independent of foreign ownership (lines 7 and 8).[17]

Overall, Table 3 tells us that changes in control of continuing establishments increase strongly in frequency with increase in foreign ownership. Changes in control occur frequently where foreign ownership is high, although the causal relationship (if any) is unknown at this stage. The turnover of firms in the high foreign-ownership tranche is less connected with the birth and death of

TABLE 4

AVERAGE EXTENT OF TURNOVER[1] OF MARKET SHARE[2] AMONG FIRMS,
BY SOURCE OF TURNOVER AND EXTENT OF FOREIGN OWNERSHIP,
1970 TO 1979 (PERCENT OF MARKET SHARE TRANSFERRED)

	FOREIGN-OWNERSHIP TRANCHE		
CATEGORY OF FIRM TURNOVER	LOW	MEDIUM	HIGH
Greenfield entry and close-down exit	26.0	18.8	12.2
Growth and decline of incumbents[3]	16.6	16.6	14.7
Total turnover[4]	42.6	35.4	26.9

[1]Turnover here is measured by a dissimilarity index that is described in the text.
[2]Market share is based on shipments data.
[3]Firms are defined in this line as all establishments including head offices under common control in a four-digit industry. Head offices are omitted from line 1.
[4]Total turnover is the sum of lines 1 and 2 and does not include the effect of acquisition entry and divestiture exit.

SOURCE: Special tabulations, Business and Labour Market Analysis Group, Statistics Canada

establishments, in that greenfield entry and close-down exit are less important.[18] One salient implication is that greenfield entry provides a weaker competitive stimulus for efficiency in industries with high foreign ownership, leaving a larger task for the market for corporate control and competition from abroad.

Table 4 elaborates on the findings of Table 3 by focussing on changes in the shares of four-digit industry shipments held by firms operating in 1970, in 1979, or in both years. Specifically, we calculated for each industry the sum of absolute value of share changes:

$$\Sigma | SH79_i - SH70_i |$$

where $SH79_i$ is the ith firm's share of industry shipments in 1979 and $SH70_i$ is its share in 1970. The calculation includes greenfield entrants that went from zero to positive shares and close-down exits that went from positive to zero. As the table shows, industries with high foreign ownership exhibit not only much less turnover arising from entry and exit but also slightly less turnover in the positions of incumbents present in the industry throughout the 1970s.

CONTROL CHANGES AND CHANGES IN SHARES AND PERFORMANCE OF ESTABLISHMENTS

TO THIS POINT OUR PAPER has addressed the structural conditions surrounding mergers and other changes in control. The main contention is that industries that harbour extensive foreign ownership provide the greatest scope for "lumpi-

TABLE 5

AVERAGE COMBINED MARKET SHARES AND AVERAGE RELATIVE PLANT SIZE OF
ESTABLISHMENTS SUBJECT TO CHANGES OF CONTROL[1] BETWEEN 1970 AND 1979,
BY NATIONALITY AND EXTENT OF FOREIGN OWNERSHIP[2]

| TYPE OF CONTROL CHANGE | YEAR | FOREIGN-OWNERSHIP TRANCHE | | | |
		LOW	MEDIUM	HIGH	TOTAL
Average Share (%)					
Domestic to domestic	1979	3.24	5.60	1.46	3.45
	1970	3.55	5.74	1.33	3.55
Domestic to foreign-controlled	1979	1.96	1.70	1.56	1.74
	1970	2.16	1.86	1.41	1.81
Foreign-controlled to domestic	1979	0.80	1.80	1.89	1.50
	1970	0.73	1.89	2.38	1.66
Foreign-controlled to foreign-controlled	1979	1.12	2.69	6.50	3.42
	1970	1.01	2.16	6.22	3.11
All divested	1979	7.14	11.79	11.41	10.10
All acquired	1970	7.44	11.66	11.33	10.14
Average Relative Plant Size[3]					
Domestic to domestic	1979	1.22	1.36	0.76	1.15
Domestic to foreign-controlled	1979	1.53	1.26	0.71	1.14
Foreign-controlled to domestic	1979	2.13	1.29	0.82	1.28
Foreign-controlled to foreign-controlled	1979	2.58	3.59	1.15	2.22
All acquired	1979	1.67	1.78	0.94	1.44

[1]For plants divested by exiting firms and acquired by entering firms — unrelated mergers.
[2]The calculations in this table are unweighted averages at the industry level.
[3]Size of plants subject to control change relative to plants that had continued between 1970 and 1979 in the same industry without a change in control.

SOURCE: Special Tabulations, Business and Labour Market Analysis Group, Statistics Canada

ness", intangible assets, and product-line complexity. The evidence indicates that these industries exhibit the most turnover of control of plants among firms and entry and exit of firms through merger transactions. We can now consider the specific effects of these control changes, both overall and by nationality of the firms involved.

We identified the establishments in each industry that continued in operation from 1970 to 1979 but underwent changes of control during the period because of divestiture by exiting firms and acquisition by entering firms; we also grouped those firms in each industry by the nationality pattern of the control change: that is, between domestic companies, between foreign companies, and between foreign and domestic companies. Market shares of the establishments in each category were summed for 1970 and for 1979 in each industry, and unweighted averages within each tranche of the resulting industry sums were calculated. The results appear in Table 5, along with the average relative plant size of acquired plant in 1979. Relative plant size is calculated in relation to plants that continued over the decade without a change in ownership.

It is well established that turnover in larger firms tends to take the form of mergers and other control changes, while greenfield entry and close-down exit tends to involve smaller firms (Baldwin and Gorecki, 1991b). This tendency for larger firms is confirmed in Table 5, in that the average size of acquired plant in 1979 is greater than that for plants that continued over the decade without a change in ownership. There is a marked difference in the relative plant size of acquired plants across the foreign-ownership tranches. Acquired plants are larger than average in the sector with the most domestic ownership and less than average in the high foreign-ownership tranche. There is also a difference in size of plants that are acquired by foreign and domestic firms. Plants that are divested and acquired by foreign firms are generally larger than plants divested and acquired by domestic firms; this difference partially reflects the differences in the underlying populations.

Because initially large plants or firms tend subsequently to lose market share (the regression process outlined in Baldwin, 1991b), we expect the shares of the larger establishments undergoing changes in control to decline, and the reverse to occur for smaller establishments that are acquired. What matters, therefore, is deviations from this expected pattern.

Changes in shares for domestic-to-domestic transfers accord with our expectations. Share losses occur in the low foreign-ownership tranche where the acquired plants are larger than continuing plants, and share gains occur in the high foreign-ownership tranche where the affected plant is smaller than other continuing plants. In contrast, the plants involved in foreign-to-foreign transfers experience a small share gain across all tranches, even though the relative size of acquired plant differs across foreign-ownership tranches in much the same way as do plants involved in domestic-to-domestic transfers. These results suggest that mergers between foreign enterprises have favourable effects generally because most such control changes involve the type of asset transfer hypothesized by the theory of the multinational firm. That transfers among domestic enterprises have unfavourable effects in industries where domestic control is high and where acquired plant is relatively large, suggests that there is a strong component here of transfers that involve difficult turnaround situations.

We checked to see whether any patterns emerge when Table 5 is recalculated using horizontal acquisitions only: that is, control changes that transfer plant from exiting firms to firms that are present in the industry throughout the decade. In the horizontal category, the success of foreign-to-foreign transfers is less in the high foreign-ownership tranche, and higher in the low foreign-ownership tranche. The direction of the other changes remains basically the same. This confirms the earlier hypothesis that closely related mergers by foreign firms may be less successful, but shows that the problems here are basically restricted to the high foreign-ownership tranche. This is probably also the sector where most of the mergers occurred that were incidental to control changes effected abroad and that had questionable effects.

The market-share changes that have been described for divested and acquired plants appear to be partially explained by the nature of the stochastic process at work in the firm population. To investigate this proposition further, a growth equation that allows for the regression to the mean phenomena was estimated for all plants in the manufacturing sector. The dependent variable chosen for the analysis was the log of the ratio of 1979 share to 1970 share for all continuing plants.[19] The dependent variable was regressed against 1970 share, a binary variable that takes on a value of one when the plant size is greater than the median in an industry. Both of these had significant and negative coefficients, indicating that growth rates were inversely related to plant size. Also included were binary variables for industry foreign-ownership tranche, the nationality of the control change (foreign-to-foreign, domestic-to-domestic, domestic-to-foreign, and foreign-to-domestic), and the extent to which the control change involved a horizontal component. Four horizontal categories were defined. These categories were based on whether the acquiring and divesting firm continued in the industry over the period. Divesting and acquiring firms were classified as: 1) entrants/exits — unrelated control changes, 2) continuing/exits — horizontal mergers, 3) entrants/continuing — unrelated spin-offs, 4) continuing/continuing — related spin-offs.

The core regression included only the initial market share and the dummy variable that divided each industry at the median. The strategy pursued was to add binary variables first for each tranche, then for each type of horizontal category, and then for nationality of the transaction. When only foreign-ownership tranche is considered, the two tranches with the highest foreign ownership have a negative co-efficient, thereby indicating more share loss for these plants than would have been expected on the basis of the regression to the mean process. This is primarily the result of the interaction with horizontal merger type. Inclusion of horizontal type along with interaction terms for ownership tranche produces a significant positive co-efficient in the lowest foreign-ownership tranche and a significant negative co-efficient on the high foreign-ownership tranche for horizontal mergers (the continuing/exiting category) and, therefore, accords with the previous finding that these mergers do well in the domestic sector and poorly in the foreign segment. On the other hand, the co-efficients attached to the unrelated control change category (entry/exits) do not show that the lowest and highest foreign-ownership tranches are markedly different from all continuing establishments. Observed differences in the share changes across all plants in the unrelated control-change category are explained by the regression to the mean process. Finally, the horizontal type, nationality and tranche variables were all entered to test whether there were significant differences in the cross-tranche performance of each horizontal type by nationality of the transfer. None of the components of the merger class on which we are focussing in this paper (unrelated control changes) showed a pattern in market share changes that could be distinguished from the general population of continuing plants.[20]

In conclusion, the micro-economic analysis demonstrates that once the regression to the mean phenomenon is considered, the pattern of share changes does not vary systematically with the level of foreign ownership. The relative changes in share following transfers of control indicate that nationality-related differences in transferred units' abilities to maintain their market shares is related to initial position. Nevertheless, it is clear that transfers in the domestic sector do differ from those in the foreign sector because the relative size of plants differs. We cannot reject the hypothesis that transfers of plants between foreign enterprises have favourable effects in industries with high foreign ownership, while transfers of plants between domestic enterprises have unfavourable effects in industries where domestic control prevails because of these plant-size effects.

We pointed out that the comparative incidence of mergers involving foreign and domestic firms should shed light on the importance of two sources of potential gain from mergers: synergies in the use of resources and improvement in managerial effectiveness. If the latter source prevails, foreign firms should be disproportionally inactive in the tranche with low foreign ownership. The data in Table 1 show that the mean foreign-ownership share in the high industries is about six times the mean foreign-ownership share in low industries in 1970; domestic ownership in the first tranche is about twice that in the third tranche. Foreign-to-foreign transfers and domestic-to-domestic transfers vary across tranches in about these same proportions. That is not the case for transfers from domestic to foreign firms, and this finding confounds our expectation that these shares should be similar or smaller in the low foreign-ownership industries. Perhaps the pattern results from the differential changes in the prevalence of foreign ownership noted in Table 1. Perhaps it reflects a division of labour in the market for corporate control not anticipated by our hypotheses — a question to be investigated below.

Market shares can change for many reasons; although according to Darwinian reasoning, an increasing share suggests an improvement in productivity, the association between the two is by no means automatic. In order to investigate the effect of control changes on productivity (and other variables), we divided each industry into those establishments that continued without a change of control between 1970 and 1979 and those that did not.[21] Characteristics of the plants that continued with no change in control (foreign and domestic taken together) were used to normalize data for plants that underwent changes: changes in control, or entry or shutdown of the plants themselves. A comprehensively weighted average (that is, both within and between industries) was computed for each foreign-ownership group by calculating the weighted average

TABLE 6

CHARACTERISTICS OF ESTABLISHMENTS SUBJECT TO CONTROL CHANGES, STARTUP,
OR SHUTDOWN BETWEEN 1970 AND 1979 NORMALIZED BY CHARACTERISTICS OF ALL
CONTINUING PLANTS, BY EXTENT OF FOREIGN OWNERSHIP (WEIGHTED MEAN RATIO)[1]

| | | FOREIGN-OWNERSHIP TRANCHE | | |
CHARACTERISTIC BY CATEGORY[2]	YEAR	LOW	MEDIUM	HIGH
Productivity (value added per employee)				
Continuing plants acquired	1979	1.02	1.03	0.80
Continuing plants divested	1970	0.97	1.04	0.69
New plants of greenfield entrants	1979	0.89	0.91	0.80
Closed plants of exiting firms	1970	0.74	0.75	0.67
New plants of continuing firms	1979	1.22	1.05	1.00
Closed plants of continuing firms	1970	0.86	0.74	0.80
Average remuneration per production worker[3]				
Continuing plants acquired	1979	1.07	0.97	0.88
Continuing plants divested	1970	1.08	1.00	0.87
New plants of greenfield entrants	1979	0.89	0.85	0.86
Closed plants of exiting firms	1970	0.87	0.80	0.81
New plants of continuing firms	1979	0.88	0.99	0.99
Closed plants of continuing firms	1970	1.00	0.89	0.92
Annual salary per non-production worker				
Continuing plants acquired	1979	1.06	0.94	0.89
Continuing plants divested	1970	1.01	0.97	0.94
New plants of greenfield entrants	1979	0.98	0.90	0.94
Closed plants of exiting firms	1970	0.93	0.87	0.89
New plants of continuing firms	1979	0.91	0.95	0.99
Closed plants of continuing firms	1970	0.90	0.87	0.92
Percentage of non-production workers[4]				
Continuing plants acquired	1979	1.53	1.48	0.77
Continuing plants divested	1970	1.76	1.48	0.78
New plants of greenfield entrants	1979	0.43	0.56	0.33
Closed plants of exiting firms	1970	0.53	0.48	0.33
New plants of continuing firms	1979	0.82	0.92	0.59
Closed plants of continuing firms	1970	1.31	1.05	0.65

[1]Each statistic presented in this table consists of the ratio of two weighted averages. Thus, for the relative salary of entrants, the numerator is the sum of all salary remuneration to non-production workers in entrant firms in a tranche divided by all non-production workers in these entrants; the denominator is the same statistic for all continuing plants that did not experience an ownership change.

[2]For a definition of the plant turnover categories, see Table 3. Only unrelated control changes were used here: plants divested by exiting firms and acquired by entering firms.

[3]Remuneration refers to gross earnings of workers from salaries and wages before deductions of any kind, such as income tax, unemployment insurance, and pension benefits. Workers are defined in person-year equivalents. For further details, see Statistics Canada.(1979, p. 26).

[4]The percentage of total industry employment (production plus salaried workers) accounted for by salaried workers. For details of the distinction between production and salaried workers, see Statistics Canada (1979, pp. 23-24).

SOURCE: Special tabulations, Business and Labour Market Analysis Group, Statistics Canada

of the variable across plants in the changed category, then across all continuing plants without changes in control, and then by dividing the former by the latter.[22]

The first section of Table 6 shows relative productivity, measured by value added per employee. Productivity changes show larger gains in the tranche where foreign ownership is highest. In the high foreign-ownership industries, plants undergoing a control change moved from only 69 percent of the productivity of the control group (column 3, line 2) to 80 per cent of the productivity of the control group (column 3, line 1) — a gain of 11 percentage points. In contrast, the gain was only five percentage points in the tranche with the highest domestic ownership. The pattern of productivity changes, as expected, corresponds to that for share changes described in Table 5. Industries with traits that dispose them toward extensive foreign ownership are those in which changes in control have the most positive effects. This pattern is fully consistent with the internalization theory of foreign investment and diversification, which marks these industries as the ones where changes in control can contribute most to the utilization of lumpy and intangible assets.

When these calculations are performed only on the horizontal component, the results are exactly the opposite. Productivity gains are 14 points in the lowest foreign-ownership tranche, 11 points in the middle tranche, and six points in the highest tranche — once more in accord with the share changes recorded for this category of mergers across ownership tranches. This pattern conforms to the interpretation offered for Table 5: where foreign ownership is low, the productivity of mergers depends on the close similarity of activities between the acquiring and acquired units.[23]

While these increases are positive, they need to be set in the context of the gains being made by plant exit and entry. The gains stemming from replacement by continuing firms of closed plants by new plants range from 13 to 20 points in the high foreign-ownership tranche and from 15 to 36 points in the lowest foreign-ownership tranche. Here the largest gains are made in the lowest foreign-ownership tranche.[24]

The remainder of Table 6 supplies evidence on certain changes relating to labour inputs and costs that might accompany changes in control. A change in control might be profitable to the acquirer because it can curb the payment of above-market wages or salaries. However, only in industries with low foreign ownership are both wages and salaries initially higher in establishments that change control than in all continuing establishments. In those industries, changes in control pull wages down toward the norm, but increase salaries. Sectors with medium and high foreign investment exhibit more containment of salaries. The normalized percentage of non-production workers decreases in plants subject to control change in industries with low foreign ownership; this decrease is consistent with new owners reaping pecuniary gains by squeezing out excess costs (staff and compensation), particularly in the domestic sector.[25] The same results are also found if the calculations are redone for the horizontal mergers. Mergers in the high domestic ownership sector are accompanied by both wage and salary declines (five and six points, respectively) and by decreases in the percentage of non-production workers (49 points). On the other hand, only the percentage of non-production workers decreases in the high foreign-ownership sector, and by much less (six points).

The indexes reported in Table 6 use plant-size-weighted averages,[26] which seems appropriate for the questions under investigation. Whether changes in control raise or lower average productivity is the question important for economic welfare; large establishments *all else being equal*, matter more for aggregate welfare, quite apart from the fact that any impairment of productivity by mergers is suspected mainly in the case of those undertaken by large enterprises, which in turn are likely to operate large establishments. These aggregate results depend both on the distribution of changes across firms and industries, and also on the sizes of the firms and the industries in which the mergers are occurring, because the average is weighted. Therefore, it seemed desirable to ask whether the results depended on the weights used. To pursue this question, we took the industry-level weighted averages[27] of the gain in productivity accruing from changes in control and correlated them with several industry attributes, overall and for industries in each foreign-investment tranche. There is relatively little association between the productivity gains and various measures of unit size. What stands out is that the productivity gains decrease with the productivity of to-be-divested plants relative to continuing plants in 1970. The shortcoming of large mergers in the domestic sector may lie not so much in limited ability to raise productivity in purchased units as in the purchase of units with little scope for improvement. This result is similar to that observed for changes in market shares.

The strategy of dividing all 4-digit industries by the degree of foreign ownership was designed to stratify industries based on the multitude of factors that are associated with foreign ownership, most of which are also predicted to affect the success of mergers. This strategy will be particularly powerful if the factors that affect foreign ownership also affect the efficacy of mergers. The results suggest that this does, in part, occur. This finding should not be misconstrued to imply that factors other than those determining foreign investment also influence the effect of mergers, nor that there are some reasons for foreign investment that might be less conducive to the success of mergers.

In order to investigate the extent to which other factors affect the success of mergers and of foreign ownership, all 4-digit manufacturing industries were divided into five groups: resource-based, labour-intensive, scale-related, product-differentiated, and science-based. These categories were based on a taxonomy outlined by the Organization for Economic Cooperation and Development (OECD) (1987, chapter 7, Annex A). Canadian industries were assigned to the classification used by the OECD using the Statistics Canada concordance between the Canadian Standard Industrial Classification (SIC) and the International Standard Industrial Classification (ISIC) used by the OECD. Then a discriminant analysis was performed using variables such as wage rate, percent

TABLE 7

CHANGES IN RELATIVE PRODUCTIVITY BETWEEN 1970 AND 1979 OF PLANTS UNDERGOING UNRELATED CONTROL CHANGES BY INDUSTRY TYPE, AND FOREIGN OWNERSHIP BY INDUSTRY TYPE[1]

| INDUSTRY TYPE[2] | FOREIGN-OWNERSHIP TRANCHE | | | |
	LOW	MEDIUM	HIGH	ALL
Panel A:				
Changes in Relative Productivity				
(value added per employee)				
Natural resources	0.08	−0.19	0.02	−0.02
Labour-intensive	−0.24	0.03	−0.06	−0.09
Scale-based	0.31	−0.01	−0.08	0.09
Product-differentiated	−0.09	0.65	0.14	0.33
Science-based		−0.14	0.28	0.22
Panel B:				
Levels of 1979 Foreign Ownership(%)				
and Number of Industries (in brackets)				
Natural resources	13 (21)	37 (15)	82 (16)	41 (52)
Labour-intensive	10 (28)	42 (18)	76 (8)	30 (54)
Scale-based	13 (6)	42 (13)	82 (14)	54 (33)
Product-differentiated	6 (1)	44 (8)	80 (8)	58 (17)
Science-based	(0)	41 (2)	83 (9)	75 (11)
All	11 (56)	41 (56)	81 (56)	44 (167)

[1]Relative productivity is defined as the productivity in plants undergoing control changes divided by the productivity of continuing plants that did not experience a control change. A weighted mean was calculated for productivity (value-added per worker) in each category and then the ratio of the two was computed. The value of the change in relative productivity is the difference in this ratio between 1979 and 1970.
[2]Industry Groupings are defined in OECD(1987).

SOURCE: Special Tabulations, Business and Labour Market Analysis Group, Statistics Canada

of value added accounted for by labour remuneration, concentration, economies of scale estimates, R&D intensity, and advertising-to-sales ratios to verify the classification. Corrections were made when the original assignment was shown to be wanting. Then the same weighted-average relative-productivity variable used in Table 6 was calculated for each of the five main industry groupings, cross-classified by foreign-ownership tranche. Changes in the relative productivity of each category are reported in Table 7, panel A. Panel B reports the number of industries classified to the cell and the percentage of foreign ownership in each.

The effect of mergers on productivity differs substantially across the sample, both for industry totals and across foreign-ownership tranches. In natural resource industries and labour-intensive industries, the overall effect of mergers on productivity is negative. Scale-based industries experience a small gain from control changes. Product-differentiated and science-based industries

TABLE 8

EFFECTS OF CHANGES IN CONTROL OF CONTINUING ESTABLISHMENTS (RELATIVE TO CONTINUING ESTABLISHMENTS WITHOUT CONTROL CHANGES), BY NATIONALITY OF FIRM AND EXTENT OF FOREIGN OWNERSHIP, 1970 AND 1979[1] (WEIGHTED MEAN RATIO)

| CHARACTERISTIC BY CATEGORY | YEAR | FOREIGN-OWNERSHIP TRANCHE | | | |
		LOW	MEDIUM	HIGH	ALL
Productivity (value added per employee)					
All continuing plants acquired	1979	1.02	1.03	0.80	0.95
All continuing plants divested	1970	0.97	1.04	0.69	0.87
Domestic acquired from domestic	1979	1.05	1.12	0.68	0.96
Domestic divested to domestic	1970	1.06	1.16	0.61	0.94
Domestic acquired from foreign	1979	1.12	1.01	0.86	1.01
Foreign divested to domestic	1970	0.86	0.95	0.55	0.76
Foreign acquired from domestic	1979	0.95	0.87	0.80	0.86
Domestic divested to foreign	1970	0.87	0.77	0.73	0.77
Foreign acquired from foreign	1979	0.93	0.92	0.83	0.89
Foreign divested to foreign	1970	0.85	0.91	0.79	0.83
Average remuneration per production worker					
All continuing plants acquired	1979	1.07	0.97	0.88	0.97
All continuing plants divested	1970	1.08	1.00	0.87	0.98
Domestic acquired from domestic	1979	1.12	1.02	0.79	0.99
Foreign divested to domestic	1970	1.20	1.05	0.79	1.02
Domestic acquired from foreign	1979	1.09	0.98	0.91	0.99
Foreign divested to domestic	1970	0.96	1.02	0.98	1.01
Foreign acquired from domestic	1979	0.99	0.80	0.88	0.89
Domestic divested to foreign	1970	0.89	0.82	0.87	0.86
Foreign acquired from foreign	1979	0.97	0.95	0.92	0.96
Foreign divested to foreign	1970	0.98	0.94	0.87	0.93
Annual salary per non-production worker					
All continuing plants acquired	1979	1.06	0.94	0.89	0.94
All continuing plants divested	1970	1.01	0.97	0.94	0.97
Domestic acquired from domestic	1979	1.14	0.94	0.85	0.96
Domestic divested to domestic	1970	1.08	0.96	0.91	0.96
Domestic acquired from foreign	1979	1.13	1.02	0.92	0.99
Foreign divested to domestic	1970	1.06	1.04	0.99	1.03
Foreign acquired from domestic	1979	0.91	0.89	0.86	0.88
Domestic divested to foreign	1970	0.91	0.91	0.98	0.93
Foreign acquired from foreign	1979	0.91	0.91	0.90	0.91
Foreign divested to foreign	1970	0.93	0.98	0.90	0.93
Percentage of non-production workers					
All continuing plants acquired	1979	1.53	1.48	0.77	1.30
All continuing plants divested	1970	1.76	1.48	0.78	1.35
Domestic acquired from domestic	1979	1.62	1.55	0.64	1.24
Domestic divested to domestic	1970	1.72	1.56	0.57	1.23

TABLE 8 *continued*

| CHARACTERISTIC BY CATEGORY | YEAR | FOREIGN-OWNERSHIP TRANCHE | | | |
		LOW	MEDIUM	HIGH	ALL
Domestic acquired from foreign	1979	1.71	1.19	1.05	1.30
Foreign divested to domestic	1970	1.46	1.39	1.39	1.40
Foreign acquired from domestic	1979	1.21	0.92	0.60	0.93
Domestic divested to foreign	1970	1.71	1.01	0.50	0.98
Foreign acquired from foreign	1979	1.78	1.95	0.80	1.57
Foreign divested to foreign	1970	2.23	1.67	0.78	1.52

[1]Only unrelated mergers were considered. For definition of control, see Table 1. All summary statistics presented here are fully weighted averages, defined in Table 6.

SOURCE: Special tabulations, Business and Labour Market Analysis Group, Statistics Canada

exhibit the greatest productivity gains. It is the assets primarily associated with marketing and innovation that generate the greatest gains from merger activity. Differences across the five sectors in the tranche with the highest foreign ownership (column 3) mirror the overall total. Few gains are made in natural resources, labour-intensive industries, or even in scale industries; all of the gains are in the product-differentiated and science-based industries. In contrast, the tranche with the highest domestic ownership (column 1) makes relatively more gains in resource and scale industries, but does poorly in the product-differentiated tranche as compared to the high foreign ownership tranche. A comparison of the high and medium foreign-ownership tranches for the science-based industries (row 5, columns 2 and 3) shows that domestic ownership leads to lower gains in this sector.

We have established the basic relation between the prevalence of foreign ownership in an industry and the character of gains that stem from changes in the control of establishments. During the 1970s, productivity gains typically resulted from changes in control. Where foreign ownership is low, there is some evidence that gains come from containing excess costs, or that they come from closely related diversification. Where foreign ownership is high, gains seem to stem from improved usage of lumpy and intangible assets. Especially for the industries with high foreign ownership, there remains the important question whether those gains come specifically from control changes involving foreign enterprises, or whether they are independent of the firms' nationalities. To answer that question, we divided the establishments into two groups: those that in 1970 were fated for control changes and those that in 1979 had undergone changes into foreign and domestic control. This division allowed us to identify those control changes subject to the four classes of changes shown in Table 8: foreign-to-foreign, foreign-to-domestic, domestic-to-foreign, and domestic-to-domestic. Table 8 reports on the same characteristics as Table 6: labour productivity, production and non-production worker remuneration, and the proportion of the workforce employed as non-production workers. In each section, we repeat the data from Table 6 on the ratios for all establishments subject to changes in control to all continuing establishments. Then, using the same control group, we report ratios for the groups subdivided by nationality of enterprise.

Several conclusions emerge from the pattern of productivity changes. First, although the largest gains are centred in the industries with high foreign ownership (Table 8, column 4), domestic-to-domestic and foreign-to-domestic transfers are also shown to perform well. Thus gains involving domestic enterprises as buyers are just as large as those which involve foreign firms as buyers. Where foreign ownership is high, the environment benefits both domestic and foreign takeovers. Second, the lowest foreign ownership tranche demonstrates a tendency for foreign firms to do well. Foreign-to-foreign and domestic-to-foreign transfers lead to gains, although domestic-to-domestic transfers lead to losses. This finding suggests that foreign transfers in all tranches involve lumpy asset transfer, whereas for the most part, lumpy assets are involved only for domestic transfers in the high foreign-ownership sector.

Exercises similar to those presented in Table 8 for productivity were also done using the five-fold classification, consisting of natural resource, labour-intensive, scale-related, product differentiated, and science-based industries. All cells where there were particularly large losses or gains were chosen, and differences between productivity gains for domestic-to-domestic and foreign-to-foreign transfers were examined. The differences were found to be small. The environment rather than nationality is the primary determining factor of success for transfers within each of the two nationality groups.

In Table 6, we found that control changes reduce above-norm wages slightly in industries with low foreign ownership, while employee compensation starts below norm in industries with high foreign ownership and increases. Table 8 shows that the "excess" wages[28] in low foreign-ownership industries appear mainly in domestic establishments and are alleviated most in domestic-to-domestic mergers. Where foreign ownership is high, changes in control tend to bring wage increases, except for transfers of control to domestic firms. Thus both industry environment and nationality affect the extent to which wages change after a transfer of control. Wages decline more in the low foreign-ownership tranche for both domestic-to-domestic and foreign-to-foreign transfers than in the high foreign-ownership tranche. In the latter tranche wages actually increase. However, the difference in the performance of domestic-to-domestic transfers is greater than the difference in the performance of foreign-to-foreign transfers when the low and high foreign-ownership tranches are compared.

In Table 6, we noted that transfers tended to increase salaries in industries with low foreign ownership and to decrease salaries in the high foreign-ownership industries. Table 8 shows that the tendency to increase salaries comes from domestic acquisitions in the low foreign-ownership sector. The compression of salaries in the high foreign-ownership industries following changes in control occurs in every category other than foreign-to-foreign changes. As occurred with wage rates, the effect of control changes on salary differs across tranches, and the differential effect is greatest in the domestic-to-domestic sector.

Also in Table 6, we saw that changes in control bring about reductions in the non-production worker component of the workforce where foreign ownership is low, but cause virtually no change where it is high. Table 8 shows that those staff reductions in firms characterized by low foreign ownership occur in all sectors except the domestic-to-foreign changes. Where foreign ownership is high, the percentage employed as non-production workers is unaffected by foreign-to-foreign control changes but increases in the classes where a domestic divestor is involved.

The descriptions provided by the weighted averages in Table 8 give a broad overview of the effects of changes in control. In order to provide a more precise test of the effect of nationality and foreign-ownership tranche on control changes, a regression using the underlying micro-units was performed. All establishments existing in 1970 and 1979 were pooled, and value-added per worker was regressed on size of plant, industry binary variables, a shift term to allow intercept and size slope to vary between 1970 and 1979, and binary variables for all entry, exit, acquisition and divestiture categories. The binary variables permit estimation of the productivity of a category relative to plants that continue over the decade without a change in control. Earlier results (Baldwin, 1991a) founded on this micro-data base, showed that there was no productivity gain, on average, for the unrelated control changes (the exit/entry category) and a significant gain for horizontal mergers (the exit/continuing category).[29]

Building on this framework, we divided each of the acquisition categories into domestic-to-domestic, foreign-to-foreign, foreign-to-domestic, and domestic-to-foreign so as to test whether the effect of a category depended on the nationalities involved in a transfer. By interacting each of these with binary variables for the foreign-ownership tranche, the hypothesis that environment (i.e., industry sector) is a matter of importance was also examined.

The analysis of unrelated control changes (plants divested by exiting firms and acquired by entering firms), indicated that differences across tranches and across nationality groupings were both insignificant. For horizontal mergers — divestitures by exiting firms that were acquired by continuing firms — foreign-ownership tranche was more important than nationality. Most of the control changes for different nationality types did better in the low foreign-ownership tranche.

In conclusion, when nationality of transaction party is examined, neither type of acquirer appears systematically to outperform the other. In the high foreign-ownership tranche, domestic-to-domestic transfers are characterized by higher productivity and non-production worker gains, but lower wage gains and greater salary losses, compared with foreign-to-foreign transfers. In the low foreign-ownership tranche, foreign-to-foreign transfers have better productivity gains and lower wage-rate losses than domestic-to-domestic transfers, but lower salary and non-production worker changes. There is also evidence of a division of labour between domestic-to-domestic and foreign-to-foreign transfers. Domestic enterprises achieve more containment of costs. When control changes across all tranches are considered, domestic-to-domestic transfers experience either a decline or no change in their relative wage, salary and non-production worker percentages; the reverse occurs in foreign-to-foreign transfers. Foreign enterprises effect more relocations of resources that might lead to synergistic gains. Their productivity gains extend across all industries, whereas these gains occur only in the high foreign-ownership tranche for domestic-to-domestic transfers. There is an evident difference between the types of opportunities for productive control changes that arise in industry structures congenial to foreign ownership and those that arise in industries uncongenial to such ownership.

Summary and Conclusions

THIS PAPER HAS INVESTIGATED the effects of mergers and other changes in the control of establishments using the comprehensive data of Statistics Canada for manufacturing establishments in 1970 and 1979. Theory and previous research on mergers suggest that the effect of changes in control might vary with the affinity of industries' structures for the operation of multinational enterprises: the same opportunities for the synergistic deployment of lumpy and intangible assets that foster foreign investment also create opportunities for beneficial changes in control. On the other hand, if mergers increase efficiency in the use of establishments' existing input flows, no such association should appear. The data support the following conclusions:

1. The proportion of establishments subject to changes in control over 1970 - 1979 increases with the importance of foreign ownership. The occurrence of greenfield entry by new firms and close-down exit decreases sharply with foreign ownership, so that industries with high foreign ownership experience less pressure from this source to improve efficiency. They also experience a little less turnover of market share among incumbents. Roughly speaking, producers in industries with high foreign ownership feel pressures to achieve efficiency more from control changes and less from domestic product-market competition than do producers in industries with low foreign ownership.
2. Industries with low and high foreign ownership differ sharply in the opportunities they afford for gains through changes in control. Where foreign ownership is high, so are opportunities for the synergistic deployment of lumpy and intangible assets. Where foreign ownership is low, the opportunities for productive changes in control lie more in cost containment and improved use of the establishment's existing input flow.

3. The favourable effects of changes in control increase with an industry's foreign ownership. Changes in control lead to increases in relative market share and relative productivity that are greater in the highest foreign-ownership tranche than the lowest foreign-ownership tranche.

4. While industries with high foreign ownership show gains in productivity associated with control changes, there is a wide variation of performance within this sector. In particular, productivity gains are larger in product-differentiated and science-based industries, and less in the natural resource sector.

5. Productivity gains in high foreign-ownership industries do not come only from foreign acquisitions. Acquisitions by domestic firms also make important contributions in this sector, though not in the sector with the highest level of domestic ownership. This finding accords with the hypothesis that the predominant reason for control change in these high foreign-ownership industries relates to the synergistic merging of assets.

6. Foreign firm productivity gains are not restricted to the high foreign-ownership sector. That they also occur in the sector with the highest level of domestic ownership supports the contention that most control changes affecting multinational firms involve the transfer of specialized assets.

7. Transfers between foreign firms in the sector with the highest foreign ownership are beneficial on several counts. Control changes involving foreign-to-foreign firms in the highest foreign-ownership sector lead to productivity gains and are not accompanied generally by wage or salary losses for production workers, nor by a decline in the proportion of the workforce employed as non-production workers.

8. There are sectoral differences in the function of transfers changing the nationality of control that suggest a specialization of function by nationality across foreign ownership tranches. On the basis of productivity, wage, salary and non-production worker gains, transfers from foreign to domestic firms do better in the domestic than the foreign sector, and transfers from domestic to foreign firms do better in the high foreign-ownership sector.

9. Domestic-to-domestic control changes in the low foreign-ownership sector have so many negative characteristics — share losses, productivity losses, wage losses, non-production worker losses — as to suggest that problems may occur with this type of transaction.

10. Once we control for the opportunities that market structures dictate for productive changes in control, there is no evidence that either foreign or domestic acquirers achieve consistently better results across the whole range of industries.

11. Foreign firms are not proportionally more active as acquirers in industries with high foreign ownership. However, acquiring firms exhibit some division of labour by nationality. Foreign control seems more oriented toward realizing synergistic use of resources, while domestic control favours cost containment. The decline in the extent of foreign control that occurred

during the 1970s has no counterpart in evidence of asymmetrical effects of shifts of establishments between domestic and foreign control.

The policy conclusions that follow from these quantitative findings are clear and largely benign. Control changes typically have favourable effects on productivity and efficiency. It is desirable to have both foreign and domestic enterprises active in the market for corporate control because both types of enterprise bring somewhat different skills to the task of resource reallocation. If any class of enterprises sports an inferior record, it is large domestic firms undertaking mergers in domestic industries; encouraging them to put their funds to other uses might be warranted. Some foreign-to-foreign changes in control in Canada (particularly horizontal mergers in the high foreign-ownership category) probably were adjuncts of similarly suspect mergers taking place outside Canada. Finally, because industries with high foreign ownership are also highly concentrated and subject to fewer pressures for efficiency from actual and potential competition, the discouragement of control changes is probably more costly than it is in industries with low foreign ownership. That consideration calls into question a procedure of public review of changes involving foreign acquirers unless the procedure recognizes the value of control changes. Little is known about the objectives actually pursued in the review of foreign control changes during this period (Rugman, 1980). The findings in general support the benign view taken of corporate mergers by the Royal Commission on Corporate Control (1978), although they do not address the question of discrepancies between private and social values that are raised by horizontal mergers and perhaps by some other types (compare Stanbury and Waverman, 1979).

ENDNOTES

1. Caves (1989) surveyed this literature as well as the positive findings based on *ex ante* market valuations. Evidence on large mergers in Great Britain leads to similar conclusions.
2. Lumpiness refers to a fixed cost or minimum capacity that may be large relative to a single market, so that declining marginal revenue deters full utilization there. An intangible asset or skill, which is a public good proprietary to the firm, is of course the limiting case of lumpy capacity.
3. See Gilbert and Newbery (1988), Caves and Mehra (1986).
4. An international merger that extends multinational control of business assets can be horizontal (that is, a geographic extension), vertical, or a diversification with regard to the product market(s) of the foreign acquirer. The available evidence indicates that a one-time prevalence of horizontal and vertical modes of expansion has given way somewhat to foreign investments that are diversifying in both geographic and product space (Hisey and Caves, 1985). It is not clear, however, what efficiency

gains, if any, underlie this trend; Davidson and McFetridge (1984) found that the sale or liquidation of a U.S. firm's Canadian affiliate is more likely if the affiliate operates in a different two-digit industry from its parent.

5. The propensity of any country's political system to lend a sympathetic ear to a domestic management threatened by a foreign enterprise's hostile takeover only reinforces the point.

6. When a Canadian business unit is (or becomes) part of a multinational enterprise, the level (change) of its reported productivity or profitability depends on transfer prices in its dealings with its corporate siblings. We assume that transfer-pricing practices may inject noise but do not systematically obscure the underlying economic relations.

7. Globerman (1977) summarized data from various issues of the *Combines Investigation Report* indicating that the foreign proportion had been about 25 percent in the late 1940s, then rose by 1953 to a plateau level varying between 35 percent and 45 percent. The apparent trend may result from the data source, however.

8. This pattern is consistent with the implication of evidence discussed below that foreign firms' entries are driven more by proprietary assets possessed by the foreign parents than by opportunities newly emerging in Canada.

9. Shapiro (1984) obtained similar conclusions for domestic and foreign new plant creation in Canadian manufacturing industries during 1972 - 1976. He did not, however, break the data down by continuing firm new plant creation and new firm plant creation.

10. Laiken (1973) found no association between acquisition activity and financial performance among Canadian firms. Lecraw (1977) found that large firms classified as unrelated diversifiers were heavily engaged in merger activity (his Table 13) and tended to report lower profits over 1960 - 1975 than did less diversified firms (Table 20). Jog and Riding (1988) and Tarasofsky and Corvari (1991), using a sample of mergers obtained from the merger register of the Department of Consumer and Corporate Affairs by acquirers that were listed on the Toronto Stock Exchange, found about equal numbers of post-merger failures and successes, where success is equated to profitability.

11. Reuber and Roseman (1967, pp.76-8) reported that the most common reasons given for mergers were the desire of the acquiree to sell and the acquirer's desire to add capacity cheaper than through *de novo* investment. They also reported that, although acquirees were no less profitable than the firms acquiring them, losses were more common among the acquirees. Lecraw (1977, pp. 16-18), generalizing from case studies of large mergers, confirmed the importance of sellers' initiatives; however, he ascribed importance to what was later named the "free cash flow" hypothesis, that large enterprises undertake mergers when their cash inflows exceed outlays on profitable reinvestments in their base activities plus normal dividends.

12. For an analysis similar to that made in this paper, but based on the subdivision of industries by research intensity, see Baldwin and Gorecki (1991d).

13. The total numbers of plants per enterprise are also shown, but they are not as good a measure of multiplant operation because those numbers vary among industries mainly with the number of single-plant firms. Not surprisingly, this suggests that single-plant firms are more common in industries where foreign ownership is low.

14. Plants, of course, produce some products that are not classified to their primary four-digit industries, and these products are included in line 4. To that extent, the lower bound shown in line 3 is not constraining. Given the typically high plant-specialization ratios (the percentage of output produced by a plant that is classified to the Standard Industrial Classification [SIC] industry to which the plant is assigned), however, the constraint is still approximately relevant.

15. Plant size is also related to diversity and to foreign-control status within industries (Caves, 1975). We therefore ascertained by a regression procedure which controls for plant size that the foreign-domestic differences in plant characteristics shown here are not solely due to plant-size differences.

16. For a description of the data and the definitions of entry and exit used, see Baldwin and Gorecki (1991a).

17. These relations were investigated extensively by Baldwin and Gorecki (1990), showing that greenfield entrants and entrants by acquisition fall into different segments of an industry's firm-size distribution. Moreover, when industries are sorted by producer concentration rather than by foreign ownership, as in Table 3, essentially the same conclusions follow about the relative place of greenfield entry as opposed to entry in contrast to entry by acquisition.

18. The inter-industry averages shown in Table 3 are unweighted. When we weight these averages by industry size, the changes in the data indicate that, except for continuing-plant turnover, the intensity of turnover is greater in smaller industries. A sufficient (but not necessary) explanation for this is the tendency for absolute sizes of plants (and firms) to be correlated to the size of the industry (market). The proportion of a plant's costs that are sunk probably increases with the plant's absolute size (capital intensity certainly increases), both within and between industries. Smaller plants in smaller industries accordingly exhibit greater turnover.

19. See Baldwin (1991b). This dependent variable allows for fixed industry effects.

20. Differences were found in the related spin-off merger component. Transfers between continuing firms both of which are foreign — spin-offs to incumbents — show a differential pattern between domestic and foreign industry tranches. These foreign-to-foreign transfers gain share in the low foreign ownership tranche and lose it in the higher tranches.

21. Recall that horizontal mergers and plants transferred between continuing firms are excluded from this analysis.

22. Thus, for example, relative output per worker was calculated as follows: the numerator is the sum of output divided by the sum of workers taken across all plants in all merged plants in one foreign-ownership group. The denominator is the sum of output divided by the sum of workers taken across all continuing plants that did not experience a control change in the same foreign-ownership group.

23. The greater productivity gain from horizontal mergers might suggest monopoly rents. However, it should be noted that firms merging purely for monopoly profits, unless they actually achieve a monopoly, generally must give up some market share to non-merging firms in order to increase their profit margins. The evidence of Table 5 indicated that horizontal mergers in industries dominated by domestic firms also achieve market-share increase.

24. See Baldwin and Gorecki (1991c) for a discussion of the contribution that plant turnover makes to productivity growth.

25. The non-production-worker percentages of plants subject to control changes in the high-foreign-ownership sector are less than those of continuing plants both before and after acquisition, and the percentages of non-production workers in plants opened and closed in general decline across groups with the extent of foreign ownership. These patterns suggest that in industries with high foreign ownership the high-ground positions of continuing units are held by foreign-controlled units employing large non-production contingents and subject to low turnover. This finding is consistent with the evidence from Table 5 on the variation of foreign-to-foreign mergers with the extent of foreign control.

26. The weights are calculated in relation to all plants in a foreign-ownership tranche, that is, value-added and labour inputs are totalled for all plants in a foreign-ownership tranche.

27. The weights are calculated for all plants in an industry, that is, the value-added and labour inputs are totalled for all plants in an industry.

28. The term should not be given a normative connotation. All we know is the level of average compensation in the control-change establishments relative to continuing establishments with no changes in control. We do not know whether compensation levels lie above or below employees' opportunity costs in either group.

29. The results were derived from an unweighted regression that used all plants existing in 1970 and 1979, and calculated productivity gains relative to plants that continued over the decade without a change in control.

BIBLIOGRAPHY

Baldwin, John R. "The Success of Mergers in the Canadian Manufacturing Sector", a paper presented at a conference, "Mergers, Oligopoly, and Trade", University of Aix-Marseille, 1991a.

_____. "Patterns of Intra-Industry Mobility in the Canadian Manufacturing Sector," Analytical Studies Branch, Research Paper #23f, Ottawa, Statistics Canada, 1991b.

Baldwin, John R. and Paul K. Gorecki. *The Role of Scale in Canada/U.S. Productivity Differences in the Manufacturing Sector, 1970 - 1979*, Royal Commission on the Economic Union and Development Prospects for Canada, Research Studies, Vol. 6, Toronto, University of Toronto Press, 1986a.

_____. "Mergers and Merger Policy in the Canadian Manufacturing Sector: 1971 - 79", Discussion Paper No. 297, Ottawa, Economic Council of Canada, 1986b.

_____. "Plant Creation versus Plant Acquisition: The Entry Process in Canadian Manufacturing", *International Journal of Industrial Organization* 5, March 1987, pp. 27-41.

_____. "Measuring the Dynamics of Market Structure", *Annales d'Economie et de Statistique* 15/16, July-December 1989, pp. 315-32.

_____. "Mergers Placed in the Context of Firm Turnover", *Proceedings of the Census Bureau 1990 Research Conference*, Washington, DC, Bureau of the Census, 1990, pp. 53-73.

_____. "Measuring Firm Entry and Exit with Panel Data", *Analysis of Data in Time: Proceedings of the 1989 International Symposium*, A. C. Singh and P. Whitridge (eds), Ottawa, Statistics Canada, 1991a, pp. 255-70.

_____. "Firm Entry and Exit in the Canadian Manufacturing Section", *Canadian Journal of Economics*, May 1991b.

_____. "Entry, Exit and Productivity Growth", in *Entry and Market Contestability: An International Comparison*, Paul Geroski and J. Scwalbach (eds), Oxford, Basil Blackwell, 1991c.

_____. "Foreign High-Technology Acquisitions in Canada's Manufacturing Sector in *Foreign Investment, Technology and Economic Growth*, Donald McFetridge (ed), Calgary, University of Calgary Press, 1991d.

Caves, Richard E. "Causes of Direct Investment: Foreign Firms' Share in Canadian and United Kingdom Manufacturing Industries", *Review of Economics and Statistics* 56, August 1974, pp. 279-93.

_____. *Diversification, Foreign Investment, and Scale in North American Manufacturing Industries*, Ottawa, Economic Council of Canada, 1975.

_____. "Mergers, Takeovers, and Economic Efficiency: Foresight vs. Hindsight", *International Journal of Industrial Organization* 7, March 1989, pp. 151-74.

Caves, Richard E. and Sanjeev Mehra. "Entry of Foreign Multinationals into U.S. Manufacturing", *Competition in Global Industries*, M.E. Porter (ed), Boston, Harvard Business School Press, 1986, pp. 449-81.

Crookell, Harold. "Subsidiary Strategy in a Free Trade Environment", Working Paper No. 1990-II, Investment Canada, 1990.

Davidson, William and Donald G. McFetridge. "Recent Directions on International Strategies", *Columbia Journal of World Business* 19, Summer 1984, pp. 95-101.

DeMelto, Dennis P., Kathryn E. McMullen and Russel M. Wills. "Preliminary Report: Innovation and Technological Change in Five Canadian Industries", Discussion Paper No. 176, Economic Council of Canada, 1980.

Eckbo, B. Espen, "The Market for Corporate Control: Policy Issues and Capital Market Evidence", *Mergers, Corporate Concentration and Power in Canada*, R.S. Khemani, D.M.

Shapiro, and W.T. Stanbury (eds), Halifax, Institute for Research in Public Policy, 1988.

Gilbert, Richard J. and David M. Newbery. "Entry, Acquisition, and the Value of Shark Repellent", Working Paper #8888, Department of Economics, University of California, Berekely, August 1988.

Globerman, Steven. Mergers and Acquisitions in Canada: A Background Report, Royal Commission on Corporate Concentration, Study No. 34, Ottawa, Supply and Services Canada, 1977.

Gorecki, Paul K. Economies of Scale and Efficient Plant Size in Canadian Manufacturing Industries, Ottawa, Bureau of Competition Policy, Department of Consumer and Corporate Affairs, n.d.

Hisey, Karen B. and Richard E. Caves. "Diversification Strategy and Choice of Country: Diversifying Acquisitions Abroad by U.S. Multinationals, 1978-1980", Journal of International Business Studies 16, Summer 1985, pp. 51-64.

Jog, Vijay M. and Allan L. Riding. "Post-Acquisition Performance of Partially Acquired Canadian Firms", Mergers Corporate Concentration and Power in Canada, R.S. Khemani, D.M. Shapiro and W.T. Stanbury (eds), Halifax, Institute for Research in Public Policy, 1988.

Kaplan, Steven N. "The Effect of Management Buyouts on Operating Performance and Value", Journal of Financial Economics 24, October 1989, pp. 217-54.

Laiken, S.N. "Financial Performance of Merging Firms in a Virtually Unconstrained Legal Environment", Antitrust Bulletin 18, Winter 1973, pp. 827-51.

Lecraw, Donald J. Conglomerate Mergers in Canada, Royal Commission on Corporate Concentration, Study No. 32, Ottawa, Supply and Services Canada, 1977.

Lichtenberg, Frank R. and Donald Siegel. "Productivity and Changes in Ownership of Manufacturing Plants", Brookings Papers on Economic Activity, 1987 (3), pp. 643-83.

Matthews, Roy A. Structural Change and Industrial Policy: The Redeployment of Canadian Manufacturing, 1960-1980, Ottawa, Supply and Services Canada, 1985.

McFetridge, Donald G. Trade Liberalization and the Multinationals, Ottawa, Economic Council of Canada, 1987.

Mueller, Dennis C. "Mergers and Market Share", Review of Economics and Statistics, 67, May 1985, pp. 259-67.

Organization for Economic Cooperation and Development. Structural Adjustment and Economic Performance, Paris, OECD, 1987.

Ravenscraft, David J. and F.M. Scherer. Mergers, Sell-Offs, and Economic Efficiency, Washington, Brookings Institution, 1987.

Royal Commission on Corporate Concentration. Report of the Royal Commission on Corporate Concentration. Ottawa, Supply and Services Canada, 1978.

Reuber, Grant L., and Frank Roseman. The Take-Over of Canadian Firms, 1945-61, Ottawa, Queen's Printer, 1969.

Rugman, Alan M. Multinationals in Canada: Theory, Performance and Economic Impact, Boston, Martinus Nijhoff, 1980.

Shapiro, Daniel M. "Entry, Exit, and the Theory of the Multinational Corporation", The Multinational Corporation in the 1980s, Charles P. Kindleberger and David B. Audretsch (eds), Cambridge, MIT Press, 1984, pp. 103-22.

Stanbury, William T., and Leonard Waverman. "Merger Policy of the Royal Commission on Corporate Concentration: Conclusions Without Evidence", Perspectives on the Royal Commission on Corporate Concentration, P.K. Gorecki and W.T. Stanbury (eds), Montreal, Butterworth & Co. for Institute for Research and Public Policy, 1979, pp. 109-31.

Tarasofsky, Abraham, with Ronald Corvari. "Corporate Merges and Acquisitions: Evidence of Profitability", unpublished manuscript, Economic Council of Canada, 1990.

Wolf, B.N. "Industrial Diversification and Internationalization: Some Empirical Evidence", *Journal of Industrial Economics*, 26, December 1977, pp. 177-91.

Michel Patry,   and   Michel Poitevin   5
Institut d'économie appliquée,   Université de Montréal et
École des Hautes Études Commerciales   Centre de recherche et développement
                                         en économique

Hostile Takeovers: The Canadian Evidence

Introduction

IN THE 1980s, a wave of hostile takeovers literally swept across the United States and, to a lesser extent, across Canada. These takeovers have invited strong reactions from the public and academics. Yet, despite the apparent curiosity that hostile takeovers generate, little is known about them. For instance, we do not know what motivates these aggressive actions, or how they differ from mergers or friendly takeovers. There have been numerous studies of mergers in the United States and Canada,[1] but most have failed to discriminate between different types of takeover and have reported only aggregate results. Because the proliferation of hostile takeovers is a fairly recent phenomenon, they have not so far been the object of extensive research.[2]

Casual reading of the business press indicates that many managers believe that the future will see fewer, larger corporations in operation. The recent world trend in trade liberalization is a sure indicator that these managers are right in their view. If managers talked about diversification and conglomerates in the 1960s and 1970s, economic integration and market globalization have become part of the language of the 1980s and 1990s. In a context of economic integration and globalization, takeovers may have an important role to play in the reallocation of resources by allowing corporations to merge and achieve the economies of scale and scope necessary to compete in international markets. The purpose of this paper is to examine the role played by hostile takeovers in this process of resource reallocation.

Hostile takeovers are characterized by the refusal of the target's management to accept the bidder's initial offer. The resistance by the target's management can take various forms, but it usually forces the bidder to increase the initial bid, often substantially, in order to secure the deal. Consequently, the acquiring firm often pays a price for the target that is significantly higher than the price at which the target was evaluated on the stock market prior to the transaction. This higher price reflects the value that the bidder attaches to the acquisition of the target. We address the question of why the bidder values the target more highly than the stock market. To understand why the bidder pays a premium above its stock-market price for the target, one must determine whether or not hostile takeovers generate value for the acquiring firm and, if they do, where these gains come from. Most studies on takeovers (see note 1) calculate the abnormal returns earned by the bidder and the target. However these studies often fail to identify the sources of these gains. To understand the impact of takeover activity on the Canadian economy, we investigate the origin of takeover premiums.

We focus on a sample of recent hostile takeovers of Canadian firms. For each transaction, we estimate the premium paid by the bidder over the target's stock-market value. We then examine the post-takeover performance of these transactions to try to explain the addition of this premium. To do so, we first identify potential factors which are known to motivate takeovers: wealth transfers between shareholders of the two firms, layoffs, investment cuts, tax savings and sell-offs.[3] We then qualitatively assess the relative importance of these factors for each transaction. As a byproduct, we can examine the role played by foreign firms in the acquisition of Canadian firms. Finally, we compare our results with those of other studies on American and Canadian takeovers.

Sample and Methodology

WE NOW TURN TO A DESCRIPTION of our sample of hostile takeovers. In the next section, we characterize the motivating factors behind hostile takeovers.

Description of the Sample

WE OPT FOR A CASE-STUDY APPROACH to the analysis of hostile takeovers. Ideally, we would prefer to consider all takeover contests above some cut-off value involving a Canadian firm during, say, a three-year period. Conclusions drawn from such a sample would be more reliable. Bhagat, Shleifer & Vishny (1989) construct such a sample for the United States, as they select all hostile takeovers worth $50 million or more over the 1984 - 1986 period. They consider a total of 62 cases. Similarly, Morck, Shleifer & Vishny (1990) study all takeovers (hostile and friendly) that involve one of the Fortune 500 firms in the United States. We do not have at our disposal a similar and exhaustive data set for Canada.

Instead, we identify ten cases of hostile takeovers worth $10 million or more, which we analyze both quantitatively and qualitatively.[4] Following the classic definition of W.T. Grimm, which is also adopted by Bhagat, Shleifer, & Vishny (1989), we consider a takeover to be hostile when the target's management, at least initially, expresses opposition (even if only to encourage higher bids).[5] We identified each case by looking at all major mergers and acquisitions between 1985 and 1989, examining the business press to determine whether the acquisition was the result of a hostile takeover, and then checking to determine that there was enough public information on the takeover to document wealth changes, layoffs, investment cuts, tax savings and sell-offs.[6] Many cases were rejected because of data limitations. For example, some takeovers involved private firms (Vidéotron buys TéléMétropole); others occurred too recently to allow for a detailed analysis of the post-takeover reorganizations (Socanav — Caisse de Dépôt buys Steinberg). A brief description of the selected targets and bidders, and some details about the transactions are given in the Appendix.

Although this list represents only a sample of all hostile takeovers, the cases we analyze cover a wide range of industries, including chemicals, communications, electronics, energy, financial services, manufacturing, and resources, and many involve a foreign bidder (Imasco — 40 percent owned by British BAT, Allied Lyons of Great Britain, France's Dumez S.A., and Indal and Motorola of the United States).

The information on each firm and takeover was gathered from various sources: the bidder's and target's annual reports, *FRI's Stocks Database*, the *Financial Post Corporate Database*, *Compustat*, *The Globe and Mail*, *The Financial Post*, and other business periodicals.

METHODOLOGY

OUR METHODOLOGY BORROWS heavily from that employed by Bhagat, Shleifer & Vishny (1989) and Bhide (1989). Following is a description of this methodology.

An understanding of the motives behind takeovers and of the sources of wealth gains to target firms' shareholders requires that we first evaluate the extent of the gains involved. To estimate these gains, we concentrate only on shareholders' gains and neglect the wealth changes experienced by non-shareholder constituencies. Although little evidence is available on this issue, recent advances in the literature found no significant abnormal returns to the target's bondholders (Dennis & McConnell, 1986). On the other hand, the literature on mergers and acquisitions in general tends to support the view that the target's shareholders frequently experience positive abnormal returns (Eckbo, 1986; Ravenscraft & Scherer, 1987; Bradley, Desai & Kim, 1988; Bhagat, Shleifer & Vishny, 1989; Asquith, Opler & Weston, 1990; Morck, Shleifer & Vishny, 1990).

We first estimate a market model of asset pricing for the target firm to forecast the value of the target firm on the day that it accepts the winning bid *as if the takeover had not occurred.* The market model simply argues that returns on the target's security, R_{it}, are linearly related to returns on a market portfolio, R_{mt}:

$$R_{it} = a_i + \beta_i R_{mt} + e_{it},$$

where R_{mt} is defined as the return on the Toronto Stock Exchange 300 index, and e_{it} is a stochastic disturbance term reflecting the effect of specific non-systematic risk on the firm's returns. We assume that e_{it} follows a normal distribution with a zero-mean. The estimated parameter β_i is a measure of the systematic risk of the firm, that is, a measure of the co-variance of the firm's returns with those of the market portfolio.

Equation (2.1) is estimated on the basis of daily observations of the closing price of the target's stock over a 200-day period. To offset the effects of any information leaks about the takeover attempt, we remove from the estimation period stock-price movements in the 80 trading days preceding the first bid. Hence, the estimation period goes from 280 trading days before the first bid is announced to 80 trading days before the announcement. This estimation strategy compares advantageously with the use of accounting data, since it takes into account the fluctuations of the stock market.

The parameter estimates are then used to compute the predicted return on the target's stock between date of the first bid minus 20 days and resolution date. The resulting predicted stock price is our forecast of the target's stock value had there been no takeover. We then compare this predicted value to the actual price paid by the bidding firm. This actual price is usually greater than the estimated market value; the difference is the premium paid by the bidding firm. If the bidding process is fairly competitive, the premium paid over the stock-market value of the target represents an estimate of the bidder's gains of acquiring the target. However, if the bidder has some idiosyncratic reasons for acquiring the target, his gains cannot be completely bid away, and the estimated premium may underestimate the bidder's gains.

The problem is to examine the post-takeover performance of the firms to see what justifies the payment of a premium. The study of post-takeover performance is complicated by the fact that in most cases the two firms merge following the takeover. Therefore, the use of accounting data does not always reflect the marginal impact of the takeover on the bidder and the target. Furthermore, accounting data are sometimes unreliable, as they may not correspond to the true economic worth of the assets. As a consequence, we rely on information sources such as stock-market prices, newspapers, business magazines and annual reports. This approach is possible because of the small sample size and the coverage that hostile takeovers get in the business press. However, since not all actions pertaining to the takeover are reported, our estimates of changes may be downward biased.

The post-takeover performance is assessed by looking at six different motivating factors that may have triggered the takeover, and that may explain the premium paid by the bidding firm. We now briefly describe these factors and provide the economic justification underlying them.

Wealth Change of Bidding Shareholders

ONCE A TAKEOVER IS ANNOUNCED, it becomes a zero-sum bargaining game between the shareholders of the two concerned firms. The transaction price is just a transfer between the two firms. One firm's gain is the other firm's loss. It is possible, then, that the bidding firm paid too much for the target. This possibility is investigated by forecasting the market value of the bidding firm *as if the transaction had never been proposed*, and comparing this forecast value to the actual value of the firm. The same methodology as that employed for the target can be adapted to assess the wealth changes of the bidder's shareholders. An estimation period of 200 trading days is also used for the bidder's empirical market model. The problem is a bit more complex in this case because there is no equivalent to the price paid to the target's shareholders. Furthermore, for reasons that have nothing to do with the takeover, many bidders' stock prices vary wildly in the often lengthy interval separating their first bid and the resolution date. For instance, some large firms pursue many acquisitions at the same time (for example, Motorola). Other firms experience regulatory shocks or go through a major reorganization (for instance, Gulf Canada Ltd. becomes Gulf Canada Corp.). We then define the abnormal change in bidding shareholders' wealth as the difference between the value of the firm three days after it has announced its first bid and its predicted value, using the market model, on that same day. We forecast the bidder's stock price three days after its bid, using the observed stock price three days before the bid and the forecast return given by the estimated market model for the seven-day period of three days before the bid to three days after the bid. This method allows us to capture the stock market's reaction to the first bid. It therefore reflects whether the market perceives the transaction as good news or bad news.

Using this forecast, we can infer the value that the stock market attributes to the takeover for the bidder. This value may be negative, in which case part of the premium is explained by a transfer of wealth between the two firms' shareholders.[7] This will be the case if, for example, managers pursue personal objectives and foresee personal gains in the takeover. Managers may then be willing to overbid somewhat for the target. On the other hand, if the bidding shareholders gain with the takeover, the amount of this gain must be added to the premium paid to reflect the total value generated by the takeover. This may be the case if the bidding firm has some sort of bargaining power which prevents the target from extracting all the rents from the transaction. For example, the target firm may have had difficulty defending itself by calling upon a white knight[8] or by threatening to undertake a recapitalization. To substantiate this point about the relative bargaining power of the two firms, we examine the relationship between, on one side, the split of the premium between the two firms and, on the other side, the level of defensive tactics undertaken by the target firm.

Layoffs

The presence of workers paid above their marginal productivity may motivate the acquiring firm better to allocate resources by firing some workers. These layoffs will then translate into cost savings and efficiency gains for the merged firm. The estimation of these cost savings will explain a portion of the premium paid by the bidder. Shleifer & Summers (1988) argue that one reason why workers may have been earning some rents before the takeover is the presence of implicit contracts between workers and shareholders. The layoffs of some of these workers by the acquiring firm can therefore be seen as a breach of contract. In that case these layoffs would represent a transfer of wealth from the workers to the bidding firm's shareholders.[9] In any case, layoffs represent a private gain to the acquiring firm that should be accounted for in the explanation of the premium. Whether or not those layoffs represent a breach of trust is not relevant for the imputation of the premium.

We proceed to estimate the present value of savings from layoffs as follows. We assume layoffs will last five years, the discount rate is 10 percent, and the pre-tax labour cost for a blue-collar worker is $35,000 per year and that for a white-collar worker is $80,000, including all benefits.[10]

Investment Cuts

Jensen (1986) argues that firms with excessive cash flows may invest in negative present-value projects. In that case, an acquiring firm may pay a premium for the target if it plans to cut back these negative present-value projects. When possible, we shall report how the acquiring firm modifies the investment projects of the target.

Tax Savings

If the target has some tax pools — that is unused tax losses — that may be realized sooner by the acquiring firm than by itself, then a premium may be justified. The reason is that in some cases, prior to the takeover, the stock market might not have valued those tax pools at the full value accruing to the acquiring firm.

Taxes might also motivate a premium if the target was underleveraged and the transaction was financed through debt. In this case, the deductibility of interest payments might reduce the target's financial costs without significantly raising expected costs of financial distress, thereby increasing the firm's market value.[11] However, this last argument may be difficult to justify, since it would also require explanation of why the target was underleveraged in the first place. Furthermore, to evaluate the importance of this source of tax savings we would need information, which we seldom have, on how quickly the debt is repaid. Thus, we shall focus mainly on the presence of tax pools, although we shall also qualify our analysis by considering how the transaction was financed.

Divestitures

The acquiring firm often dismantles part of the target firm by selling off some assets. Frequently, the sum of the dismantled assets may be worth more than the target as a whole.[12] The bidder may then generate value by selling these assets one by one, in a piecemeal fashion. For example, these assets may be sold to an incentive organization, such as a management group, or to an industry-related buyer. An incentive organization is willing to pay more for the assets because it improves their efficiency by managing them better. On the other hand, some assets may be worth more to a related buyer if their acquisition realizes economies of scale, or improves the market position with respect to competitors. These gains can be accounted for by looking at the industry and identifying the type of organization that acquires the assets put up for sale.

It is often argued that the market for corporate control acts as a watchdog to eliminate managerial inefficiencies.[13] These inefficiencies may be classified in one of two categories. First, inefficiencies may result from the mismanagement of existing assets. Second, inefficiencies may result from a misallocation of assets. In the first instance, the assets may be expected to be sold to an incentive organization; in the second, assets are most likely to be sold to a firm in a closely related industry.

Strategic Acquisitions

In the 1960s and 1970s, most mergers seemed to be undertaken by large conglomerates and motivated by diversification (Asquith, Opler & Weston, 1990). In the 1980s, the proportion of horizontal and vertical mergers[14] increased both in the United States and in Canada.[15] These horizontal acquisitions may increase the efficiency of the industry as the merged firms share production, marketing, distribution, research and development (R&D) and/or administrative facilities. They may also serve the purpose of increasing market power by reducing the number of firms in the industry, although this latter argument seems less convincing in a globalization context. These two effects, referred to as strategic, are difficult to quantify. It is therefore rather difficult to determine whether consumers are better off with or without the takeover. There is some evidence in Eckbo (1983) and Stillman (1983) that competitors' stock prices rise when a horizontal merger is announced; this move is consistent with the increased market power of the firms in the industry as a result of a greater concentration. Jensen (1988) cites evidence that in some cases competitors' stock prices have also risen when the government chal-

TABLE 1

CHANGES IN THE WEALTH OF TARGET AND BIDDING SHAREHOLDERS[1] ($ MIL)

DEAL	CHANGE IN TARGET'S WEALTH		CHANGE IN BIDDER'S WEALTH		TOTAL PREMIUM[2]
	$	%	$	%	
Imasco – Genstar	624.8	41.1	358.0	9.8	982.8
TCPL – Encor	149.2	20.7	–137.0	–6.8	12.2
Nova – Polysar	987.3	134.7	201.2	7.9	1188.5
Cambior – Sullivan	13.0	36.4	80.7	14.4	93.7
Dumez – Westburne	66.5	33.9	n/a	n/a	66.5
Gulf – Hiram Walker	510.0	22.5	n/a	n/a	510.0
Unicorp – Union	7.6	3.1	–4.8	–4.7	2.8
Fleet Aerospace – Fathom	6.5	157.6	0.4	2.9	6.9
Motorola – MDI	44.1	72.4	n/a	n/a	44.1
Noranda & Trelleborg – Falconbridge	250.6	14.7	155.8[3]	3.7	406.4[3]
Total[2]	2659.6	35.6	654.3	3.4	3313.9

1. Changes in wealth could not be estimated for Dumez, Motorola, and Trelleborg because these firms were engaged in other ventures or were not listed on the TSE at the time of the take-over or for Gulf which underwent a major financial reorganization, making the estimation of the market model impossible. The premium for Fathom was not estimated by the market model because no value could be attributed to the medium of exchange (warrants). We used market analysts' opinions of the value of the warrants and stock offer as reported in the business press.
2. For each row and column, the total was calculated for the firms for which changes were computed.
3. This represents only Noranda's wealth changes. Trelleborg's wealth changes were not estimated. Thus the actual total premium is likely to have been larger.

lenges the takeover on antitrust grounds. This may not be contradictory to previous evidence, as in some cases an increase in concentration may result in competitors being worse off if the merged firm becomes an undisputed leader of the industry.[16] Whether or not a takeover was motivated by strategic reasons will be assessed by looking at the bidder's and target's industries and, equally important, at that of subsequent buyers if the original bidder divests itself of some or all assets.

VALUE CREATION AND SOURCES OF GAINS

THIS SECTION PRESENTS the results of the detailed analysis of the ten cases of our sample. We first investigate whether or not the takeovers created value and, if they did, we then consider the sources of these gains. We delay the comparisons of our results with those of other studies in the literature to the following section.

VALUE CREATION

TABLE 1 PRESENTS the wealth changes estimated for each transaction using the market model presented in the previous section. For each firm, the $-column gives the dollar value of the wealth change while the %-column gives the premium as a percentage of the estimated value of the firm if no takeover had taken place. The last column gives the total premium for both firms. For all cases for which it was possible to estimate the wealth changes, a total of $3,314 million was created in value. As expected, this value was split unevenly between targets' and bidders' shareholders. The targets' shareholders fare very well, as they gain on average 35.6 percent over their estimated market value if no bid had occurred. The bidders' shareholders do less well, as the takeovers increase their value by a mere 3.4 percent on average.

In most cases the target's premium ranged between 20 percent and 42 percent. In three cases the premium represented an important proportion over the estimated market value. In the Fleet-Fathom transaction, Fleet paid an impressive 157.6 percent over Fathom's market price. Nova paid a premium of 134.7 percent to Polysar's shareholders, a premium close to $1 billion. Motorola paid a 72.4 percent premium for MDI. In one case, the premium was quite low; Unicorp paid only 3.1 percent over Union's estimated value, a mere $7.6 million.[17]

In most transactions, bidder's wealth changes were positive but small, usually less than 10 percent. Cambior was the only bidder to break that mark with an increase in value of 14.4 percent. In two cases, the bidders realized negative but small returns. Shareholders of TCPL and Unicorp lost in their transaction respectively 6.8 percent and 4.7 percent in value. These negative returns may occur if the bidder's managers attribute a personal value to the takeover, in which case they may overpay for the target.

The distribution of the wealth gains varies markedly across all cases. We now try to relate the distribution of wealth gains to the importance of defensive tactics and the level of competition in the bidding for the target.

DEFENSIVE TACTICS AND THE DISTRIBUTION OF THE GAINS

THE TARGET'S SHAREHOLDERS seem to receive the bulk of the value generated by the takeovers. Jarrell, Brickley & Netter (1988) attribute the secular decline in bidder's returns partially to the improvement of anti-takeover defences. The bargaining process between the bidder and the target which determines how the gains will be split is rather complex. The number of bidders, the height and nature of the defences against takeovers, and other structural factors that have an impact on the competition in the market for corporate control are key determinants of the distribution of gains. Most of these factors are unobservable or non-measurable. However, in Table 2, we summarize qualitatively our findings on the anti-takeover defences used by the targets.

There are basically two types of defence. First, preventive tactics may not have a strong impact on the distribution of the gains, as they are designed

---

TABLE 2

SUMMARY OF ANTI-TAKEOVER DEFENCES[1]

Preventive Tactics
  Bylaws
    Super-majority   F
    Fair-price amendment   F, FB
    Golden parachute   P, F, M

Aggressive Tactics
  Dilution of equity capital   P, F
  Share Buy-back   E, FB
  Distribution to Shareholders   P, FB

Defensive Tactics
  White Knight   E, S, H, U, M, FB
  Selling the Crown Jewel   H
  Managed Buy Out   G, H
  Proxy Battle   P, M, FB
  Poison Pill   U

Judicial Tactics
  Federal & Provincial Tribunals   H, U
  Antitrust   P
  T.S.E.   H, F
  O.S.C.   H, U, F, M, FB

---

1. In the table, G stands for Genstar; E, for Encor; P, for Polysar; S, for Sullivan; H, for Hiram Walker; U, for Union; F, for Fathom; M, for MDI; FB, for Falconbridge. United Westburne did not use defensive tactics.

to deter takeovers rather than to increase shareholders' wealth once a bid has been made. They may, in fact, reduce the shareholders' wealth given that a takeover is occurring. Such tactics include varying bylaws and golden parachutes. Second, another type of tactic is developed after the initial bid, to entice the bidder to increase the offer. These include what we call aggressive tactics, defensive tactics, and judicial tactics. Capital dilution, poison pills and white knights are among the better-known of these.

Preventive tactics do not appear to be as popular as defences used after the initial bid. This finding may, however, be attributed to a self-selection problem. Preventive tactics are supposed to deter takeovers. Since our sample contains successful bids, it is not surprising that the use of preventive tactics was low. In the matter of post-bid tactics, some targets appear to have put up strong defensive lines, using a wide range of tactics. Table 2 shows that Falconbridge, Fathom, Hiram Walker, MDI, and Polysar were among the most actively defensive firms. Some defences proved highly popular. We found white knights playing an active role in four cases. Two white knights became the actual acquirer: Cambior, which successfully fought Ste-Geneviève to gain control of Sullivan; and Motorola which fought off Glenayre in the battle for MDI. In two cases the white knights did not win: Amax failed to rescue Falconbridge, and TCPL could not stop Gulf from acquiring Hiram Walker. In two other cases, Union and Encor frantically searched for a white knight but found none.

Among the seven cases for which we could estimate wealth changes for both firms involved, two targets could extract a large part of the rents created by the takeover. Despite its inability to find a white knight, Encor was actually able to actually get 1 223 percent of the total value created as TCPL's wealth decreased. This achievement resulted from a combination of two factors. First, Encor engaged in a buy-back program of its own shares. Second, the success of that program was guaranteed by the fact that some important shareholders were sympathetic to Encor. A few days before the final offer, 47.7 percent of Encor's stock was in friendly hands, with Dome and Sam Belzberg holding respectively 35 percent and five percent. This concentration of the target's stock weakened TCPL's bargaining power, and it was forced to increase its offer substantially until the group led by Dome and Sam Belzberg finally tendered. In another case, Polysar extracted 83 percent of the total gains. Polysar was certainly one of the hardest fought takeovers in the sample. Polysar engaged in two large distributions of dividends to shareholders, which accounted for the difference. Despite these distributions, Nova did not lower its bid price, thus conferring a direct gain to Polysar's shareholders.

The description of these cases offers weak evidence that appropriate defensive tactics have a positive impact on the target's share of the total value created by the takeover. The more aggressive tactics usually yield the higher share of the rents. We examined the effect of the number of independent players in the bidding war and found no significant correlation with the percentage of the premium going to the target. Given the small sample size, we could not get enough variation to draw any conclusions.

Finally, this description also provides some evidence that the market for corporate control is not perfect. The fact that the bargaining power of each party may be affected by defensive tactics and idiosyncratic motivations indicates that the market for corporate control is not truly competitive. If, for example, there are costs for the bidder to put up a bid, the expected distribution of the rents may affect the bidder's incentives to invest in a takeover, thus resulting in fewer takeovers than is optimal. Grossman & Hart's (1980) model suggests that this result will not occur if the target can commit not to defend itself too aggressively. But as we see, this does not always occur, implying that the market for corporate control may not be a perfect mechanism for the elimination of managerial inefficiencies or the reallocation of assets.

Since hostile takeovers generate important wealth changes, we now try to identify which factors may explain this wealth creation.

The Sources of Wealth Gains

In the section on Sample and Methodology we presented various factors that might explain the premium usually paid to the target's shareholders in hostile takeovers. We now present the evidence concerning each of these factors. We have already discussed a potential redistribution of wealth between the shareholders of the two firms involved in the transaction. Although transfers of wealth occurred in some cases, they only explain a small portion of the total value created by the takeover. We now turn to the other potential sources of value creation.

Layoffs

We could find evidence of layoffs in only two cases. In the TCPL - Encor transaction, TCPL undertook a corporate restructuring of Encor and cut its overhead by 24 percent, a proportion that amounted to a net present-value cost savings of about $90 million. In November 1989, in the Nova - Polysar transaction, Nova laid off 45 white-collar workers from Polysar's petrochemicals research & development division, and more cuts were announced for January 1990. The 45 laid-off workers represented an estimated cost savings of $13.6 million. This estimate is conservative, as we could find no evidence of the layoffs announced for 1990. In these two cases layoffs resulted in savings in what may be considered fixed expenditures. It appears, then, that these cost savings were the result of economies of scale rather than of overpaid workers being laid off.

Overall, layoffs did not represent a significant source of gains. Total cost savings accruing from layoffs amounted to approximately $110 million, while the total premium paid exceeded $3.3 billion. Thus our calculations suggest that layoffs explain roughly three percent of the average premium in our sample. Although they are important in one case — TCPL buys Encor — layoffs do not appear to play a very significant role in Canada. Note that our estimate is likely to be somewhat downward biased, since not all layoffs are reported. It is also difficult to check for wage reductions or changes in forms of compensation. However, it is unlikely that the bias may account for the difference between the estimated savings and the total premium.

Investment Cuts

It is difficult to obtain evidence of investment cuts, and when such evidence is obtained, to investigate whether or not they were the result of a takeover. For example, in May 1990, Nova announced that it was cutting its pipeline capital budget by $135 million. This decision was the result of delays in TCPL's expansion plans. Therefore the cut does not seem to be related to the takeover. In the TCPL - Encor transaction, we have soft evidence that investment cuts may have had some effect. When TCPL was restructuring Encor, it cut its overhead by 24 percent (as we saw above), and it also cut Encor's exploration budget. It was not possible to estimate the cost savings resulting from this rationalization. In the other transactions, no evidence was found showing that investment cuts were of major importance in the takeover.

TABLE 3

FINANCIAL STRUCTURE OF THE TAKEOVERS ($ MILLIONS)

DEAL	TOTAL VALUE	DEBT	COMMON SHARES	PREFERRED SHARES	WARRANTS	SHARE SWAP	CASH	% DEBT
Imasco - Genstar	2145	1600	345	200	–	–	–	74.6
TCPL - Encor	871	221	250	–	–	–	400	25.4
Nova - Polysar	1721	1349	372	–	–	–	–	78.4
Cambior - Sullivan	49	16	–	–	–	–	33	32.7
Dumez - Westburne	263	150	–	–	–	–	113	57.0
Gulf - Hiram W.	2774	1924	–	–	–	–	850	69.4
Unicorp - Union	253	59	–	← 194→		–	–	23.3
Fleet A. - Fathom	11	–	–	–	←11→		–	0.0
Motorola - MDI	105	105	–	–	–	–	–	100.0
Noranda - Falconbridge	1952	1952	–	–	–	–	–	100.0
TOTAL	10144	7376	967	← 405 →			1396	72.7

Tax Savings and the Medium of Exchange

It has been argued that the recent wave of leveraged buy-outs is largely attributable to the asymmetric fiscal treatment of debt and equity.[18] In order to realize tax savings, the bidder must assume medium- or long-term debt, or use its target's tax losses. We try to ascertain the relevance of tax savings by documenting those two sources of gains.

Table 3 gives us some indications concerning the importance of debt in the financing of the acquisitions. The total value of the acquisitions we consider is $10.1 billion. Debt accounts for $7.4 billion of this value, or 73 percent. Although there is considerable variation in the percentage of debt used to finance each transaction, it is clear that debt as a medium of exchange plays a key role in the hostile takeovers of our sample. Some of this debt was repaid rapidly, through sell-offs or issues of equity. We roughly estimate at between $5 billion and $6 billion the level of long-term debt carried to finance the acquisitions.

This represents more than 50 percent of the total value of the transactions and more than 65 percent of the total debt issued.

Debt financing is considered to be a source of gains if the target was underleveraged and the bidder used the financing of the takeover to attain an optimal debt/equity ratio for the newly acquired assets. In one case, this clearly happened. Westburne was virtually debt-free, and Dumez acquired it with a 57 percent debt financing over Westburne's assets. The takeover thus allowed Westburne to attain a presumably optimal debt/equity ratio, and consequently Dumez's cost of acquisition was reduced by the amount of the tax savings. Four other bidders, Imasco, Nova, Gulf, and Noranda, realized tax savings through the leverage and deductibility of interest payments on the long-term debt they carried following the takeover. However, in these cases, the debt load incurred for the acquisition seemed non-optimal. In these cases, debt does not appear to represent tax savings but rather excessive risk taking by the bidder. Tax savings are thus temporary and last only until debt is repaid and the optimal financial structure is restored. For example, Nova considerably increased its debt/equity ratio to acquire Polysar. This has induced Nova to divest many subsidiaries to raise cash and lessen its debt load. It is therefore unlikely that Nova used the takeover to attain an optimal debt/equity ratio. In any case, the size of the premium paid by the bidders (over \$500 million in three of the five cases) rules out the possibility that tax savings were the primary source of gain.

Tax pools may be a less risky source of gains in a takeover involving a tax-liable bidder. In the ten transactions that form our sample, we found tax pools for a value in excess of \$1.6 billion. Encor had a tax pool reserve estimated at \$400 million, Sullivan had one of \$29 million, while Polysar's tax reserves amounted to over \$1.2 billion. In these three cases, the bidders were profitable enterprises that could use the tax pools within a relatively short time span. For these firms, those tax pools may well have represented tax savings of over \$650 million. It is hard to quantify how much of this gain was already capitalized in the target's share price prior to the transaction, but it appears that the presence of tax pools was an important factor in at least the Nova - Polysar transaction. Ever since Nova made its first bid, analysts referred to the \$1.2 billion tax pool of Polysar's petrochemicals division as one clear gain accruing to Nova. Two years after the takeover, Nova finally divested itself almost completely of its Polysar subsidiaries. These divestitures were made partly to reduce its debt load but are also an indication that Nova was not too eager to keep the Polysar assets.[19]

Table 3 reports how bidders financed their transaction, but does not reflect fully how the target's shareholders were paid for their shares. In three cases, the target's shareholders received more than cash for their shares. Polysar's shareholders were paid in cash and shares of Nova. The shares they received amounted to about 22 percent of the total payment. Union's shareholders received cash in conjunction with preferred shares and warrants of Unicorp. These shares and warrants represented about 77 percent of the total payment. Finally, Fathom's shareholders were paid entirely with securities of Fleet Aerospace. Bensaïd and Garella (1990) argue that a bidding firm is most likely to pay with securities of the new venture if it values the transaction less than the target's shareholders. There is some weak evidence of this occurring in the Fleet - Fathom transaction. The business press was quite optimistic, and it expected that Fleet's stock would be volatile, implying that it was attributing a high value to Fleet's warrants (valid for five years). However, the acquisition was followed by a dark period for Fleet, which forced it to divest from Fathom at a price lower than the acquisition price. It appears as though Fleet used the optimistic expectations of the market to pay Fathom's shareholders with securities that the latter overvalued. This strategy considerably reduced the cost of the acquisition.

In summary, tax savings are important in two cases (Nova, Dumez), negligible in four more cases (Imasco, TCPL, Gulf, Noranda), and nearly irrelevant in the remaining cases. The factors surveyed in this section, even taken together, cannot completely explain the high premiums paid to the target's shareholders. The object of the next section is to focus on what we believe was the driving force behind most of the hostile takeovers in our sample.

SELL-OFFS AND STRATEGIC ACQUISITIONS

AS POINTED OUT IN THE INTRODUCTION, the current context of economic integration and globalization motivates firms to restructure and expand. If that willingness to grow is real, hostile takeovers are most likely to reflect it. The first line in Table 4A presents the percentage distribution of the initially acquired assets by category of buyer. At the time of acquisition, 44.5 percent of the traded assets was acquired by a conglomerate buyer, 8.6 percent went to a vertical acquirer, 44.4 percent was acquired by a horizontal buyer, while 2.5 percent was acquired by an incentive organization. The vertical acquisition was the TCPL - Encor transaction. The incentive acquisition was the Unicorp - Union transaction in which Unicorp, a holding company, had a single majority owner. These numbers suggest that horizontal acquisition is a major factor in Canadian hostile takeovers.

Although these numbers indicate that there is a tendency for Canadian firms to expand in related industries, a more striking picture emerges when we compute sell-offs by the initial acquirer. The second line in Table 4A takes into account sell-offs that followed the takeover and presents the final distribution of the traded assets by category of buyer. The share of traded assets that falls into the horizontal-acquisition category jumps to 70.7 percent from 44.4 percent. Conglomerate acquisitions now account for only 19.1 percent, while the asset shares of vertical and incentive acquisitions stay approximately the same. Horizontal and vertical acquisitions taken together, which we call strategic acquisitions, account for more than three-quarters of the value of all traded assets. Once sell-offs are incorporated into the picture, it appears that these

TABLE 4 A

DISTRIBUTION OF ASSETS[1] BY BUYER TYPE (%)

DATE	CONGLOMERATE	VERTICAL	HORIZONTAL	INCENTIVE
Acquisition	44.5	8.6	44.4	2.5
Final	19.1	6.9	70.7	3.4

1. A conglomerate buyer acquires a target in an unrelated industry. A vertical acquisition is one which involves vertical integration. An horizontal buyer is a firm which is in the same industry as the target. An incentive acquisition is made by a management-intensive firm. For each transaction, the target's assets were split and allocated to the relevant category.

TABLE 4 B

DISTRIBUTION OF ASSETS BY BUYER NATIONALITY (%)

DATE	CANADIAN	AMERICAN	EUROPEAN
Acquisition	87.1	1.0	11.9
Final	63.0	2.8	34.2

acquisitions are a dominant factor in explaining hostile takeovers. Furthermore, the striking differences between the two lines of Table 4A show that to achieve a better understanding of hostile takeovers, it is important to continue the investigation in order to determine into which hands all the assets ultimately fall. This finding clearly contradicts Jensen's (1988) statement that divestitures following mergers are a sign that market concentration does not increase with takeover activity.

Horizontal acquisitions allow firms to control more assets, to reach their efficient size, and possibly to become important players in their industry. Larger firms presumably will more easily survive the opening of Canadian borders and the subsequent harsh international competition. Although the contribution of this restructuring of assets is difficult to quantify precisely, it represents a source of gains that can account for a potentially significant proportion of the premium. Whether the acquisition was initially horizontal — in which case the premium is justified directly — or whether sell-offs of some newly acquired assets to horizontal buyers are expected to take place — in which case profits accrue from these divestitures — a premium can often be paid by the initial bidder. We now investigate the characteristics of the sell-offs and the profits that they might have generated for the initial bidder.

We tabulate in Table 5 the total value of divestitures and the percentage of the acquired assets they represent. The ten initial transactions involved assets evaluated at $10.1 billion. In the months (sometimes years) that followed the acquisitions, 32.7 percent of the assets changed hands as sell-offs totalled $5.9 billion. In four cases out of ten, sell-offs exceeded 50

TABLE 5

MOVEMENT OF ASSETS ($ MILLIONS)

DEAL	TOTAL SELL-OFFS	% OF ACQUISITION[1]	STRATEGIC $	%	INCENTIVE $	%	CONGLOMERATE $	%
Imasco - Genstar	2950	50.0	2407	81.6	233	7.9	310	10.5
TCPL - Encor	207.4	20.0	207.4	100.0	0	0.0	0	0.0
Nova - Polysar	1855	70.6	1855	100.0	0	0.0	0	0.0
Cambior - Sullivan	52	65.0	52	100.0	0	0.0	0	0.0
Dumez - Westburne	25	15.0	25	100.0	0	0.0	0	0.0
Gulf - Hiram W.	837	28.0	837	100.0	0	0.0	0	0.0
Unicorp - Union	0	0.0	–	–	–	–	–	–
Fleet A. - Fathom	7.5	100.0	7.5	100.0	0	0.0	0	0.0
Motorola - MDI	0	0.0	–	–	–	–	–	–
Noranda - Falconbridge	0	0.0	–	–	–	–	–	–
TOTAL	5934	32.7	5391	90.8	233	3.9	310	5.2

1. To maintain comparability and avoid problems caused by inflation, the percentage of acquisition is calculated with respect to the value of the assets at the acquisition date. For example, Imasco's sell-offs of Genstar's assets amount to $2.95 billion. This price is more than the initial acquisition price of $2.145 billion. However, these sell-offs represent about 50 percent of all assets acquired through the takeover.

percent of the acquired assets. On the other hand, we found no sell-offs in three transactions.

Sell-offs may generate profits if the assets are sold to a strategic buyer; that is, to a horizontal or vertical buyer, or to an incentive organization, or possibly even to an interested party in an unrelated field of business. If the traded divisions ultimately fall under the control of existing players in the same industry, thus reallocating the assets of the target to horizontal or vertical buyers, the sell-offs may command a high price because the buyers may internalize externalities, or may use their excess capacity more efficiently, or may increase their market power. When the divisions are sold to a management team or become private, the sell-offs are called incentive-intensive. These types of sell-offs may generate profits if the assets were poorly managed and their sale improves efficiency. Finally, it is possible that some units were sold to unrelated (conglomerate) businesses. In this case, a premium may still be generated if assets are valued more when independent than when held by the target. We identify the type of buyer in the last three columns of Table 5: strategic, incentive-intensive or conglomerate.

We find that $5.4 billion of the $5.9 billion in divested assets were bought by strategic buyers; that is, competitors or technologically-related enterprises acquired 90.8 percent of the assets, leaving four percent to incentive-intensive organizations, and 5.2 percent to diversified buyers.

Examples of strategic divestitures are: the sale of Hiram Walker-Gooderham & Worts, the "jewel" in the Gulf-Hiram Walker transaction, to Allied Lyons, a leading British liquor producer; the sale of Nova's rubber division to Germany's Bayer AG, thus making Bayer an international leader in the production of rubber; the sale of Genstar's cement division to S.A. Cimenteries of Belgium, of Genstar's stone division to the United Kingdom's Redland PLC, (a firm also involved in building products), and of GSX Corp. to Laidlaw Transportation Ltd., two companies involved in waste management; and the sale of Fathom Oceanology to Indal.

Selling off newly acquired divisions can be very profitable. In three cases (Imasco, Nova, Cambior) the sale of less than three-quarters of the newly acquired assets generated more revenue than the cost of the original takeover. In these cases, most of the divested assets went from a conglomerate owner (the initial acquirer) to strategic hands. The example of Imasco is illustrative of this type of behaviour. In the Fleet-Fathom case, the resale of Fathom was made at a price lower than the acquisition price, reflecting the fact that the acquisition of Fathom did not turn out well for Fleet.

Thus, strategic aspects appear to be very important in the hostile takeovers that we have analyzed. The results reported here suggest that a reallocation of assets toward strategically interested parties creates value. Over $3.3 billion of wealth appears to have been created in our sample of takeovers. Wealth transfers, tax savings, layoffs, and gains through increased incentives cannot explain the greater part of this wealth creation. At most, the latter factors explain the greater part of the gains in two or three cases (Nova-Polysar and TCPL-Encor are the two best examples). Hostile takeovers primarily allocate assets to businesses in the same or related lines of business. This fact suggests that the consolidation of assets is central to the acquisition process.

We think, on the basis of the evidence presented here, that this consolidation of assets is likely to be the principal source of gains. It is possible that we have underestimated the other sources of gains, and since we treat the strategic character of the transactions as a residual factor, that we have overestimated the importance of strategic acquisitions as a source of value creation. But, on the whole, the margin of error would have to be very large indeed to offset the gains that we attribute to consolidation.

However, the channel through which that value is generated is still difficult to identify. We cannot at this point determine precisely how important in accounting for the premium are cost savings resulting from economies of scale and scope, integration of management, purchasing, distribution, and other factors. Perhaps a more detailed analysis of the profitability and productivity of the units sold could shed some light on the origins of the savings. Sometimes the overlapping of operations is well documented. For instance, Cambior had a mill that was underutilized, but which now runs at full capacity thanks to the takeover by Sullivan. This is one type of realized efficiency gain through the joint use of some indivisible input. In other examples, Fleet and Fathom both produce sonar equipment; and MDI will definitely benefit from Motorola's technological capabilities. At the same time, MDI was one of Motorola's few competitors in the communications business.

THE ROLE OF FOREIGN FIRMS

FOREIGN FIRMS PLAY AN IMPORTANT ROLE in the transactions we have analyzed. Three acquirers are foreign-owned: Dumez (France), Motorola (United States), and Trelleborg (Sweden). In addition, 40 percent of Imasco is controlled by BAT Industries (United Kingdom).

Table 4B shows that the share of assets acquired by foreign firms is 13 percent at the date of acquisition.[20] As assets are reorganized and spun off, this share climbs to 37 percent. The value of sell-offs to foreign-owned firms exceeds $3.5 billion, or 59 percent of all sell-offs. Imasco was one of the largest sellers of assets to foreign firms. It sold Genstar's cement and building products divisions to European firms for nearly $900 million, and other assets for $470 million to American interests; half of the latter amount was obtained through management buyouts. In another case, following Nova's takeover of Polysar, Bayer (Germany) acquired Polysar's rubber division for $1.48 billion. Furthermore, the sale of Polysar's latex division to Germany's BASF for $500 million during the negotiations between Nova and Polysar is not tabulated in the Nova-Polysar transaction. Gulf sold 51 percent interest in Hiram Walker's distillery division to Allied Lyons (United Kingdom) for $837 million. Note that over 95 percent of all foreign acquisitions and sell-offs are of the strategic type.

The share of assets that came under foreign control appears to be in line with the overall level of foreign control in the Canadian industry. For example, in 1984, the extent of foreign control in the Canadian manufacturing industry was estimated at 44 percent (Green, 1990).

European firms were much more active in the Canadian market for corporate control than were American firms.[21] In our sample, American firms play a minor role in the restructuring of Canadian assets. American firms acquired a mere 2.8 percent of all traded assets, while European firms bought nearly 35 percent of traded assets, thus accounting for more than 92 percent of all assets that went to foreign firms. This may indicate that it is easier for European firms to enter the Canadian market than for American firms which are often already present in Canada and may not satisfy the requirements of the new Competition Act. It may also be a response by European firms to the new opening of the North American market, as European firms can use Canadian firms as a basis for entering the American market.

Overall, the impact of foreign firms appears to be significant in the hostile takeovers of our sample. More than one-third of traded assets ultimately came into foreign hands.[22] Foreign firms were central in the largest contests: Imasco-Genstar, Nova-Polysar, Gulf-Hiram Walker, and Noranda & Trelleborg-Falconbridge. Besides, foreign firms can play a major role as white knights in the contests for Canadian firms. For example, Amax was a foreign, but defeated, white knight.

This completes the description and analysis of the takeovers of our sample. In the next section we will compare some of our results with those of other studies.

COMPARISONS WITH OTHER STUDIES

WE ESTIMATED THAT TARGETS earned an average premium of 35.6 percent over their market value, while acquirers gained a mere 3.4 percent. Our results parallel the calculation of Bhagat, Shleifer & Vishny (1989) for hostile takeovers in the United States for the period 1982 - 1984. Jensen (1988) points out that targets' shareholders in hostile takeovers earn premiums exceeding 30 percent on average, while acquiring firms' shareholders on average obtain an abnormal return of about four percent. Copeland and Weston (1988) survey empirical studies of mergers and acquisitions, and conclude that acquired and acquiring firms in tender-offer studies experience abnormal positive returns of 35 percent and three percent to five percent respectively. In a study of Canadian mergers over the period 1964 - 1983, Eckbo (1986) found that targets earned an abnormal return of about 15 percent while bidders gained more than three percent. Our results clearly fall in line with those found in the literature.

When comparing our results to Eckbo's (1986), we cannot draw the conclusion that in Canada hostile takeovers confer higher gains to targets than do friendly mergers. This conclusion would overlook the evidence of Bradley, Desai & Kim (1988), who found premiums similar to ours in a study of all types of mergers in the United States in the 1980s. Their study also shows that targets' premiums have been increasing over time. This may explain why our results differ from Eckbo's (1986).

Few studies of mergers examine the sources of value creation. The reason is that it requires a case-by-case approach to gather all relevant information. Since most studies of takeover activity deal with very large samples, finding the sources of gains would represent a Herculean task. By focussing on an interesting but small subsample of all mergers, it becomes possible to undertake such an examination. Our results, then, can best be compared with those of Bhagat, Shleifer & Vishny (1989). No similar study is available for Canada.

The similarity between the results of the two studies is striking. We found that 71 percent of all traded assets ultimately came into the hands of a horizontal acquirer, while Bhagat, Shleifer & Vishny (1989) found that 72 percent of sell-offs came into the same or closely related lines of business. Sell-offs are very important in reallocating resources after the takeover. In both studies, about 30 percent of the newly acquired assets were resold. Our results, like those of Bhagat, Shleifer & Vishny (1989), suggest that cost savings from joint operations are a potentially important source of gains in hostile takeovers.[23]

Tax savings also seemed to have performed a similar function in Canada and the United States. As in Auerbach & Reishus (1988), Jarrell, Brickley, & Netter (1988), and Bhagat, Shleifer & Vishny (1989), tax savings are of key importance in a small number of cases. They are therefore not a major factor in most takeovers, friendly or hostile.

The two studies differ on other grounds. In the United States, Bhagat, Shleifer & Vishny (1989) estimate that layoffs explain about 10 percent to 20 percent of the average premium, while they seem to be almost insignificant in Canada. How can this difference be explained? First, we may have underestimated the extent of layoffs, but so might researchers in the United States. Like the researchers in the U.S., we depend on publications to report layoffs. Yet, in many cases, we can make sure that very little change has occurred on the employment front. Second, it is possible that layoffs are more important in the United States because more American transactions are initiated by raiders, highly leveraged firms, or other incentive-intensive organizations. These organizations are aggressive and benefit from the reduction of inefficiencies. Nearly 15 percent of assets came into the hands of incentive-intensive organizations in the United States. The corresponding figure in our sample is a paltry four percent. Finally, since many assets in Canada were acquired by foreigners, it is possible that the acquirers committed themselves not to lay off workers in order to obtain Investment Canada's permission to invest in Canada. If this were so, we should be faced with a self-selection phenomenon: only foreign takeovers that did not result in layoffs were observed.

Overall, our results are similar in many ways to those of other studies of mergers and hostile takeovers in the United States and Canada. This indicates that even though our sample is small, it is probably representative of the Canadian market for corporate control.

CONCLUSION

OUR PRINCIPAL FINDINGS are summarized in Table 6. Strategic considerations appear to be driving the acquisition process. Be it increased efficiency or market power, the integration of production and the coordination of the

TABLE 6

CLASSIFICATION OF TRANSACTIONS BY SOURCE OF GAINS[1]

DEAL	STRATEGIC FACTORS IMPORTANT	SELL-OFFS IMPORTANT	LAYOFFS IMPORTANT	TAX SAVINGS IMPORTANT	INVESTMENT CUTS IMPORTANT	FOREIGN ACQUISITIONS IMPORTANT
Imasco - Genstar	–	B (50%) B → S (81%)	–	Debt	–	B (23%)
TCPL - Encor	S	–	$90M	$400M tax pool	maybe	–
Nova - Polysar	S	B (70.6%) B → S (100%)	$21M	Debt $1200M tax pool	–	B (48.9%)
Cambior - Sullivan	S	B (65%) B → S (100%)	–	$29M tax pool	–	–
Dumez - Westburne	S	–	–	Debt	–	A (85%)
Gulf - Hiram Walker	S	–	–	Debt	–	B (28%)
Unicorp - Union	–	–	–	–	–	–
Fleet Aerospace - Fathom	S	B (100%) B → S (100%)	–	–	–	B (100%)
Motorola - MDI	S	–	–	–	–	A (100%)
Noranda - Falconbridge	S	–	–	Debt	–	·A (50%)

1. S means Strategic; B stands for Bustup (sell-offs), and A for initial Acquisition. An acquisition is strategic if more than 50 percent of the assets were initially acquired by a bidder in a related industry. It therefore includes horizontal and vertical acquisitions. Sell-offs are important if more than 50 percent of the assets were resold. Debt is a tax-savings factor if the deal was financed by at least 50 percent long-term debt. All tax pools are reported. Every foreign acquisition is reported. The assets can be initially acquired by a foreign firm (A), or through a sell-off (B).

decision-making processes are of key importance in all but one transaction.[24] Overall, conglomerate diversification and vertical integration fade in the background, and the gains through tax savings, layoffs, etc., are too small to explain the important premiums.

Strategic factors seem to be important whether or not the bidder sells off a division. When we found sell-offs, horizontal buyers accounted for over 90 percent of the value of the assets involved. Overall, 70 percent of the traded assets came into the hands of horizontal buyers. This finding parallels Bhagat, Shleifer, & Vishny's (1989) results for hostile takeovers in the United States. Most likely, hostile takeovers serve to reorganize industries as markets in the United States and Canada are opening up and enlarging. A typical example of this is the Dumez-Westburne transaction. Montreal-based Westburne was the largest Canadian manufacturer and distributor of plumbing, heating and electrical supplies. Dumez is a French company in the same industry. Before the transaction, Westburne held 11 percent of its business in the United States. Two years after the transaction, it was investing close to $100 million to expand its business south of the border. The Canada-U.S. Free Trade Agreement (FTA) seems to have been instrumental in facilitating the entry in the American market of a French company through a Canadian acquisition. This illustrates the economic pressures that are facing Canadian firms today.

Strategic factors also appear to be just as important when foreign acquirers are involved as when the buyers are Canadian. Tax savings, bidding shareholders' losses, and layoffs are occasionally important, but were not of primary importance in the cases we examined.

Finally, it is often argued that the market for corporate control acts as a watchdog for managerial inefficiencies. From the cases studied here, however, as well as in the light of other studies citing experience in the United States, it appears that these inefficiencies arise because of misallocation of assets rather than because existing asset structures are mismanaged. Therefore the market for corporate control seems more to serve the purpose of restructuring the assets of Canadian companies than of eliminating possible managerial inefficiencies. In other words, the motivation for the reallocation of corporate control has more to do with industrial organization than with internal organization inefficiencies.

ENDNOTES

1. For example, see Ravenscraft & Scherer (1987), Bradley, Desai & Kim (1988), Asquith, Opler & Weston (1990) for the United States, and Eckbo (1986) for Canada.
2. Bhagat, Shleifer & Vishny (1989) study the factors behind hostile takeovers in the United States. To our knowledge, there is no such study for Canada.
3. These motivating factors are described at greater length in the next section.
4. Although we do not know precisely how many hostile takeovers worth more than $10 million there were in Canada between 1985 and 1989, we think the total number might be 20 or so cases. Our sample can be compared somewhat advantageously to the sample of 62 hostile takeovers reported by Bhagat, Shleifer & Vishny (1989) in the more active American market over a similar period.
5. Notice that this definition of hostile takeovers is somewhat broader than the one commonly used by the business community. The advantage of our definition is that it offers an objective criterion to determine whether or not a takeover is hostile.
6. For more recent takeovers, not enough data are available to make a detailed analysis of post-takeover performance.
7. This is not as unusual as it appears. In the United States, some studies have shown that a transfer of wealth often occurred in all types of mergers (Ravenscraft & Scherer, 1987; Bradley, Desai & Kim, 1988; Asquith,

Opler & Weston, 1990), as well as in hostile takeovers (Bhagat, Shleifer & Vishny, 1989).

8. A "white knight" is a friendly firm called upon by the target to bid against the bidder.

9. Shleifer & Summers (1988) illustrate this argument using the Icahn - TWA case in the United States.

10. See Bhagat, Shleifer, & Vishny (1989), p. 21. We think these numbers roughly reflect the Canadian situation. Our results are not sensitive to reasonable changes in these values. See section on The Sources of Wealth Gains.

11. This hypothesis is based on the theory of financial structure in the presence of corporate and personal taxes. This theory is summarized in Copeland & Weston (1988).

12. This may be the case if the sell-off implies some sort of complementarity in management or assets.

13. For example, see Grossman & Hart (1980).

14. A horizontal merger refers to a merger involving two firms competing in the same industry. A vertical merger involves a firm and its supplier or its client.

15. Shyam Khemani, in his contribution to this volume, provides evidence that horizontal mergers in Canada increased from about 56 percent of all mergers in 1978 - 79 and 1983 - 84 to about 66 percent in 1988 - 89.

16. See Farrell & Shapiro (1990) for a theoretical analysis of the effects of mergers on prices, profits and welfare.

17. Note that Union is in a field unrelated to Unicorp's, and that the merger was strongly opposed by Union's management, who went so far as to swallow a poison pill. Union, a utility company, bought an unrelated food-processing business. It is possible that this pill was too poisonous and that they paid too much for this company, thus lowering the acquisition price. (A "poison pill" is an action undertaken by the target's management to make its firm less attractive to the bidder.)

18. For example, see Kaplan (1989).

19. It may also be noted that Nova's debt load became unbearable, as the takeover was followed by a drop in petrochemical prices.

20. Imasco's acquisition is not considered as foreign. Therefore 13 percent is a lower bound.

21. This was pointed out to us by Dan Shapiro.

22. Note that the treatment of Imasco as being under foreign control would push the share of assets ultimately controlled by foreigners to roughly 51 percent.

23. The assumption that strategic acquisitions are motivated by the desire to increase market power becomes less attractive when one considers the globalization of markets.

24. Unicorp-Union is a classic case of diversification into an unrelated line of business. In the Imasco-Genstar transaction, the acquisition was for the purpose of product diversification, as none of the assets was strategically

acquired initially. However, through sell-offs, 40 percent of Genstar's assets came into strategic hands.

APPENDIX

DESCRIPTION OF THE CASES

1) **Imasco buys Genstar.** $2.1 billion, 74.6 percent debt financing. August 1986.

Imasco is a Montréal-based tobacco products, fast food, and drugstore conglomerate, 40 percent owned by BAT Industries of London, England.

Genstar Corp., based in Vancouver but operating from San Francisco, has activities in building, real estate development, waste disposal, and financial services (with its subsidiary, Canada Trust Co.).

In March 1986, Imasco made a $54 bid for each Genstar share. It had to accept some conditions concerning the management of the financial subsidiary of Genstar, and to sweeten its offer to $58 to complete the acquisition of 100 percent of Genstar on August 1, 1986. Since the acquisition of Genstar, the sell-offs totalled $2.8 billion, as Imasco divested itself of all Genstar's assets except its real target: Canada Trust Co.

2) **TransCanada PipeLines buys Encor Energy.** $871 million, 25.4 percent debt financing. December 1987.

TCPL, a Toronto-based company, owns and operates a pipeline for the transportation of natural gas from Western Canada to Eastern Canada and export markets.

Encor, a Calgary-based company, is engaged in the exploration and production of crude oil, natural gas, and related products, in Western Canada and internationally.

During the period from February 1987 to mid-November 1987, TCPL purchased 13 percent of the common shares of Encor. On November 16, 1987, TCPL made a cash offer of $8.75 a share for all the shares of Encor. Encor rejected the offer. But its efforts to find a white knight were made more difficult by the Federal Government rules preventing foreign take-overs of healthy Canadian energy companies. Finally TCPL increased its offer to $9.37 to take control of 97 percent of Encor on December 23, 1987. Tax pools were about $400 million. TCPL cut Encor's overhead by 24 percent. In January 1989, TCPL spun off its oil and gas subsidiary, Encor Energy. BCE, TCPL's main shareholder, now holds 67 percent of Encor's shares; the remaining 33 percent is publicly held.

3) **Nova Corporation buys Polysar Energy and Chemical Corporation.** $1.7 billion, 78.4 percent debt financing. September 1988.

Calgary-based Nova Corporation is in the energy industry, including petrochemicals, pipelines, gas marketing, petroleum, and related engineering and manufacturing.

Toronto-based Polysar is a management company involved in the exploration and production of oil, gas and sulphur, and in the development of related downstream petrochemical products.

In October 1987, Nova bought 9.7 percent of Polysar. In January 1988, Nova offered to buy 24.8 percent of Polysar. The offer was rejected. Polysar granted golden parachutes to its president and nine other executives, and made two very generous extraordinary distributions of dividends to its shareholders. In June 1988, both firms agreed in principle to the acquisition of Polysar by Nova. The transaction was completed on September 7, 1988.

Tax pools were about $1.2 billion. 45 white-collar workers subsequently lost their jobs. In May 1990, Nova sold its rubber division to Bayer AG, making Bayer one of the world's leaders in the production of rubber. This division was considered to be the "crown jewel" in the Polysar takeover.

4) Cambior buys Sullivan Mines. $49 million, 32.7 percent debt financing. October 1987.

Cambior, based in Val d'Or, Québec, is engaged in the exploration and development of mineral properties (principally gold).

Sullivan Mines is a Montréal-based gold producer.

In July 1986, Cambior acquired 30.9 percent of Sullivan in exchange for common and preferred shares. In July 1987, Ste Geneviève, a Montréal-based mining exploration company, made an offer to buy a minimum of 51 percent and a maximum of 70 percent of Sullivan. The offer was rejected. In October 1987, Cambior acquired 100 percent of Sullivan. Tax pools were estimated at $29 million. With this acquisition, Cambior increased the production of one of its mills, which was underutilized. In June 1988, Cambior sold its stake in Arthur W. White gold mine (acquired through the merger with Sullivan).

5) Dumez Investment buys Westburne International Industries. $263 million, 57 percent debt financing. May 1987.

Dumez SA, a Paris-based multinational construction company, owns 70 percent of Dumez Investment and 30 percent is owned by Unicorp Canada Corp., a holding company operating in energy production, marketing and transportation, U.S. financial services and real estate, and merchant banking.

Westburne International Industries is a Calgary-based oil and gas company which owns 94 percent of United Westburne Industries, a Montréal-based holding company whose subsidiaries are engaged in wholesale distribution of plumbing, heating, water works, and air conditioning equipment.

In April 1987, after three unsuccessful attempts since September 1986, Dumez Investment made an offer of $25 a share for Westburne. In May 1987, Dumez became the sole shareholder of Westburne. The transaction was financed with 57 percent debt as Westburne was virtually debt free. In the summer of 1988, Unicorp had sold out its participation in Dumez Investment which is now held by Dumez SA (71.3 percent), the Caisse de Dépôts (7.3 percent), the BNP (6.4 percent), and employees and directors (8.1 percent).

Dumez Investment has since divested itself of the oil and gas division of Westburne. Two years after the deal, Dumez was investing $100 million to expand its business in the United States.

6) Gulf buys Hiram Walker. $2.8 billion, 69.4 percent debt financing. April 1986.

Gulf, a subsidiary of Olympia and York (O&Y), has activities in the energy sector.

Hiram Walker is a conglomerate, operating in the gas and the distillery sectors, among others.

In March 1986, Gulf offered to buy 39 percent, then 60 percent, of Hiram Walker at $32 a share; later the offer reached 100 percent at $35 a share. TransCanada PipeLines appeared as a white knight, with an offer of $36.50 a share. Gulf responded by offering $38 for the shares not held by O&Y, for a total of $3 billion. The distillery division of Hiram Walker was the object of a bid by Allied Lyons, a British distillery. Finally, in September 1986, Gulf acquired Hiram Walker. At present, Gulf holds 49 percent of the distillery, with the remaining 51 percent under Allied Lyons' control.

7) Unicorp Canada Corporation buys Union Enterprises Ltd. $253 million, 23.3 percent debt financing. March 1985.

Unicorp Canada Corporation is an operations-oriented holding company active in the sectors of energy production, marketing and transportation, U.S. financial services and real estate, and merchant banking.

Union Enterprises Ltd, a management holding company, is the parent company of Union Gas, the second-largest gas utility in Canada.

In January 1985, Unicorp bought 13.8 percent of Union on the market. On January 31, 1985, Unicorp made a takeover bid for Union, offering a share exchange. Union tried to stop Unicorp's takeover by taking a poison pill, as it acquired Burns Foods for $125 million. This operation diluted Union shares, and Unicorp's stake decreased from 36 percent to 31 percent. In March 1985, Unicorp held 60 percent of Union. After the transaction, Unicorp sold off Burns Foods.

8) Fleet Aerospace Corporation buys Fathom Oceanology Ltd. $10.7 million, no debt financing. March 1985.

Fleet is a designer and manufacturer of components and subsystems for the aerospace, marine, and communications industries.

Fathom provides custom-engineered equipment, products, and technical services for defence and commercial marine applications.

In February 1985, Fleet made a take-over bid for Fathom, which rejected the offer. In March 1985, 11 Fathom senior officials signed contracts containing employment extensions (golden parachutes). Later the same month Fleet obtained control of Fathom. Fathom's shares were exchanged for Fleet's shares and warrants. In November 1989, Fleet sold Fathom to Indal, a diversified industrial company.

9) Motorola buys MDI (Mobile Data International). $105 million, 100 percent debt financing. July 1988.

Motorola is a U.S. corporation, providing electronic equipment to many sectors, including two-way radio and data communications industries.

MDI, a Canadian company based in British Columbia, is a manufacturer of communications equipment used in police cars, firefighting equipment and taxis.

In April 1988, BCE Mobile Communications (85.5 percent owned by BCE), made an offer for 64 percent of MDI at $9.75 a share. In May, Motorola offered $13.50 a share for all of the company's common stock. Two months later, Motorola had taken over 98 percent of MDI, despite the golden parachutes given to MDI's senior executives.

10) Noranda buys Falconbridge. $1.9 billion, 100 percent debt financing. September 1989.

Noranda has activities in several sectors, including minerals and metals, forest products, energy and manufacturing.

Falconbridge is an international resource corporation engaged in the exploration, development, mining, processing, and marketing of minerals and metals.

In the summer of 1988, Noranda offered to buy 10 percent of the common shares of Falconbridge, gaining — a full year later — control (95 percent) of its target, in a joint venture with Trelleborg AB, a Swedish company. Falconbridge had tried to find a white knight in Amax, by signing an agreement with this U.S. company. However, Noranda-Trelleborg AB finally outbid Amax. The transaction was financed with loans from the six largest Canadian chartered banks and a $500-million bank letter of credit.

ACKNOWLEDGEMENT

THIS IS A REVISED VERSION of a paper presented at Investment Canada's Authors' Conference on *Corporate Globalization through Mergers and Acquisitions* held in Toronto November 29 - 30, 1990. We wish to thank Derek Rolfe, Zulfie Sadeque, Pierre St-Laurent, Daniel Shapiro, François Vaillancourt and Len Waverman for many helpful comments. We are also grateful to our research assistants Nayla Béchir, Harold Coulombe, Alia Karouani and Claude Pedneault. Finally, we wish to acknowledge financial support from Investment Canada.

BIBLIOGRAPHY

Asquith, D., T.C. Opler and J.F. Weston. "The Size and Distribution of Shareholder Wealth Gains from Mergers: Evidence from the Takeover Boom of the 1980's", University of California at Los Angeles, Discussion Paper No. 11, 1990.

Auerbach, A.J. and D. Reishus. "Effects of Taxation on the Merger Decision", in *Corporate Takeovers: Causes and Consequences*, A. J. Auerbach (ed), Chicago, University of Chicago Press, 1988.

Bensaïd, B. and P.G. Garella. "Tendering for Cash or for Shares in Takeover Bids", Banque de France, Mimeo, 1990.

Bhagat, S., A. Shleifer and R.W. Vishny. "The Aftermath of Hostile Takeovers", Mimeo, 1989.

Bhide, A. "The Causes and Consequences of Hostile Takeovers", *Journal of Applied Corporate Finance*, 2, 1989, pp. 36-59.

Bradley, M., A. Desai, and E.H. Kim. "Synergistic Gains from Corporate Acquisitions and their Division between the Stockholders of Target and Acquiring Firm", *Journal of Financial Economics*, 21, 1988, pp. 3-40.

Copeland, T.E. and J.F. Weston. *Financial Theory and Corporate Policy*, Reading, MA, Addison-Wesley Publishing Co., 1988.

Dennis, D.K. and J.J. McConnell. "Corporate Mergers and Security Returns", *Journal of Financial Economics*, 16, 1986, pp. 143-87.

Eckbo, B.E. "Horizontal Mergers, Collusion, and Stockholder Wealth", *Journal of Financial Economics*, 11, 1983, pp. 241-74.

_____. "Mergers and the Market for Corporate Control: The Canadian Evidence", *Canadian Journal of Economics*, 19, 1986, pp. 236-60.

Farrell, J. and C. Shapiro. "Asset Ownership and Market Structure in Oligopoly", *Rand Journal of Economics*, 21, 1990.

Green, C. *Canadian Industrial Organization and Policy*, Toronto, McGraw-Hill Ryerson, 1990.

Grossman, S.J. and O.D. Hart. "Takeover Bids, the Free-Rider Problem and the Theory of the Corporation", *Bell Journal of Economics*, 11, 1980, pp. 42-64.

Jarrell, G.A., J.A. Brickley and J.M. Netter. "The Market for Corporate Control: The Empirical Evidence since 1980", *Journal of Economic Perspectives*, 2, 1988, pp. 49-68.

Jensen, M.C. "Agency Costs of Free Cash Flow, Corporate Finance, and Takeovers", *American Economic Review*, 76, 1986, pp. 323-29.

_____. "Takeovers: Their Causes and Consequences", *Journal of Economic Perspectives*, 2, 1988, pp. 21-48.

Kaplan, S.N. "Management Buyouts: Evidence on Taxes as a Source of Value", *Journal of Finance*, 44, 1989, pp. 611-32.

Morck, R., A. Shleifer and R.W. Vishny. "Do Managerial Objectives Drive Bad Acquisitions", *Journal of Finance*, forthcoming, 1990.

Ravenscraft, D.J. and F.M. Scherer. *Mergers, Selloffs and Economic Efficiency*. Washington, 1987.

Shleifer, A. and L. Summers, "Breach of Trust in Hostile Takeovers" in *Corporate Takeovers: Causes and Consequences*, A.J. Auerbach (ed), Chicago, University of Chicago Press, 1988.

Stillman, R. "Examining Antitrust Policy Toward Horizontal Mergers", *Journal of Financial Economics*, 11, 1983, pp. 225-40.

Paul Halpern and Jack Mintz
Faculty of Management
University of Toronto

6

Taxation and Canada-U.S. Cross-Border Acquisitions

INTRODUCTION

THIS PAPER EXAMINES the impact of taxes on the incidence, form and method of cross-border transactions between Canada and the United States. The literature on domestic mergers and takeovers in the United States and Canada presents tax attributes that may affect takeovers; the attributes identified include tax losses, the deductibility of interest payments, tax-free rollovers and, in the United States prior to 1986, step-up provisions for asset values. A general conclusion based on this literature is that, at the margin, taxation is an important variable.[1] The structure of the transaction and the resulting impact on wealth for the shareholders of the companies involved, while they are not the primary incentive for the transaction, will be affected, to some degree, by relevant tax provisions.

Our primary interest is focussed on cross-border acquisitions — the purchase of existing domestic operations by a foreign company. This is not the only form in which foreign direct investment (FDI) takes place. Other forms are de novo entry, joint venturing with a foreign partner of either a new or an existing operation, further transfers of funds by the parent to its foreign operation, and the retention of funds within the foreign operation. Unfortunately, since data are not collected for each of these categories, it is not possible to determine the extent to which foreign companies in a domestic market prefer cross-border acquisitions over other forms of entry. All methods of entry are affected by the tax regime under which both the foreign and domestic operations of the parent are taxed, and by any tax treaties in existence among countries. The taxation impacts are described in a subsequent section. In this paper, we focus on cross-border acquisitions between Canada and the United States, but the literature review is drawn from analysis undertaken for other countries as well.

With increased capital mobility at the international level, the function of taxes in cross-border transactions has become a new topic for analysis. Much of the current economics literature deals with the effect of taxation on foreign direct investment of multinationals (e.g. Hartman, 1985; Hines, 1988; Grubert and Mutti, 1989). As yet, however, little work has been undertaken to clarify the role of taxes in affecting cross-border acquisitions. Cross-border acquisitions involve a highly complex part of tax law, not just of one but of many countries. We examine only the tax law related to U.S.-Canada cross-border acquisitions and draw some conclusions with respect to the effect of taxes on economic behaviour. Testing of propositions is a very difficult task, given the paucity of data, as we discuss below.

As a general point, we suggest that the following cross-border transactions are affected by taxes:

— Taking into account differential statutory tax rates, depreciation allowances and inventory deductions, the relatively higher effective tax rates on capital in Canada encourage companies to establish in the United States relative to Canada.

— Generally speaking, tax rules relating to the tax-free rollovers and the transfer of pre-acquisition tax losses from one entity to another, favour mergers and acquisitions over de novo entry if the acquiring and acquired companies are incorporated in the same jurisdiction. However, some tax benefits that are advantageous to domestic-owned companies may not apply if the acquiring company is incorporated in a different country.

— Tax rules tend to encourage the establishment of a subsidiary rather than a branch in another country because taxes paid to the capital-exporting country on foreign-source earnings can be partly avoided with the subsidiary form of enterprise. Under certain circumstances, however, it may be better to set up a branch for tax purposes — particularly if there are initial losses, or if the home country tax on foreign-source earnings is more generous than the host country tax regime.

— Tax rules also encourage share-for-share exchanges rather than cash-for-share exchanges, since the former allow relief from capital gains taxes paid by vendors of shares.

— Tax rules affect the decision to issue debt in one country relative to the other. At present, it is generally better to issue more debt in Canada, where the statutory corporate tax rate and inflation rate are higher.

This paper is organized as follows: Initially, some characteristics of Canada-U.S. cross-border acquisitions are presented. Next, the rationales for cross-border acquisitions are described, along with a discussion of the form and method of entry. Thereafter, the taxation issues and the impact on acquisitions for both U.S. and Canadian cross-border acquisitions are presented. A review of the empirical results in other papers and their consistency with tax motivations follows, with conclusions presented last. An appendix provides a detailed discussion of tax law relevant to cross-border acquisitions.

TABLE 1
(PANEL A)

CHARACTERISTICS OF CROSS-BORDER ACQUISITIONS
(YEAR ENDING DECEMBER 1988)

	PURCHASES BY CANADIAN FIRMS			SALES OF CANADIAN FIRMS		
	NO. OF DEALS	$US (MIL.)	AVERAGE	NO. OF DEALS	$US (MIL.)	AVERAGE
Total	79	$10 708	135.5	517	$3 548	6.9
Transaction Size						
Mid-Market	69	548	7.9	510	961	1.9
>$100M	10	10 160	1 016.0	7	2 587	370.0
Country Group						
European Community	13	1 051	80.8	138	1 073	7.8
	(16%)	(10%)		(27%)	(30%)	
United States	60	9 589	159.8	304	2 188	7.2
	(76%)	(90%)		(59%)	(62%)	
Rest of the World	6	70	11.7	75	287	3.8
	(8%)	(0%)		(14%)	(8%)	

NOTE: Numbers in parentheses are percentages of total amounts by country group.

SOURCE: KPMG Peat Marwick Thorne, *Deal Watch*, various issues.

TABLE 1
(PANEL B)

CHARACTERISTICS OF CROSS-BORDER ACQUISITIONS
(YEAR ENDING DECEMBER 1989)

	PURCHASES BY CANADIAN FIRMS			SALES OF CANADIAN FIRMS		
	NO. OF DEALS	$US (MIL)	AVERAGE	NO. OF DEALS	$US (MIL)	AVERAGE
Total	90	$4 173	46.4	212	$11 927	56.3
Transaction Size						
Mid-Market	81	1 025	12.7	199	1 514	7.6
>$100M	9	3 148	350.0	13	10 413	801.0
Country Group						
European Community	12	165	13.8	67	2 419	36.1
	(14%)	(4%)		(32%)	(20%)	
United States	76	3 973	52.3	105	7 760	73.9
	(84%)	(95%)		(50%)	(65%)	
Rest of the World	2	35	17.5	40	1 748	43.7
	(2%)	(1%)		(18%)	(15%)	

NOTE: Numbers in parentheses are percentages of total amounts by country group.

SOURCE: KPMG Peat Marwick Thorne, *Deal Watch*, various issues.

CHARACTERISTICS OF CROSS-BORDER ACQUISITIONS

IT IS VERY DIFFICULT TO OBTAIN INFORMATION about the amount and composition of cross-border acquisitions. Some comparative statistics for the 12 months ending with December 1988 and December 1989, for Canada and the United States are presented in Tables 1 and 2 respectively. In Table 1, statistics on the purchases by and the sales of Canadian companies in cross-border acquisitions are presented for 1988 (Panel A) and 1989 (Panel B). In Table 2, comparable statistics for U.S. cross-border acquisitions are supplied. The transactions are identified by the number of deals and their value in American dollars. The acquisitions cover all transactions, and reflect both private and public offerings. The data were obtained from KMPG *Deal Watch* (various issues).

Table 1 (Panel B) shows that in 1989, there were 90 cross-border acquisitions by Canadian firms and that these firms had an average dollar value of $46.4 million. Most deals were in the mid-market category (less than $100 million), but the dollar value of transactions was largest in the over-$100 million category. These figures reflect the small number of very large transactions. The 1988 data and the sales of Canadian companies reflect the same phenomenon. The total value of acquisitions is sensitive to a small number of large transactions. For example, in 1988 Canadian companies effected three large cross-border acquisitions with a total value of approximately $10 billion.

In both years, the acquisition of American firms by Canadian companies was the major element in both number and dollar value of transactions. In fact, purchases in dollar amounts were worth much more than sales of companies in 1988 ($10 billion as compared to $2 billion) but worth less than sales in 1989 ($4 billion as compared to $8 billion).

The sales of Canadian companies in these transactions show that the major purchaser of Canadian companies was the United States, which accounted for 50 percent of the deals and 65 percent of the dollar value of the transactions in 1989; the results for 1988 were approximately the same. In 1988, sales of Canadian firms to companies in the European Community (EC) constituted about 30 percent of the deals, while the rest of the world segment comprised about 14 percent by number and eight percent by value. For 1989, even with a smaller number of deals, there were increases in the average size of acquisition and proportion of value for the category "Rest of the World" (which includes Japan).

Table 2, Panels A and B, which shows the sales of American firms for 1988 and 1989, demonstrates that the major region, in terms of dollar value of transactions, was the EC with 62 percent of deals in 1988 and 55 percent in 1989. Most of these transactions are likely to involve firms in the United Kingdom. The "Rest of the World" group, which includes the Far East, made up approximately 38 percent of the value of transactions in 1989, and 25 percent in 1988.

In 1989, the United States experienced a reduction in total number of deals and their dollar value as compared to the 1988 figures. The major acquiring area

TABLE 2
(PANEL A)

CHARACTERISTICS OF CROSS-BORDER ACQUISITIONS
(YEAR ENDING DECEMBER 1988)

	PURCHASES BY AMERICAN FIRMS			SALES OF AMERICAN FIRMS		
	NO. OF DEALS	$US (MIL)	AVERAGE	NO. OF DEALS	$US (MIL)	AVERAGE
Total	471	$9 354	19.9	729	$71 976	98.7
Transaction Size						
Mid-Market	445	1 254	2.8	626	8 223	13.7
>$100M	26	8 100	311.5	103	63 753	619.0
Country Group						
EC	121 (26%)	6 435 (69%)	53.1	536 (74%)	44 669 (62%)	83.3
Canada	305 (65%)	2 195 (23%)	7.2	61 (8%)	9 594 (13%)	157.3
Rest of the World	45 (9%)	724 (8%)	16.1	132 (18%)	17 713 (25%)	134.2

NOTE: Numbers in parentheses are percentages of total amounts by country group.

SOURCE: KPMG Peat Marwick Thorne, *Deal Watch*, various issues.

TABLE 2
(PANEL B)

CHARACTERISTICS OF CROSS-BORDER ACQUISITIONS
(YEAR ENDING DECEMBER 1989)

	PURCHASES BY AMERICAN FIRMS			SALES OF AMERICAN FIRMS		
	NO. OF DEALS	$US (MIL.)	AVERAGE	NO. OF DEALS	$US (MIL.)	AVERAGE
Total	366	$23 278	63.6	700	$55 665	79.5
Transaction Size						
Mid-Market	327	2 582	7.9	588	8 048	13.7
>$100M	39	20 696	530.7	112	47 617	425.2
Country Group						
EC	205 (56%)	12 907 (55%)	63.0	444 (63%)	30 488 (55%)	68.7
Canada	105 (29%)	7 760 (33%)	73.9	76 (11%)	3 973 (7%)	52.3
Rest of the World	56 (15%)	2 611 (11%)	46.6	180 (26%)	21 204 (38%)	117.8

NOTE: Numbers in parentheses are percentages of total amounts by country group.

SOURCE: KPMG Peat Marwick Thorne, *Deal Watch*, various issues.

of American firms is the EC, but its importance diminished from 1988 to 1989. The "Rest of the World" component has experienced a significant increase in cross-border acquisitions of American firms.

These tables contain some indirect evidence about the impact of the Free Trade Agreement (FTA) on cross-border acquisitions. In 1988, purchases by American firms of Canadian firms made up, in terms of value, 23 percent of the total acquisitions and 65 percent of the total number of deals (Table 2, Panel A). While the value of the transactions increased to 33 percent in 1989, the number of deals fell to 29 percent of the total. After the FTA was struck, it was no longer necessary for businesses to enter the Canadian market through the purchase of small firms. From that point, the value of the average transaction increased from $7.2 million in 1988 to $73.9 million in 1989. Acquisitions are now larger and are likely to be targeted at establishments that could be part of a continent-wide industrial strategy.

Evidence (not reported here) relating to the nine months ending with September 1990 shows that the number and value of sales of Canadian companies is down from the same period in 1989. Surprisingly, Europe was the major player, accounting for 40 percent of the value of the transactions; the United States accounted for 37 percent and Japan and Hong Kong for nine percent. The size of the European presence is primarily related to Canadian-German acquisitions.

Evidence dating from 1988 and 1989 suggests that the composition of the country groups acquiring American companies in cross-border acquisitions is generally similar to findings recorded in other studies that investigated cross-border transactions. Harris and Ravenscraft (1989) observed that of 159 cross-border acquisitions of American firms made over the period from 1970 to 1987, 67 percent originated in Europe (where the United Kingdom represented 38 percent of the total number of acquisitions), 21 percent originated in Canada and 12 percent in "Rest of the World". Since the study based its analysis on stock market data, only those acquired companies which had listed common equity were included in the sample, while data reported in Tables 1 and 2 include private transactions as well. This distinction could account for some of the differences in the importance of the various acquiring-country groups. The importance of the companies in the "Rest of the World" category has been increasing as well.

In the United States, Harris and Ravenscraft report that for 1986, 63 percent of the foreign direct investment in the U.S. was made up of cross-border transactions.

RATIONALES FOR CROSS-BORDER ACQUISITIONS

THE ARGUMENTS PRESENTED to explain foreign direct investment (FDI) in general and cross-border acquisitions in particular, are based primarily on wealth-maximizing behaviour on the part of parent companies. The criteria used by the acquiring company in making a decision to purchase would incorporate the opportunity costs of the investment and would provide sufficient means to cover the significant transactions and monitoring costs that arise from foreign acquisitions.

The gains from multinational investments are expected to be positive to all participants in the transaction. These gains would be reflected in the security prices of the parent/acquiring firm.[2] Unless the management of the parent company derives significant benefit from managing a multinational enterprise, in contrast to a purely domestic firm, the effect on the price of the acquirer's common equity should be positive. The alternative hypothesis of management utility maximization, with utility based, in part, on managerial preferences for security or non-pecuniary benefits, suggests a negative effect on the common equity prices of the parent firm.

The effect on common equity prices could be observed in relation to a specific foreign investment (acquisition) event or to the expected profitability of all foreign operations and would be reflected in the deviation of the parent company's share price from a benchmark value. The deviation would reflect the expected accumulated cash flow or risk-reduction benefits of cross-border and domestic acquisitions, as well as of continuing domestic operations.

Two major areas of interest in the FDI literature are rationales for foreign direct investment and the form and method by which it is undertaken in the host country. Both of these streams of literature rely quite heavily on transactions costs to rationalize their position. In addition, in each of these areas taxation can exercise influence.

Corporations develop myriad rationales for new cross-border investment to capture the wealth gains. These rationales range from the simplistic to the sophisticated, embodying arguments that include the following: imperfections in capital markets and the function of diversification;[3] imperfections in factor and product markets;[4] the transfer of intangible assets or of assets for which there is proprietary information across borders, through the use of acquisitions and not the more conventional markets;[5] and taxation, the area of direct interest to us. Our discussion will deal only with the taxation issue, although we shall touch upon some of the other areas in the review of the literature. In the following section we discuss not only the structuring of the transaction to capture the taxation benefits, but also the influence of taxation on the method of acquisition and form of entry into another country.

TAXATION AND SPECIAL BENEFITS

THE EXISTENCE OF DIFFERENTIAL TAX RATES, especially in the presence of a tax haven, and the current method of taxation for multinational firms in their home country both affect cross-border transactions. Many multinationals' home countries will provide specific tax incentives or disincentives for direct investment abroad.[6] Other countries, such as the United States, have taken a different approach. American tax law does not grant fast write-offs for depreciation and investment tax credits for foreign investment undertaken by

American multinationals; these write-offs are applicable only to domestic investments.

Many host countries provide tax and other incentives to improve the economic environment in an effort to attract foreign business operations. These incentives include tax holidays (Mintz, 1990), fast write-offs for depreciation, investment allowances and credits. In fact, some developed countries (the U.S. is a notable exception) grant "tax sparing", an arrangement that allows multinationals to benefit from tax incentives given in a developing economy without increasing the level of foreign-source taxes imposed on the home country when income is remitted to the parent firm.

FORM AND METHOD OF ENTRY

NEW FOREIGN DIRECT INVESTMENT (excluding the retention of profits within the subsidiary and the transfer of funds directly from parent to subsidiary) may occur through an acquisition (total or partial) of an existing company in the host country, the establishment of a new company (referred to as a greenfield investment), or the use of a joint venture. In the literature, the joint venture is evaluated either as an acquisition with shared control or as a case distinct from a (partial) acquisition, since the structure of the managerial relationships and the influence of the host-country partners is an important factor in this form of entry. In either the greenfield or the acquisition form of entry, the entering company must choose the method of entry. The choice lies between setting up a branch and/or establishing a subsidiary.

A number of studies have investigated the factors that determine the choice of the form of entry. Kogut and Singh (1988) is one recent work in which entry choice is viewed as a function of cultural, firm and industry variables. The firm variables include asset size, diversification and experience of the parent firm in the country of entry. The industry variables include R&D and advertising intensity.

The results of the investigation suggest that cultural differences increase the probability that entry will be made by joint venture or greenfield investment rather than by acquisition. Similarly, the greater the uncertainty of the parent about organizational relationships in the foreign country, the greater the probability that entry will not be by acquisition. However, there is no variable that takes into account the possibility that different income tax consequences may result from the form of entry. For example, does the tax treatment of a joint venture, a subsidiary, or a greenfield investment, whether established by de novo entry or by acquisition, have any bearing on the entry choice?

Again, this literature does not consider the influence of taxation in the home and foreign countries on the method of entry. For example, do income tax provisions of the host and home countries influence firms' decisions to establish a foreign operation as a subsidiary, with its own management team and board of directors, or as a branch plant? This paper, however, does discuss the influence of taxation on the method and form of entry.

CROSS-BORDER TAX ISSUES AND ACQUISITIONS

THIS SECTION PROVIDES AN OVERVIEW of the primary effects that taxes may have on merger and acquisition decisions in the United States and Canada. We use "may" because many of the tax effects are too difficult for us to test by means of the data currently available. At best, we only speculate on the most important tax factors that might influence the number and types of cross-border acquisitions. To the extent that we can rely on data to support or negate various propositions, we shall present such information in the section on Empirical Analysis.

We consider four broad issues:

- the effect of taxes on cross-border acquisitions that may be viewed as a substitute for de novo entry;
- the choice between branch and subsidiary forms of acquisitions;
- the choice of the type of acquisition: share-for-share exchange (mergers), amalgamation, and share-for-cash exchange;
- the choice of the location of debt by the parent when financing acquisitions in the other country.

DE NOVO ENTRY VS. ACQUISITION

SUPPOSE A COMPANY DECIDES TO LOCATE in the United States or Canada, most likely for non-tax reasons. The company has a choice of creating a new operation from scratch (de novo entry) or purchasing an existing business. To keep the example simple, we generally assume that the owner of assets or businesses acquired in the country is a resident, rather than a non-resident.

The choice of investing in capital through de novo entry or acquisition in Canada or the United States depends on a number of tax factors.

First, there is the domestic tax paid on business income earned in each country on new investments after the purchaser has established the new company. This effective tax rate will apply on de novo investments and new capital projects of a company that may have been started through acquisition of another company. With respect to Canada-U.S. cross-border transactions, differences in domestic effective tax rates affect, in part, the location of new capital for production purposes.

Second, the establishment of the business by asset purchases or acquisition of companies will affect the level of taxes paid by the vendor or purchaser on assets held at the time of sale. The decision to locate in a particular country will be affected not only by the taxation of new capital but also by the tax impacts on purchasing old capital obtained through acquisitions. If the tax system encourages the acquisition of companies and old assets, then there are additional incentives, over and above the domestic taxation of new capital projects, to locate investments in a particular country.

Domestic Effective Tax Rate on Capital after Establishment of the Company

A company investing in Canada or the United States pays taxes in accordance with domestic tax law. The most important tax to influence the location of capital investment is the corporate income tax.[7] Companies also pay corporate taxes to their resident country on foreign-source earnings. This topic is reserved for discussion below of subsidiaries and branches.

Depending on the type of investment activity, the company might find that the American *domestic* effective tax rate on capital is higher or lower than one computed for a similar investment made in Canada. The American corporate statutory tax rate, including state corporate income taxes, is approximately 38 percent, generally less than the Canadian combined federal and provincial statutory tax rates, which vary from a low of 34 percent for Quebec manufacturing to a high of 45 percent for non-manufacturing companies in several provinces. The average statutory corporate tax rate is about 42 percent in Canada. However, statutory tax rates are not the only relevant statistic by which to compare the impact of taxation on capital investment in both countries. Other considerations include differences in capital cost allowances given for depreciable capital, inventory cost deductions (FIFO in Canada and LIFO in the United States), and other tax provisions that affect the effective tax rate on investments in Canada and the United States.

McKenzie and Mintz (1990) have estimated, on the basis of a number of different assumptions, the effective tax rate on capital for American and Canadian companies. In Table 3, below, estimates of the effective *domestic* corporate tax rates in both countries[8] suggest that Canadian effective tax rates on capital investments are higher than the American effective tax rates on investments for most industries. This suggests that, for *de novo* entry, there is a corporate tax bias in favour of locating investments in the United States rather than Canada. The source of this bias is the higher statutory tax rate in Canada, less generous treatment of inventory costs in Canada (FIFO accounting) as compared to the United States (LIFO accounting), and lower capital cost allowances for equipment in Canada as compared to the United States.

These numbers suggest that cross-border acquisitions tend to be "one way" for tax reasons: that is, Canadian businesses tend to establish production facilities in the United States. In the matter of corporate taxes, at least, there is little incentive for American firms to establish themselves in Canada, except in a few cases (such as communications).

TABLE 3

COMPARISON OF EFFECTIVE TAX RATES ON CAPITAL IN THE UNITED STATES AND
CANADA FOR 1990 (%)

	CANADA	UNITED STATES
Agriculture, Forestry & Fishing	27.6	26.2
Manufacturing	31.1	27.0
Construction	43.4	24.0
Transportation & Storage	21.7	8.3
Communications	17.5	25.2
Public Utilities	19.8	12.5
Wholesale Trade	34.9	24.8
Retail Trade	30.5	21.3
Services	22.9	16.1
Buildings and Structures	21.1	17.6
Machinery and Equipment	25.6	18.9
Inventories	43.2	28.0
Land	20.2	19.0
TOTAL	28.9	20.4

SOURCE: McKenzie and Mintz (1990)

Tax Impacts on Asset Purchases and Acquisitions

When a company decides to enter the market, it may choose to purchase assets through *de novo* entry or by acquiring an existing company. Cross-border transactions will be affected by the taxation of acquired assets when new firms are established. Two particular issues arise: tax-free rollovers and the treatment of tax losses. We have reviewed in the Appendix the specific rules used in Canada and the United States. Here, we simply suggest how tax factors might influence acquisition decisions.

Tax-Free Rollovers   In both Canada and the United States, vendors who sell an acquirer a company, rather than individual assets, are able, subject to certain limitations, to defer the payment of capital gains taxes on non-depreciable property and recapture of depreciation on depreciable property. However, the purchaser of the company must then carry depreciable assets at historical cost rather than bumping up the cost basis to fair market value. This regulation reduces the value of capital cost allowances in the future. By contrast, with assets disposals as in the *de novo* entry, the vendor pays taxes on capital gains and recapture of depreciation, while the purchaser of depreciable property is able to bump up asset values for depreciation purposes.

When acquisitions are made in the United States, a tax benefit to the vendor and/or purchaser is generally arranged through the exchange of assets by means of an acquisition that can enjoy a tax-free rollover. By deferring the tax on capital gains and recapture of depreciation, the vendor generally saves more taxes than are paid by the purchaser, who is unable to depreciate assets at a higher stepped-up value.[9]

When acquisitions are made in Canada, there is a tax benefit in seeking a tax-free rollover for non-depreciable assets. With respect to depreciable assets, however, no clear conclusion can be reached. Since only three-quarters of the difference between the sale value and the original cost of the asset is included in income (i.e., the capital gain component of recapture of depreciation), it may be better for a vendor to sell an asset at its fair market price and allow the purchaser to deduct capital cost allowances based on the bumped-up value of the asset. However, American firms directly purchasing Canadian companies cannot provide a tax-free rollover to the Canadian shareholders.

Tax Losses   One of the important advantages of an acquisition is the possibility it confers offsetting pre-acquisition operating (non-capital) losses of the acquired or acquiring company against the taxable income of the other company. In recent years, the United States has restricted the use of pre-acquisition operating losses, although there remains an incentive to acquire companies if losses in one entity can be written off more quickly by the combined company.

Tax losses are particularly important in Canada, where over one-half the corporations are in a non-taxpaying position (Glenday and Mintz, 1991). Pre-acquisition tax losses can be written off more quickly as long as certain tests (as reviewed in the Appendix) are satisfied. One of the important restrictions is that pre-acquisition losses can be written off only against income earned in the same line of activity.[10] In addition, unused deductions, such as exploration and development expenditures and capital cost allowances, must be declared in the year in which a change of ownership is made. This latter provision makes an acquisition of a company with tax losses less desirable than simply purchasing the assets as in the case of *de novo* entry.

In conclusion, there are tax benefits associated with tax-free rollovers and pre-acquisition tax losses that arise in a cross-border acquisition. However, the benefits do not accrue in all situations so that *de novo* entry may be preferred in some situations.

SUBSIDIARY OR BRANCH

SO FAR, WE HAVE NOT REMARKED on the implications of American and Canadian taxes that apply to foreign-source income of parent companies residing in a particular country. This level of taxation can affect cross-border transactions, not only in terms of the effective tax rates calculated in Table 3 above, but also in terms of the tax benefits arising from acquisitions of companies and assets in another country.

The United States taxes the branch profits and remitted earnings of its own multinationals on a worldwide basis. A credit is given for worldwide corporate income and withholding taxes paid to foreign governments. If the foreign tax credit is more (less) than the underlying U.S. tax on foreign-source income, the parent is said to be in an "excess credit" ("deficient credit") position. Branch profits are taxed on an "accrual basis", while subsidiary income is taxed only on a remitted basis (reinvested profits are exempt from U.S. tax).

The right of subsidiaries to defer U.S. tax by not remitting income to the parent has been an important reason for operating subsidiary enterprises in another country. However, in certain situations, a branch form of enterprise may be preferable. In particular, branch losses may be used to reduce world-wide foreign-source income. Moreover, depending on tax provisions in each country, a branch may be preferable to a subsidiary. For example, if Canadian capital cost allowances are less generous than American allowances, it might be better for a parent firm to organize a Canadian company as a branch rather than as a subsidiary, since with a branch, only U.S. tax provisions matter to the American multinational's investment decision.[11]

Canadian tax law is somewhat different from American law with respect to the treatment of foreign-source income of resident multinational parents. Canadian taxes apply to foreign-source branch profits and remitted income of subsidiaries. However, if a parent owns at least 10 percent of any class of shares, dividends remitted from foreign affiliates are exempt from Canadian tax. Although this exemption tends to promote the subsidiary form of enterprise, there are three situations in which branches may be preferred. First, dividends remitted from foreign affiliates are not exempt from U.S. withholding taxes. If the dividends are remitted and are exempt from Canadian tax, the Canadian parent cannot credit the U.S. withholding tax against qualifying taxes on foreign-source income. Second, only branch losses in the United States are directly written off worldwide income for tax purposes. Third, certain tax write-offs for capital may be more generous under Canadian law, making the branch a better form of organization for taxation purposes. However, a number of tax penalties arise from using the branch method as discussed in the Appendix.

In Table 4, we compute effective tax rates on subsidiary and branch forms of Canada-U.S. cross-border transactions for investments, excluding inventories.[12] The subsidiary effective tax rates are based on McKenzie and Mintz (1990), while the branch effective tax rates are computed according to theoretical results derived by Leechor and Mintz (1991). Both sets of effective tax rates take into account Canadian and American taxes owing on income earned in each of the two countries.

The numbers given in Table 4 illustrate significant differences in branch and subsidiary effective tax rates. For Canadian investments in the United States, the branch form of enterprise, according to these calculations, is somewhat preferable on average, particularly with respect to manufacturing, retail trade and service industries. The reason is that the branch form of enterprise can take better advantage of higher capital cost deductions for retail trade and services and a lower statutory tax rate on manufacturing in Canada, assuming that the parent is in a "deficient tax credit" position. These calculations, however,

TABLE 4

COMBINED U.S.-CANADIAN EFFECTIVE TAX RATES ON CAPITAL BRANCH AND
SUBSIDARY FORMS FOR 1990 (%)

I CANADIAN INVESTMENT IN THE UNITED STATES

	SUBSIDIARY	BRANCH[1]
Manufacturing	30.9	22.6
Construction	30.0	34.4
Transport & Storage	–1.8	17.4
Communications	–2.1	10.4
Utilities	4.2	13.3
Wholesale Trade	4.4	19.7
Retail Trade	14.4	12.2
Services	31.2	19.9
AGGREGATE	19.8	19.3

[1]Deficient Credit case only. If the parent is in excess credit, the effective tax rate is the same as for the subsidiary case.

II AMERICAN INVESTMENT IN CANADA

	SUBSIDIARY[1]		EXCESS CREDIT	BRANCH[1]	
	$ U.S.	$ CAN		$ U.S.	$ CAN
Manufacturing	29.1	35.3	26.1	36.9	39.0
Construction	40.6	47.7	38.1	39.9	42.1
Transport & Storage	20.6	15.2	25.0	12.2	15.2
Communications	16.6	17.4	19.2	11.2	13.8
Utilities	18.8	20.6	20.7	14.3	16.4
Wholesale Trade	23.1	19.5	26.0	12.3	14.7
Retail Trade	21.7	24.6	19.7	22.8	24.7
Services	31.7	37.0	27.7	38.6	40.5
AGGREGATE	25.4	28.6	25.7	28.0	30.3

[1]Case of percent in deficient credit position.

SOURCE: Data taken from McKenzie and Mintz (1990)

ignore other important factors that limit the use of branches as compared to
subsidiaries. In particular, the interest allocation rules in the United States,
which are not included in these calculations, make the branch method less
attractive to a Canadian business, since American interest deductions may be
lost to the Canadian company.

Effective tax rates are also calculated for U.S. multinational investments
in Canada for the deficient tax credit position (subsidiary and branch) and
excess tax credit position. The branch and subsidiary cases are broken down to
take into account optional treatment given to American companies in the
matter of using a specific currency to convert profit and asset values in Canada

for U.S. tax purposes. American rules require firms to use the foreign currency as the "functional currency"; assets are maintained in their foreign currency values while profits, including capital cost allowances, are converted to U.S. currency values when income is remitted. However, the American parent may use the U.S. dollar as the "functional currency" for Canadian investments; asset values are converted to U.S. dollars at time of purchase and depreciation deductions are denominated in U.S. dollars. The important difference is that the use of the weaker currency, the Canadian dollar, as a functional currency, implies that the U.S. dollar value of capital cost allowances will fall, over time, as the Canadian dollar depreciates. In general, we find that the use of the Canadian dollar as the functional currency implies a higher effective tax rate on U.S. investments when the parent is in a deficient tax credit position.

The calculations provided in Table 4 suggest that the subsidiary form of enterprise is generally preferable to a branch for U.S. investment in Canada. In fact, it may also be preferable for the American parent to be in a deficient tax credit position, to minimize corporate taxes paid to both Canadian and American parents. The reason for this last result is that the statutory tax rates in Canada are generally higher than those in the United States (except for manufacturing). Thus, it is better to deduct expenses in Canada and to keep Canadian taxes below American taxes paid on remitted income.

TYPE OF MERGER

A COMPANY MAY BE PURCHASED by the acquiring company issuing shares for shares, or paying cash for shares, of the acquired company. Or, two companies may be amalgamated into one. When acquiring and acquired companies are resident in the same jurisdiction, shareholders can defer capital gains taxation if there is a share-for-share exchange or an amalgamation, as long as there is a change in control of the acquired company. This deferral is not permitted with cash-for-share exchanges.

With cross-border transactions, direct amalgamation of incorporated American and Canadian companies is difficult; instead, amalgamations are generally achieved through affiliate companies that are residents of the same jurisdiction.[13] In addition, Canada does not permit a tax-free rollover for vendors when a share-for-share exchange involves the sale of a Canadian company to a non-Canadian company. The United States does permit a tax-free rollover for vendors if a foreign buyer is involved, although permission may be required and a "toll" charge may be assessed.

LOCATION OF DEBT

A COMPANY CAN ISSUE DEBT in Canada or the United States to finance investments in either country. Under Canadian law, a Canadian parent can issue debt to finance equity acquisitions in the United States while an American branch or subsidiary in Canada may deduct interest incurred in Canada, subject to certain limitations. Under U.S law, interest costs are also deductible, although there are several restrictions on both American parents and foreign subsidiaries and branches in the United States relating to the deductibility of interest expense incurred in that country. These limitations are discussed in the Appendix.

Leaving aside these limitations, what is the best choice for the parent?

If the parent is Canadian, the cost of debt finance in Canada and the United States is as follows. If the parent incurs the debt in Canada at the nominal interest rate, i, the net-of-tax cost of the debt is $i(1-u)$, u denoting the corporate tax rate in Canada. The cost of debt raised in the United States depends on whether the parent operates as a subsidiary or branch in the United States. Let i^* be the nominal interest rate of debt incurred in the United States and x the expected appreciation of the American dollar relative to the Canadian dollar, which is assumed to be untaxed.[14] The cost of debt finance raised in the United States is $i^*(1-u^*) + x$, u^* denoting the effective tax rate at which interest costs are deductible. For a subsidiary, u^* can be interpreted as the American corporate rate and, for a branch, u^* may be interpreted as either the Canadian corporate tax rate (if American foreign tax credits are less than the Canadian tax) or the American corporate tax (if there are excess credits).

Taxes have two effects on the decision to incur debt in either the United States or Canada. First, it is better to incur the debt in the country with the highest corporate tax rate (i.e., Canada in most situations at the present time). Second, it may also be better to incur the debt in the country with the higher nominal interest rate because of inflation (see Booth, 1990; and Leechor and Mintz, 1990). To understand the latter case, assume that without corporate taxation, nominal interest rates are the same $(i=i^*+x)$.[15] With corporate taxation, the cost of debt finance in Canada is reduced from i to $i(1-u)$, and in the United States, from i^* to $i^*(1-u^*)$. Note that even where corporate tax rates are the same, the debt deduction is more valuable in the country with the higher nominal interest rate. With nominal interest deductibility of interest costs, a company enjoys a tax benefit accruing from inflation, since the interest costs include compensation to the lender for the reduction in the real value of the debt's principal. The cost of debt finance, adjusted for taxes and inflation, is less in the country with the higher inflation rate.[16]

For an American parent, these considerations are essentially the same, except for an American subsidiary operating in Canada while the American parent is in a deficient tax credit position. When the American subsidiary issues more debt in Canada, both Canadian corporate taxes and American taxes owing on remitted dividends are affected. In fact, the issuing of more local debt in Canada can drive up the rate of American tax on each dollar of remitted dividends, thereby reducing the value of debt deductions incurred in Canada.[17]

TABLE 5

COMBINED U.S.-CANADIAN EFFECTIVE TAX REBATES ON CAPITAL ACCORDING
TO PLACEMENT OF DEBT (%)

I CANADIAN INVESTMENT IN THE UNITED STATES

	DEBT IN CANADA	ALL DEBT IN U.S.
Manufacturing	30.9	31.7
Construction	29.9	32.0
Transport & Storage	-1.8	6.0
Communications	-2.1	5.2
Utilities	4.2	10.2
Wholesale Trade	4.4	9.6
Retail Trade	14.4	19.3
Service	31.2	35.0
AGGREGATE	19.8	22.8

II AMERICAN INVESTMENT IN CANADA

	DEFICIENT TAX CREDIT				EXCESS TAX CREDIT	
	$ US		$ CAN			
	DEBT IN CAN.	DEBT IN U.S.	DEBT IN CAN.	DEBT IN U.S.	DEBT IN CAN.	DEBT IN U.S.
Manufacturing	29.1	29.3	35.3	35.5	25.2	26.1
Construction	40.6	40.7	47.7	47.5	37.1	38.8
Transport & Storage	20.6	20.2	15.2	14.5	20.4	25.0
Communications	16.6	16.4	12.4	17.0	13.4	19.2
Utilities	18.8	18.7	20.0	19.8	15.7	20.7
Wholesale Trade	23.1	23.0	19.5	19.3	22.0	26.0
Retail Trade	21.7	21.7	24.6	24.7	14.9	19.7
Services	31.7	32.2	37.0	37.5	23.3	27.7
AGGREGATE	25.5	25.5	28.6	28.6	22.0	25.0

In Table 5, calculations are provided for Canadian parents that issue
debt either in Canada or in the United States to fund subsidiary investments
in the United States. As the Canadian inflation rate is assumed to be higher
than the American rate for these calculations, and as, for most sectors,
Canadian corporate tax rates are higher than the American rates, we find that
the effective tax rate on capital is lower when more debt is issued in Canada.

As for American investments in Canada, the issuing of more debt in
Canada decreases the effective tax rate in the excess tax credit case, as in
results obtained for Canadian parents. However, in the case of deficient tax
credits, the tax rate imposed on remitted dividends increases with the increase
in debt issued in Canada. As a result, there is no significant benefit in issuing

debt in Canada. These calculations, however, do not take into account special restrictions that limit the deductibility of interest expenses in the United States. The incentive to issue debt in Canada is stronger for tax reasons, given these limitations.

EMPIRICAL ANALYSIS AND REVIEW OF THE LITERATURE

IN THIS SECTION, we review the empirical evidence relating to the effect of taxes on the value of cross-border acquisitions. Most studies do not deal directly with taxes. Instead, they examine whether foreign acquisitions improve the after-tax profitability of the multinationals. This possibility could be influenced by either non-tax factors as discussed earlier, or tax factors as discussed above.

From the literature review, we observe that no direct evidence has been presented on the influence of taxation, and the indirect evidence, while not consistent with any effect of taxation, has some methodological problems.

TESTING METHODOLOGIES

ALL STUDIES THAT WE REVIEWED consider the impact of multinational operations and taxation on the market value of the firms engaged in a transaction. Researchers use two general approaches. The first identifies the effect of the aggregate multinational operations on the share price. The second looks to a specific acquisition event and assesses its effect.

In identifying the effect of aggregate multinational operations on the value of a multinational firm, three different measures are used. The first two measure the extent to which multinational operations provide profitable opportunities to the firm and result in the share price (or market value of the firm) exceeding the benchmark value that would exist without these opportunities. The measures used to reflect this "above normal" valuation are either Tobin's "q", which is the ratio of the current market value of the company's equity to its replacement value, or the difference between the current market and book values of the equity of the firm, scaled by a size variable (usually dollar sales). In the literature, the second measure is referred to as "excess valuation". A third measure looks directly at the realized holding period rates of return on the common equity of the multinational company relative to its risk as measured by stock market-based data. This method is based on measurements of conventional portfolio performance.

Each measure is intended to determine three components: the above-normal returns created by international operations through real investment decisions, at rates of return in excess of the relevant cost of capital; the effect of intangible assets as evident through international operations; and the effect of diversification where a premium is found in the stock price to reflect the firm's ability to diversify more effectively than investors. Since this approach utilizes the level of share prices relative to a benchmark, it reflects total firm operations and makes it difficult to isolate the impact of cross border acquisitions *per se.*

The second general approach utilizes an event study methodology which identifies the effect that a specific international acquisition has on the abnormal return on either the acquiring or acquired company's equity close to the announcement of the acquisition. The abnormal return may not only reflect the effect of the acquisition in question but also, for the initial foreign acquisitions of a firm, serve as a signal of the direction of future growth.[18] In some of the empirical studies researchers attempt to adjust for this signal effect, although its impact is likely to be small, since it is applicable only to a subset of firms in the sample. Subject to this qualification, the "event study" approach reflects the market's expectation of the effect of a specific acquisition on the wealth of the equity investors of the companies participating in the transaction. By isolating the effect of an acquisition on the participants' share prices, this approach reflects marginal effects of a cross-border acquisition. A major problem with this approach is that the marginal effect may be small because the acquired firm is small in relation to the multinational acquiring firm.

For a number of reasons, the event study approach is preferred to the "above normal" valuation "q" and holding period risk-return methods. First, "above normal" valuation captures all influences on the value of the firm, including but not limited to the extent and effect of cross-border multinational operations. Thus, it reflects average but not marginal influences. Second, this valuation is sensitive to the accounting treatment of the foreign operations. Accounting methodologies differ among countries, and the variables used in the above normal valuation approaches are based on either book values or book values adjusted to reflect replacement values. This results in the potential for measurement biases in the "above normal" value measures for firms with significant multinational operations. With the holding period approach, even if multinationality affects the share prices and hence the rate of return adjusted for risk for any of the reasons noted, the effect will be reflected immediately in the stock price, and the firm will then earn a normal rate of return on equity as adjusted by risk. Thus it would be surprising if companies with substantial foreign operations did outperform those with exclusively domestic operations. Any deviations from this normal rate of return, usually measured through portfolio performance, may result not from internationalization or diversification, but from events in the operations of the firms. It is unlikely that these events will be concentrated only in the foreign subsidiaries of the firm.

EMPIRICAL RESULTS

SINCE THE EVENT STUDIES MEASURE the marginal effect of specific cross-border acquisitions and permit the testing of hypotheses concerning the sources of any abnormal returns, we review these studies in some depth.

Event Studies

Doukas and Travlos (1988) investigate the daily abnormal common equity returns close to the announcement of the acquisition for American *bidding* firms which are involved in international acquisitions during the period from 1975 to 1983. Over the eleven-day event period surrounding the announcement date, no significant abnormal return was associated with the announcements. However, dividing the sample into categories related to the acquiring company's experience in multinational operations produces very different results. For companies for which this is the first foreign acquisition, the abnormal return on the announcement date is positive but insignificant. However, on dates two days before and after the announcement date, the abnormal returns were negative and significant. This result is consistent with the hypothesis that human capital is generated by international experience and the lack of such experience suggests to the market that transactions costs will dominate any excess profits. Moreover, any signal of future profitable opportunities stemming from international growth buried in the acquisition does not offset the negative effect of inexperience!

The other categories indicate whether the firm has any prior operating experience in the host country through previous acquisitions. If the firm is already operating in the host country, there are no significant abnormal returns on the announcement date or over the event period. However, if the company is making its first entry into the country but already has foreign operational experience, there is a positive and significant impact on the announcement date. This finding is consistent with wealth maximization and the internalization hypothesis, since the gains are obtained only when the technology is applied to a new country.

Doukas and Travlos also regress the cumulative abnormal return for each acquisition against variables identifying the experience of the company in the host country and determining whether the acquisition is in the same line of business. The result is that the cumulative abnormal returns are significantly higher if the company is not already operating in the host country, and if the host country is a developing country. A further refinement of the research technique determined that the gains were higher for entry into a developing country if the entering company was not already present. Again, these results are consistent with the internalization hypothesis.

Fatemi (1984) used a limited sample of 18 firms to identify through a questionnaire survey, the month and year of the *first* foreign operations for each company. The observed abnormal returns around this announcement date should reflect the effect of both the specific transaction and the policy of engaging in multinational acquisitions. Fatemi found a small average abnormal return for the sample around the event date; over the fourteen months preceding the initial foreign diversification, there was an 18 percent return. The results of this study are not illuminating because the sample was small and the value of the first cross-border transaction relative to the parent company may have been small.

Harris and Ravenscraft considered abnormal returns for American *acquired* firms over the period from 1970 to 1987. The sample includes both cross-border and domestic transactions. The analysis considers a set of variables that explains the abnormal return for acquired firms in cross-border acquisitions and provides some comparisons of domestic and cross-border transactions. Since shareholders or boards of directors of the acquired firm must agree to the terms of the acquisition, it is no surprise that the abnormal returns are large. The result is that the premiums for cross-border transactions are approximately 10 percent higher than the premiums for domestic acquisitions. Restricting attention to the acquired firms does not address the question of whether the acquisitions are wealth-creating for the buyer or for the economy. The abnormal return to the acquiring firms depends on the premium paid, and if the acquiring firm is not following a value-maximizing strategy, this premium may be unrelated to value-enhancing variables.

Harris and Ravenscraft also observe that cash is used in approximately 88 percent of the cases; this incidence is greater than that recorded in domestic acquisitions and so may reflect either problems of liquidity of the acquiring companies in the stock markets, or regulatory constraints on the holding of foreign shares by the acquiring firm's investors. However, the abnormal returns on cash transactions for domestic and cross-border transactions are similar. Looking only at the cross-border transactions, abnormal returns are higher if the acquirer is Asian and is operating in an unrelated field, and if the acquired firm is in an industry which is heavily engaged in research and development. Previous experience of the acquirer in the country appears to have no effect on the abnormal return to the acquired firm.

Considering the sample of 159 cross-border transactions, Harris and Ravenscroft regress the abnormal return for each firm on a number of firm- and industry-level variables. They find that the abnormal return is significantly larger if the American industry is heavily involved in R&D, and if the acquiring firm is located in Japan, Hong Kong, Kuwait, or Rhodesia.[19] The latter observation is consistent with a practice of foreign firms paying a premium to circumvent cultural problems of starting up a new enterprise in the foreign country. It is surprising, however, that a variable identifying purchasing companies from Europe, excluding the United Kingdom, did not have the same effect. If the parties to the cross-border transaction were in related industries (about two-thirds of the sample), the abnormal return was negative and significant. Thus, premiums paid for unrelated company cross-border transactions are higher. This result may reflect the benefits to an international network or a payment to obtain access to new technology. The presence of the acquirer in the United States prior to the transaction in question has no effect. This study is consistent with the internalization approach and the effect of cultural factors. However, a number of factors have been left out; an important one is the "tax difference between the U.S. and bidder's home country" (Harris and Ravenscroft, p. 26).

"Above normal" Valuation Studies

A number of studies have used either the "excess market value" or the "q" approach to investigate the effect of foreign involvement on share prices. Kim and Lyn (1986) describe the link between the "q" ratio and the excess valuation approach, and specifically identify the necessity for each of the approaches to include some constraint on entry by other firms; otherwise, any rents created will be competed away.

Errunza and Senbet (1981, 1984) also acknowledge this problem and used this approach in their 1981 paper. They defined excess valuation as the difference between the market and book values of the shares of a firm scaled by the dollar amount of sales. They argued that economic gains were available in multinational operations from imperfections resulting from taxation, real asset investments and, in their second paper, they introduced a security to the market which did not previously exist. This last argument reflects either capital market diversification or market completion by adding a new security. Setting aside the thorny measurement problems for the book values of the multinational companies Errunza and Senbet found, in the data relating to individual firms, that there was a positive relationship between excess valuation, and current involvement in foreign operations measured as the fraction of sales from foreign subsidiaries. The second paper adjusts for the relative sizes of companies by comparing the size of the multinational and the extent of foreign investment compared to averages. In both papers, the major problem is the impossibility of identifying the contribution of the various factors to the excess market value.

Kim and Lyn, using the excess value approach, hypothesize that the excess value for an individual firm is a function of investment in R&D and advertising, monopoly power and international involvement. The last factor is measured either as dollar sales or through a dummy variable identifying the number of foreign affiliates. Monopoly power is measured as the gross (profit) margin for the multinational. Using 158 U.S.-based multinationals, Kim and Lyn find that R&D and advertising expenditures and the gross margin are the most important variables in explaining the excess valuation. The extent of foreign involvement was not! While R&D and advertising are expected to generate the base from which internalization gains are to flow, the insignificance of the foreign involvement variable is puzzling.

The "q" approach is used in an innovative paper by Morck and Yeung (1989) which presents a direct test of a number of the theories of sources of value in multinational operations including diversification, internalization and taxation. The contribution of this paper is the specification of a test for the effect of internalization. Given the premise of this theory, that gains occur in conjunction with the extent of foreign operations, the authors introduce a variable which reflects the interaction of the extent of foreign involvement; the variables are expected to provide the base for the intangible gains: R&D and advertising.

A sample of 1,644 U.S. firms over the period from 1976 to 1980 was identified with the companies ranging from pure domestic firms (62 percent of the sample) to those with significant foreign operations. Most of the companies with foreign operations were in the subset of 1 to 4 subsidiaries (20 percent); companies with more than 20 subsidiaries comprised six percent of the sample. The extent of foreign involvement was measured either according to number of subsidiaries or number of nations hosting subsidiaries (or dummy variables derived from these measures). Unfortunately, these variables may be only weakly related to the true variable of interest: the investment in subsidiary operations.

Morck and Yeung also determined that in the total sample, R&D and extent of foreign operations measured by either variable are positive and significant. The extent of the foreign involvement variable, which introduces the interaction effect, is no longer significant. The variable reflecting the interaction of foreign operations and advertising and the R&D variable are significant, however. Adding a variable for growth in labour force to capture expected profitability, the authors find that the interaction variables with R&D and advertising, R&D and growth, are positive and significant. They also found that, when the individual year cross-section regressions were undertaken, the variable used to measure multinational operations was negative, and only the interaction terms were significant. This result, along with those for the whole sample, suggests that multinational operations are costly and *per se* reduce wealth unless accompanied by the internalization factors.

Evidence on Taxation

THE ONLY DIRECT EVIDENCE of the effect of taxation on cross-border capital flows is related to aggregate foreign direct investment (FDI) and its components but not specifically at cross-border acquisitions. The empirical evidence concerning FDI in the United States is reviewed in Slemrod (1990), who reports that most researchers observe that while investments financed by retained earnings within the foreign operation are sensitive to host-country taxes, investments financed by new transfers of funds are not sensitive to this factor.[20] However, the results are mixed and different measurement methods and time periods raise a problem as to comparability among the studies. A new paper by Slemrod (as reported in his 1990 publication) observes that American effective tax rates have a negative effect on total FDI and new transfers of funds, but not on retained earnings.

Indirect evidence for cross-border acquisitions, exclusively, is probably the best that the studies reviewed can provide. The results of the Doukas and

Travlos (1988) study were consistent not only with the internalization argument but also with the effect of taxation in cross-border transactions. To the extent that first-time entrants to a country — especially a developing country — receive significant tax advantages either through lower tax rates, favourable provisions for tax losses or depreciation, or outright subsidies or tax holidays, there will be a significant effect on the share price of the entering firm.

Morck and Yeung (1989) also provide an indirect test of the influence of taxation by regressing the q ratio on variables reflecting the number of subsidiaries in developed countries, less-developed countries and tax havens. Only the number of subsidiaries in developed countries has any effect on the q ratio. There appear to be no benefits from investing in tax havens or less-developed countries. Of course, a company can obtain tax benefits without investing in a tax haven, and the extent of the effect on the q ratio will be related to the investment in the country and not to the number of subsidiaries in those countries. In addition, the q ratio as a measure of the impact of all events that affect wealth and the continued operations of the firm may not pick up the specific tax-induced benefit.

Method of Payment

Harris and Ravenscraft observe that the incidence of cash offers in cross-border transactions (88 percent) is much larger than in purely domestic transactions (49 percent) in the United States. This observation is consistent with certain limitations on tax-free rollovers that apply when a foreign company is involved in an acquisition. Under American laws, however, it is possible for a share-for-share exchange to realize tax benefits for vendors of shares to foreign companies. Why, therefore, are cash-for-share transactions much more frequent?

Harris and Ravenscraft argue that since the acquiring foreign firm's shares are probably not traded on the U.S. market, transactions are more likely to be financed with cash. However, provided that the acquirer has shares traded on its home-country stock exchange, these securities could be used to finance the transaction. In view of the countries most active in the cross-border transactions (U.K., Canada, Germany, Switzerland), securities markets are unlikely to be so imperfect that the American target would not want shares of the acquiring company. Barring capital restrictions on dividends or withholding taxes, the decision to use cash rather than share-for-share transfers must be made on other bases.

One possible argument, related to asymmetric information (signals), is the following. With wealth maximization, the bidding company will use a share-for-share exchange when its management believes that its shares are overvalued relative to the true value of the acquiring firm. In this circumstance, the new shareholders are accepting securities of too high a value, and this constitutes a wealth transfer to current shareholders. Obviously, when management believes the securities to be undervalued, the firm will use cash. Given that we do observe share-for-share exchanges, and that they are used primarily in mergers, other variables must be involved to reinforce or negate the undervaluation signal of the cash-for-share exchange.

If the true value of the target company is uncertain, that company uses stock, since the stock value will depend on the outcome. By using a share-for-share exchange, the target company shareholders risk overvaluation. If the probability of overbidding is high because of asymmetric information, then shares will be used for risk bearing purposes. When no risk is involved because there is a low probability of overbidding, cash is used.

Why do we observe that a larger number of cross-border transactions involve cash, especially in the United States? First, the issue of securities in the home country may be costly, or the liquidity of the market may be insufficient to allow for the target company shareholders to liquidate their position without significant transactions costs. Second, the use of shares forces the shareholders of the target company to accept exchange rate risk in their investment portfolio. Finally, cross-border mergers may make it more difficult for the target company shareholders to monitor management, evaluate the risk of the acquirer, and determine whether the shares are over- or undervalued. The use of cash removes this risk.

CONCLUSIONS

THE CONCLUSIONS that will be stated in this paper are tentative. We raise a number of issues about the possible effect of taxes on cross-border transactions. However, given the lack of available data, none of the propositions stated could be tested.

Nonetheless, a review of the literature and of tax law applicable to cross-border transactions has provided a useful background for further research in this area. Some of the issues that would be useful to consider are the following:

1. To what degree do taxes on cross-border acquisitions affect the number of acquisitions?
2. Is *de novo* entry less preferable than the acquisition of a company for both non-tax and tax reasons?
3. To what extent is the subsidiary usually the preferred form of organization for a foreign acquisition? Is this preference caused by tax or non-tax factors?
4. Why are cash-for-share distributions so common for cross-border acquisitions in the United States, even though the tax system is biased towards share-for-share exchanges?
5. Is debt incurred in the high-statutory, high-inflation country to finance cross-border acquisitions?

Although these issues are addressed to some extent in this paper, it is clear, at least to us, that much work remains to develop data bases for testing various hypotheses.

ENDNOTES

1. A review of the literature on tax attributes in American and Canadian settings is found in Halpern and Mintz (1991).

2. Of course, the change in the stock price will depend on the size of the gain accruing from the acquisition, relative to the size of the firm. An acquisition which provides a large expected rate of return to the parent may not affect the stock price, since the gain is small relative to the value of the equity of the acquirer.

3. This original argument for international acquisitions was related to the belief that investment portfolios of multinational firms could not be replicated by domestic investors. Errunza and Senbet (1984) extended this argument, claiming that such acquisitions provide the capital market with an asset that was not previously available. The net result should be a reduction of risk in the shares of the multinational firm.

4. This argument suggests that multinational companies acquire economic rents and improved cash flows from the exploitation of imperfections in the product and factor markets. While there may be some truth in this contention, it does not serve to explain entry into developed countries by acquisitions of companies in those countries. This is the pattern observed in cross-border transactions in Canada and the United States.

5. This position, also called the internalization hypothesis, states that intangible assets, such as skills in production, marketing, finance and consumer goodwill, can be used without any capacity constraints internal to the firm. Since their value to the firm increases directly with their use, they include a public good component. Intangible assets can include research and development and advertising investments. Assets with patents are transferred and not sold since there is concern by the transferring company that the information will not be used to their benefit alone. By utilizing foreign operations and not sales of the assets or licensing, the scale benefits of using the intangible assets can be obtained without any reduction in the cash flows of home-country operations.

6. Examples noted in Sadeque (1990) include Singapore which provides tax write-offs for losses incurred abroad, and France, which makes certain French businesses established abroad eligible for lower taxes.

7. Other taxes, such as those on personal income, payroll and sales, would not influence capital investment decisions if the burden of these taxes falls on individuals, workers and consumers, irrespective of the location of investment. Our assumption is that with open economies, these taxes make no impact on the location of capital investment. Only taxes on capital, such as the corporate income tax, paid-up capital taxes, property taxes and sales taxes on capital inputs, influence the cost of capital. The effective tax rates presented below are for corporate income taxes only, as no data are available to enable us to include other taxes in computations. However,

we doubt that our conclusions about higher rates of taxation in Canada would be much affected if other taxes on capital were included.

8. The domestic effective tax rate calculations in Table 3 ignore taxation of cross-border flows of income from one country to the other. McKenzie and Mintz estimate effective tax rates for multinational companies for various cases (excess or deficient tax credit positions). These rates are reported later.

9. In general, the present value of taxes reduced by increased capital cost allowances on the bumped-up value of assets is less than the additional tax paid by the vendor. See the Appendix for a discussion of exceptions to this observation.

10. As discussed in the Appendix, Canadian rules are slightly less restrictive than American rules when a substantial change in ownership is involved. American rules restrict the use of pre-acquisition operating losses by using an "earnings" limitation that is equal to an interest rate multiplied by the value of equity purchased.

11. This statement assumes that the parent company is in a deficient tax credit position. If the parent is in an excess tax credit position, no tax is owing to the U.S. government, so only the Canadian tax is relevant.

12. Inventory costs of capital for multinational firms in a deficient tax credit position have not been included. As a result, Canadian effective tax rates in Table 4 look lower than they should be, relative to those in the United States, since the most important American tax advantage found by McKenzie and Mintz (1990), is the LIFO treatment afforded to inventories in the United States.

13. Special rules in Wyoming and Alberta allow for amalgamations between American and Canadian companies.

14. Actually, capital gains taxes might apply if the American debt is held by the Canadian parent. We assume the debt is held by an American taxpayer. We also ignore "double dip" interest deductions that arise when companies issue debt in two countries to finance the same investment in the other by routing interest income through a third "tax haven" country.

15. Under purchasing power parity, the appreciation in U.S. currency (x) is equal to the Canadian inflation rate minus the American inflation rate. Equal nominal interest rates, corrected for expected appreciation in U.S. currency, imply that real interest rates are the same.

16. The condition for this result is more complicated since it must take into account the position of the lender who pays taxes on nominal interest income. As is shown in the literature, higher inflation can cause the nominal interest rate to go up, depending on the lender's personal tax rates. To show that the real cost of debt falls with inflation, nominal interest rates must go up by less than one (unity) divided by the corporate tax rate. In general, this condition holds in a capital market equilibrium for an open economy (see Boadway, Bruce and Mintz (1984) and Gordon (1986).

17. Leechor and Mintz (1991) derive exact conditions for this result. The result pertains to the measure of taxable income for Canadian tax purposes

relative to that used for U.S. tax purposes, in defining the Canadian sub-sidiary's income.

18. Schipper and Thompson (1983) argue that the capital market incorporates information of a company beginning a growth period through the use of domestic mergers. Morck and Yeung (1989) suggest that a similar signal, which will be reflected in the share prices, may be present in a cross-border transaction.

19. This set of companies is the residual after European countries, Canada, Australia, and the United Kingdom were accounted for.

20. This view was declared by Hartman (1985), who argued that only the host-country tax rates influence investment financed by retentions. In a recent paper by Leechor and Mintz (1990), the Hartman argument is shown to be incorrect if tax bases used by host and home countries for the taxation of the subsidiary are dissimilar. Both host and home tax systems influence investment financed by retentions of the subsidiary.

APPENDIX

THIS APPENDIX PROVIDES some detail on tax law relevant to the text. It is presented in summary form, first for Canadian acquisitions in the United States, and then for American acquisitions in Canada.

CANADIAN ACQUISITION OF AMERICAN BUSINESSES

Treatment of Asset Sales and Purchases

U.S. Taxes Imposed on the Sale and Purchase of Assets   If a Canadian company is establishing a business in the United States, it may purchase assets, such as structures and equipment, sold by American companies. To evaluate the effect of taxes imposed on investments in the United States, it is appropriate to consider the taxes imposed on vendors of capital. The relevant American tax considerations follow:

   Recapture of Depreciation   When an American taxpayer sells a depreciable asset, the asset sale will be taxed in accordance with the following rules. A tax is levied at the statutory tax rate on the difference between the sale price and the undepreciated value of the asset.[1] If the difference is negative, the amount is treated as an ordinary loss. The vendor also loses the depreciation deductions that remain after disposing of the asset.

   The purchaser may depreciate the asset at the transacted value, or as it is more commonly called, the stepped-up basis of the asset. Under current American law, the present value of depreciation allowances given to the purchaser is less than the recapture tax and the tax value of lost depreciation deductions available to the vendor when the asset is disposed of at a price greater than its undepreciated value. Thus, an additional tax is levied on the disposed asset if the asset is sold at a gain.[2]

Capital Gains Taxation   When non-depreciable or financial assets are sold, the vendor pays capital gains taxes on the sale of the asset. As discussed above, capital gain income earned by a company is fully taxed at the corporate tax rate in the United States. If there is a loss on the sale of the asset, the capital loss can only be written off capital gains, carried back for three years or forward for five years.

Distributions of Asset Disposals to Shareholders   If income from the sale of the asset is distributed, the income may be taxed as dividend and fully included in the taxpayer's income. If the shareholder is another U.S. corporation, 80 percent of the dividend is exempt from taxation. However, if the company has exhausted its retentions and the distribution reduces the paid-up capital of the company, no personal tax may be imposed on the distribution. If the shareholder is a Canadian non-resident, a withholding tax rate may apply to the dividend remitted to Canada. Canadian branch profits are also subject to U.S. withholding taxes.

Asset Disposals Arising from Liquidation   If assets are purchased from a company that is not owned by the purchaser and the company is liquidated, capital gains and recapture taxes are generally paid on asset disposals by liquidating companies.[3] (An exception that is made for liquidations of controlled subsidiaries is discussed below.)

Canadian Taxes Paid on U.S Income   A company entering the American market pays taxes on its U.S. income, depending on the form of business created in the United States. Canadian companies pay taxes on foreign-source income of controlled businesses operating in the United States and receive credit for any underlying American corporate income taxes and U.S. withholding taxes on income patriated to Canada.[4] If foreign tax credits are more than the Canadian taxes payable on qualifying foreign-source income, the credits, if associated with business income, may be carried back three years or forward seven years. If foreign tax credits are associated with "non-business income" (i.e., disposal of assets), no carry forward or carry back of unused foreign tax credits is permitted.

In addition, a provision in Canadian tax law (Section 110.5) allows companies to create a taxable loss to be carried forward seven years by declaring "phantom" foreign-source business or non-business income in the current year. By reporting additional foreign-source income, the company can use up all foreign tax credits in the current year. This arrangement can be particularly important for non-business income that arises from the disposal of assets. For business income too, this discretionary feature of the Canadian tax law effectively allows Canadian companies to carry forward business income foreign tax credits for up to 14 years.

Canadian tax law distinguishes between branches and subsidiaries. For branches, the "accrual" method of taxation applies in which all profits, whether patriated or not, are taxable in Canada. Thus, it is possible that an extra tax, payable to Canada, is owing on branch investments in the United States. However, if a branch is incurring a loss in the United States, this loss can be used to reduce taxes payable to Canada on worldwide income, a provision which may be an important consideration during the start-up phase of the business.

Alternatively, a Canadian company can create a subsidiary in the United States. If it does so, only remitted income from the subsidiary is taxable. For American subsidiaries (and those in other treaty countries) an additional important source of foreign-source income may be exempt from Canadian tax. If the subsidiary is a foreign affiliate (owning more than 10 percent of any class of shares) dividends may be remitted back to Canada free from taxation. (No foreign tax credit is given for the American taxes). Moreover, when the dividends are distributed from the Canadian parent to the Canadian shareholder, the investor may claim a dividend tax credit to offset part of the American corporate taxes. Thus, dividend income earned by a subsidiary in the United States could be exempt from Canadian taxes. However, any losses incurred by the subsidiary cannot be used directly to reduce the world-wide income of the parent firm.

As a result, companies that decide to enter the United States choose between branch and subsidiary forms of organization. The tax implications associated with each form of organization also differ with respect to other aspects, such as the treatment of interest and the sale of assets. These issues, which are discussed below, must be taken into account by firms when contemplating *de novo* entry or acquisitions.

Acquisition or Merger

To acquire control of an existing business, the acquirer may exchange shares for the shares of the acquired firm or exchange cash for the shares so that the cash can be distributed to the acquired company's shareholders. It is also possible that the parent and acquired company, once control reaches more than 80 percent, may be reorganized, often on a tax-free basis as discussed below.

U.S. Tax Factors   Depending on whether a company acquires more than 50 percent or 80 percent of the shares of another, special rules apply. These rules affect taxes paid with respect to recapture of depreciation, capital gains, and the use of tax losses held by the acquired firm.

Deferral of Recapture and Capital Gains Taxes   Under U.S. law, a company that acquires at least 50 percent of the stock of the acquired company is entitled to treat assets of the acquired firm on a tax-free rollover basis as long as the transaction was deemed not to have been made for the purpose of avoiding taxes. In addition, tax-free reorganizations are possible if the acquired firm's shareholders retain a "continuity of interest" and the reorganization satisfies the "continuity of business enterprise" test. No recapture of depreciation or capital gains taxes are paid and the pre-acquisition cost basis of assets of the acquired firm is carried forward without a step-up to market value.

Depending on the structure of the acquisition, shareholders of the acquired firm may also be affected. If the purchaser pays cash to the acquired firm's shareholders, taxes apply to capital gains that are realized and included in income.[5] If, however, there is an exchange of the acquiring firm's shares for the acquired firm's shares, capital gains are deferred until shares are sold by the shareholders.

Companies that acquire more than 80 percent control of the acquired company may elect to treat the acquisition as if the assets have been purchased and the acquired company has been liquidated (Section 338). Under this election, the value of the acquired firm's assets is stepped up to their market value, and the purchaser is responsible for recapture of depreciation and capital gains taxes. As noted above, an acquiring company now gains little in the United States by using this election, since more taxes are paid on present value basis by stepping up the cost basis of an asset. An exception exists, however, where the market value of a company's assets is valued at less than their undepreciated cost.

Tax Losses   When one company acquires another in the United States, an important issue is the extent to which pre-acquisition tax losses of the acquired or acquiring company can be used as a deduction against income earned by the other. If the pre-acquisition tax losses are deductible a gain results, in present value terms, if the losses can be used up more quickly.

American tax law has become more restrictive on the use of net operating losses (NOL) and other carry forwards upon acquisition. An acquiring company may consolidate new profits or losses of an acquired company if it assumes more than 80 percent ownership of the acquired company and the "continuity of business enterprise" test is satisfied. The entire pre-acquisition NOL, however, may be disallowed as a deduction if selling shareholders retain a limited interest in the acquired company (less than 20 percent). Under recent tax reform, the NOL of an acquired company that has undergone substantial change in ownership is restricted to an "earnings limitation". If the shift in ownership by five percent of the shareholders is more than 50 percent in aggregate, the pre-acquisition NOL of the acquiring firm claimed each year may not be more than the value of common stock in the acquired firm (adjusted for passive assets) multiplied by the federal longer-term tax-exempt interest rate. Moreover, the acquiring firms must operate for at least two years, and the pre-acquisition losses may only be applied against the income of the acquired company. (The income generated by new assets must be transferred to the acquiring company.) In addition, interest deductions arising from debt incurred to purchase more than 50 percent of the stock of a company and resulting in an increase or creation of a net oper-ating loss prevents that loss from being carried back.[6]

Canadian Tax Impacts on U.S. Acquisitions   The taxation of acquisition of American companies depends on whether the Canadian acquirer operates in the United States as a branch or as a subsidiary. As discussed above, branch income of an acquired company is taxable in Canada as foreign-source income. Branch losses could be used to reduce taxes on world-wide income. Income from a subsidiary is taxable on a remitted basis, except for dividends of foreign affiliates that are exempt from taxation in Canada.

In certain situations, a Canadian parent may enjoy tax benefits that are not available to an American domestic company in acquiring assets in the United States. For example, as argued above, there is now little incentive in the United States to bump the value of assets under Section 338. However, a Canadian branch may find that it is better to step up the value of the asset. This situation may arise if the tax value of capital cost allowance (CCA) deductions taken by the parent amounts to more than the tax by the U.S. vendor because of a higher tax rate in Canada relative to the tax payable by the American investor.

Another advantage for Canadian firms arises when these firms dispose of assets in the United States. If a Canadian resident disposes of the stock in a subsidiary, the capital gains earned on sold shares may be free of U.S. tax under American domestic law or the Canada-U.S. treaty. The proceeds of the sale of shares of a foreign subsidiary may, in part, be treated as a tax-free divi-dend in Canada rather than as proceeds of the disposition. In some cases, the gain is treated as a dividend, even though the dividend is not actually paid, thereby allowing the parent to avoid paying U.S. withholding taxes.

A Canadian company may have certain disadvantages in other situa-tions. Pre-acquisition U.S. tax losses of an acquired firm are not applicable against the Canadian income of the parent. To use up these losses of the acquired firm, the Canadian parent may need to transfer income-earning assets to the American subsidiary or branch.

If the Canadian company disposes of assets of a branch, American, as well as Canadian, recapture and capital gains taxes may be triggered (with appropri-ate crediting of American taxes against Canadian taxes). It is possible for the Canadian company to reduce Canadian taxes on disposition of depreciable assets in the United States if the Canadian and American establishments are operated as one business. In this case, American and Canadian assets are held in one common pool: the U.S. disposition could reduce the capital cost allowance of the asset pool without leading to recapture of depreciation.

Interest Deductions

In an acquisition, the Canadian parent has a choice of issuing debt in Canada or in the United States. A Canadian parent that issues debt in Canada to finance the acquisition of shares of American companies may deduct interest from the parent's taxable income. The American subsidiary may also deduct interest on debt incurred in the United States, subject to new American "thin capitalization" rules. These rules imply that certain interest is disallowed on debt held by a foreigner who has more than 50 percent of the control or ownership of stock in an American company. For interest to be disallowed, the recipient must be taxed at a reduced or zero U.S. withholding tax rate, the corporation's debt/equity ratio must exceed three to two, and "net interest expense" must exceed 50 percent of adjusted taxable income plus the three previous years' unused taxable income. When interest is disallowed, it is treated as dividend, subject to the dividend withholding tax. Redemption of the debt is also treated as a dividend which will be exempt from withholding tax only if the dividends paid out in the past have exceeded accumulated retentions.

A Canadian parent, when purchasing assets through a branch in the United States, may deduct interest on borrowed funds from American taxable income if the debt is raised in the United States. However, there may be a limitation on the amount of interest cost that is deductible for U.S. tax purposes. The American authorities may disallow interest deductions by the branch, by allocating interest deductions to the parent in Canada according to the distribution of assets in the United States and other countries. In addition, the Canadian parent may not be permitted to deduct the interest incurred in the United States from Canadian taxable income.

The parent may deduct interest on debt incurred in Canada from Canadian taxable income if the debt is raised in Canada. As long as the company is borrowing funds to earn income, interest deductions in Canada for investments in the United States are deductible. Interest deductions in Canada are disallowed if the parent does not expect to earn profit on its investment in the United States. For example, if the parent lends to its subsidiary and the interest cost of the loan, net of U.S. withholding taxes, is less than the borrowed financing costs incurred by the parent, the interest deduction may be denied.

AMERICAN ACQUISITIONS OF CANADIAN BUSINESSES

IN THIS SECTION, we examine tax effects on the American acquisitions of Canadian businesses. Our discussion of this topic is briefer since many similar points have already been discussed in the previous section dealing with Canadian acquisitions in the United States.

Treatment of Asset Sales and Purchases

If an American company is contemplating entry into Canada, both Canadian domestic taxation and American taxation of foreign-source income will affect entry decisions.

Canadian Tax Factors   If the American company establishes a new business by purchasing assets from Canadian companies without acquiring another company, the following tax rules apply:

Recapture of Depreciation   There are a number of important differences between the United States and Canada with respect to recapture of depreciation. Canadian tax law generally allows companies to pool assets for the purpose of calculating depreciation for aggregate value of the asset class. If a company sells an asset, the value of the disposal is first written off the aggregate value of the class. In effect, the vendor loses the present value of capital cost allowances remaining on the asset. If, however, the value of the disposal is more than the remaining value of the undepreciated capital cost allowance base of the asset class, recapture of depreciation operates as follows.

- If the sale price is less than the original cost of the asset (adjusted for the investment tax credit), the difference between the sale price and the undepreciated cost of the asset is fully included in taxable income.
- If the sale price is more than the original cost of the asset, the difference between the original cost and the undepreciated capital cost is fully included in income, while the difference between the sale price and the original cost is treated as a capital gain, of which three-quarters is included in income.
- If the sale price is less than the undepreciated capital cost base, the difference is treated as a terminal loss and is deductible against income.

Thus, when assets are transferred from one business to another, the tax generated depends on the sale price, the original cost of the asset, the undepreciated value of the asset, and the size of the asset class when one asset is sold. It can also depend on differences in corporate tax rates faced by the two companies exchanging assets: for now, however, we shall assume that the tax rates are the same on both sides of the transaction.

Conclusions follow:

- If the value of the asset class is merely written down after the disposal, the tax savings of the purchaser who is able to depreciate the asset at higher price are just equal to the additional taxes paid by the vendor.
- If the disposal price is more than the undepreciated capital cost of the whole class, but less than the original cost, the vendor will pay more tax relative to the tax savings of the purchaser.
- The vendor pays either more or fewer taxes relative to the tax savings of the purchaser when the sale price is greater than the original price.

The latter will depend on how quickly assets are written off: the more quickly the asset is written off, the more likely that the present value of tax savings for the purchaser with depreciation write-offs will be more than the capital gains tax on the excess of the sale price over the original cost.

This conclusion is further complicated by differences in corporate tax rates across provinces, as well as in sizes of companies and industries, since manufacturing and processing profits are taxed at a lower rate than non-manufacturing profits. If the tax rate is higher for the purchaser than for the vendor, and if the asset is used for a different line of activity (e.g., a shift from manufacturing to non-manufacturing or a change in location), the tax savings for the purchaser may be more than the additional taxes paid by the vendor.

Capital Gains Taxation   With non-depreciable assets, a vendor pays capital gains taxes on the sale of the asset: three-quarters of the asset's capital gains are included in income. If there is a capital loss, the loss may be carried back three years or forward indefinitely against capital gains income only.

Disposition of Income from Asset Disposals to Shareholders   If the proceeds of an asset disposal are distributed to the shareholders of the vendor company as a dividend, the dividend may be treated on a taxable or tax-exempt basis. In general, the dividend received by individuals is taxable, but a dividend tax credit is allowed as an offset for corporate income taxes. However, shareholders from private corporations may elect to declare the dividend a "capital dividend" for qualifying dividends, which are exempt from personal taxation, including the loss of the dividend tax credit. A dividend paid to another corporation is also exempt from taxation.

When income is distributed to an American non-resident, the amount may be treated as a dividend subject to a Canadian withholding tax of 15 percent (10 percent if paid to an American parent). American branch profits earned in Canada are also subject to 10 percent tax rate. Moreover, the first $500 000 of accumulated branch profits are exempt from Canadian withholding tax. In addition, distributions of dividends from the paid-up capital of a subsidiary may be exempt from Canadian withholding tax.

U.S. Tax Factors   American treatment of foreign-source earnings of branches of U.S. multinationals is similar to Canada's, but the treatment of earnings of subsidiaries is quite different. The United States taxes foreign-source income on a worldwide basis: income earned abroad is aggregated and a tax credit for foreign taxes paid abroad is deductible against U.S. tax.[7] Taxes apply to branch profits earned abroad, as well as to remitted income, including dividends paid by foreign affiliates of American corporations. When dividends are remitted from an American subsidiary, the withholding taxes and deemed corporate income taxes paid in the foreign jurisdiction are deductible from U.S. tax liabilities on foreign-source income. As in Canadian law, when foreign tax credits are more than American tax liabilities, excess credits may be carried back for two years or forward for five years.

The treatment of foreign losses is considerably complicated under American rules. The essential principle is that losses earned abroad must be applied to foreign-source earnings first, *before* they can be applied against U.S. income. The loss earned must be attributed to different baskets according to the distribution of income earned across baskets. In addition, U.S. domestic losses may be applied against foreign-source income on a proportional basis, *after* application of foreign losses.

Acquisition or Merger

Instead of establishing a new business, an American firm may acquire a Canadian firm. Again, many of the tax issues that arise are similar to those found in Canadian acquisitions of American businesses. There are, however, some important distinctions between the two cross-border transactions.

Canadian Tax Factors   In general, a Canadian company may be acquired by another Canadian company on a tax-free basis, and the cost basis of assets may be carried forward at their pre-acquisition historic values. The companies choose the rollover — it is not mandatory. The implications of the rollover follow:

Recapture of Depreciation and Capital Gains Taxes   By purchasing a Canadian company, recapture of depreciation and capital gains taxes can be deferred if the acquiring company is also resident in Canada. The tax savings associated with deferral must be weighed against the loss to the purchaser if it bumps up the value of assets for tax depreciation purposes. As discussed above, the tax-free rollover is not necessarily advantageous to the vendor and the purchaser, so may not be used.

Tax-free rollovers are also possible when two Canadian companies amalgamate or when a Canadian company owning at least 90 percent of its shares is liquidated and its assets transferred to the parent. If the liquidated company is not Canadian, the liquidation will trigger Canadian taxes on real property, as no tax-free rollover is applicable in this case. This consideration is important if the American parent wishes to liquidate a branch but create a subsidiary at a later time. In addition, if a Canadian company is liquidated and sold to a non-resident parent, no tax-free rollover of assets is permitted.

It is possible for non-depreciable property to be sold and the asset bumped up from its cost to fair market value without triggering capital gains taxes. This is achieved by winding up the company immediately after acquisition by a Canadian company. (The bump-up is not generally available to non-resident companies, except in certain situations as described below.) The cost of the non-depreciable capital may be increased to the extent that the cost of all assets owned by the liquidated subsidiary, net of debt, is less than the purchase price of shares.

An acquiring company may use the pre-acquisition tax losses, subject to certain restrictions. Non-capital losses must be used within seven years and must be applied against eligible income of the post-acquisition companies as discussed below. Capital losses, which are normally carried forward indefinitely and applied against capital gains, cannot be deducted if there is a change of control.

To use pre-acquisition non-capital losses, a company must meet two "tests". First, it must continue in the same line of activity ; second, there must be a change of control whereby more than 50 percent of the voting stock of the company is purchased by the acquiring company. Losses may be applied only against (i) income earned on a line of activity that is continued in a substantial way; ("substantial" is defined as continuing to generate 90 percent or more of customary income) and (ii) capital gains in excess of capital losses and allowable business losses.

A transfer of control may make it more difficult for companies to carry forward unused deductions. Under Canadian tax law, a number of deductions, such as depreciation and exploration, are discretionary, allowing the company to carry forward the deduction for an indefinite period, rather than requiring the loss to be declared. The acquired company must take deductions prior to the transfer of control. As a result, losses may be created by mandatory deductions that might expire seven years after the transfer of control.

Distribution of Dividends to Shareholders In general, shareholders of acquired firms realize dividends or capital gains that are taxable according to the usual rules. Intercorporate dividends transferred between Canadian companies are exempt from taxation. Dividends paid to non-resident companies are subject to Canadian withholding taxes. Capital gains earned by non-residents are exempt from Canadian taxes (Article 13 of the Canada-U.S. treaty), although they are subject to U.S. capital gains taxes.

Under certain circumstances, it is possible for dividends distributed to be exempt from taxation. In particular, dividends paid to shareholders as a result of a windup of a Canadian company that is at least 90 percent owned by the Canadian parent may be exempt from taxation if the dividend reduces the paid-up capital of the firm. Unlike American law, Canadian law treats dividends in a favourable way: they may be viewed as reducing the paid-up capital of the firm prior to reduction of the firm's taxable surplus. Moreover, net assets transferred to a company may increase the paid-up capital of the firm, and a subsequent distribution of dividends may be accomplished without triggering taxes. This treatment has been an important component of "butterfly" reorganizations that allow assets to be transferred to new subsidiaries that are wound up, thereby effecting a tax-free reorganization of the firm.

A foreign company, after acquiring a subsidiary, may receive dividends from the acquired company free of Canadian withholding taxes up to the historical paid-up capital of the acquired company. To maximize the distribution of withholding tax-exempt dividends from Canadian subsidiaries, the foreign parent may establish a Canadian holding company that owns the shares of an acquired company with a paid-up capital equal to the fair market value of the subsidiary's assets.[8] A windup or payment of dividend from the Canadian operating company to the Canadian holding company may be made on a tax-free basis, and the payment of the dividend from the holding company to the foreign parent may be exempt from Canadian withholding tax up to the paid-up capital of the holding company, which is much greater than that of the subsidiary. In addition, the sale of non-depreciable property can be made on a stepped-up basis, exempt from capital gains taxation, by the Canadian operating subsidiary when the Canadian withholding company purchases the asset.

U.S Tax Factors   Acquisitions by American companies of Canadian companies have different U.S. tax implications, depending on whether the company operates as a Canadian subsidiary or is eventually absorbed as a branch. The taxation of branch profits and remitted income of subsidiaries have been discussed above and the statements made will not be repeated here.

If an American company disposes of assets in Canada, it's action could trigger U.S. taxes on the capital gains as "passive" income. Whether or not the capital gain is distributed to the parent, the income is taxable in the United States as Subpart F income. Recapture of depreciation also applies for the foreign branch or subsidiary although, for the latter, only to the extent that the dividends are remitted from the subsidiary to the parent. A credit is given for Canadian taxes against American taxes which include withholding taxes levied on dividends in excess of paid-up capital distributed by the subsidiary to the parent. If the American parent is in an excess credit position, the savings of Canadian withholding taxes on the distribution of dividends, as described above, becomes important to the avoidance of Canadian taxes.

Interest Deductions

If the American parent operates a branch in Canada, interest that the branch pays in Canada is generally deductible from the taxable income of the branch. "Thin-capitalization" rules that limit interest deductions, as discussed below, do not apply to U.S. branches.

Since and American branch is non-resident, it may be required to pay Canadian withholding taxes unless it obtains a certificate showing that the payment is connected to Canadian business and the withholding tax is therefore not applicable. If the withholding tax is paid by the branch, it may not be creditable against U.S. taxes, since the income earned by the American branch may be viewed as Canadian domestic income, not U.S. foreign-source income.

If the American company operates a subsidiary in Canada, "arm's-length" interest on debt incurred in Canada is deductible from Canadian taxable income. "Non-arm's-length" interest payable to an American parent is also deductible but might be limited by the "thin-capitalization" rules. Interest is restricted to the extent that outstanding debt to non-residents owing 25 percent or more of issued shares, must be more than three times the aggregate of retained earnings and the paid-up capital of the firm.

The American parent may deduct interest incurred in the United States to fund acquisitions, except for one important limitation. Under U.S. law, interest deductions incurred in the United States are allocated to a branch or a subsidiary in accordance with the distribution of assets. The American parent may have to allocate interest costs incurred in the United States to its branches or subsidiaries, thereby increasing American taxes on domestic income and reducing the amount of American foreign-source taxes to which Canadian taxes can be charged.

ENDNOTES

1. In principle, the gain includes two components. The first is the difference between the sale price and original cost of the asset (adjusted for the investment tax credit; the general credit is no longer available in the United States). This amount is treated as a capital gain. Because of recent American tax reform, this capital gain is now fully included in income. The second component is the difference between the original cost of the asset and the undepreciated value. This gain is treated as ordinary taxable income. Prior to 1988, the capital gain component, like other forms of capital gain income, was treated at a preferential rate. In addition, real estate property, depreciated according to straight-line methods, was preferentially treated in that no recapture of depreciation applied.

2. The present value of tax savings to the purchaser is equal to $S = uaQ/(a+R)$, with "u" denoting the corporate tax rate, "a" the capital cost allowance rate (assumed here to be a declining balance rate), "Q" the transacted price of capital, and "R" the nominal discount rate. The tax paid by the vendor is $T = u(Q\text{-}Z) + uZa/(a+R)$, with Z denoting the undepreciated value of the asset at the time of the transaction. The second term of T is the present value of lost depreciation deductions arising from the disposal of the asset. The difference between the tax paid by the vendor and tax savings of the purchaser — assuming the discount rate and the corporate tax rate are the same for both firms — is $T\text{-}S = u(Q\text{--}Z)(1\text{--}X)$, $X = a/(a+R)$. Since X is less than one for any positive nominal discount rate, and if Q is greater than Z (gain on the sale), then $T\text{--}S$ is positive. If there is a loss ($Q < Z$), tax savings arise from the disposal of assets. For a richer result derived in a stochastic framework, see McKenzie (1990).

3. Distribution of proceeds to shareholders of a liquidated company are taxed as dividend income unless the proceeds reduce the original investment made by shareholders in the firm. (This investment is referred to as "paid-up capital", a term explicitly used in Canadian law.) Payments reducing paid-up capital are exempt from taxation. Under U.S. law, the ordering of dividends requires the proceeds distributed to shareholders to dilute retentions before reducing paid-up capital.

4. If certain forms of foreign-source income are exempt from Canadian tax (e.g., dividends from foreign affiliates as discussed below) no credit is given for underlying U.S. taxes.

5. There is an important distinction here between U.S. residents and non-residents selling shares of an acquired company. If the non-resident is exempt from capital gain taxation in the United States (e.g., under the Canada-U.S. tax treaty), a cash distribution to a non-resident could also be exempt from taxation. In fact, under Section 93 of the *Income Tax Act*, Canada allows the parent to treat the capital gain as a dividend exempt from Canadian taxation. Moreover, the dividend need not be paid to the parent, which allows the parent to escape any U.S. withholding tax on the capital gain income.

6. The restriction applies if the Section 338 election is used, and if the aggregate interest deduction for the year is less than the average of interest deductions claimed three years before the acquisition.

7. American tax laws require taxes on foreign-source income to be calculated for certain baskets. As a result, certain forms of income, such as dividends from companies with less than 50 percent ownership and interest from high withholding tax countries, cannot be aggregated with other sources of income to calculate the overall U.S. tax. In addition, U.S. law requires the crediting of a current year's corporate taxes deemed to have been paid on dividends to be based on the cumulative dividend and profits earned abroad, beginning in 1987.

8. Another possibility is to establish a non-resident-owned (NRO) company.

Acknowledgement

THIS PAPER WAS PREPARED for the conference on "Corporate Globalization Through Mergers and Acquisitions" sponsored by the Centre for International Studies and Investment Canada. We are particularly indebted to Stephen Richardson and Leonard Waverman for their comments. We also appreciate the co-operation of Ken McKenzie, who provided data for the construction of Tables 3, 4 and 5.

BIBLIOGRAPHY

Arnold, B. *The Taxation of Controlled Foreign Corporations: An International Comparison*, Toronto, Canadian Tax Foundation, Canadian Tax Paper No. 78, 1986.

Bicksler, J. "Discussion" of Errunza and Senbet 1984, *Journal of Finance*, July 1984, pp. 744-46.

Boadway, Robin, Neil Bruce and Jack M. Mintz. "Taxation, Inflation and the Effective Marginal Tax Rate of Capital in Canada", *Canadian Journal of Economics*, Vol. 17, 1984, pp. 62-79.

Booth, Laurence D. "Taxes, Funds Positioning and the Cost of Capital for Multinationals", in *Advances in Financial Planning and Forecasting*, Vol. 4, Part B, Greenwich, CT, JAI Press Inc., 1990.

Brean, D. *International Issues in Taxation: The Canadian Perspective*, Toronto, Canadian Tax Foundation, Canadian Tax Paper No. 75, 1984.

Brewer, H. "Investor Benefits from Corporate International Diversification", *Journal of Financial and Quantitative Analysis*, March 1981, pp. 113-26.

Buckley, P.J. "The Limits of Explanation: Testing the Internalization Theory of the Multi-national Enterprise", *Journal of International Business Studies*, Summer 1988, pp. 181-93.

Collins, J.M. "A Market Performance Comparison of U.S. Firms Active in Domestic, Developed, and Developing Countries", *Journal of International Business Studies*, 1990, pp. 271-87.

Deal Watch, KPMG Peat Marwick Thorne, various issues.

Doukas, J. and N. Travlos. "The Effect of Corporate Multinationalism on Shareholders' Wealth: Evidence from International Acquisitions", *Journal of Finance*, December 1988, pp. 1161-75.

Errunza, V. and L. Senbet. "The Effects of International Operations on the Market Value of the Firm: Theory and Evidence", *Journal of Finance*, May 1981, pp. 401-17.

_____. "International Corporate Diversification, Market Valuation, and Size Adjusted Evidence", *Journal of Finance*, July 1984, pp. 727-43.

Fatemi, A. "Shareholder Benefits from Corporate International Diversification", *Journal of Finance*, December 1984, pp. 1325-44.

Glenday, Graham and Jack Mintz. "The Nature and Magnitude of Tax Losses of Canadian Corporation", in *Tax Loss Utilization*, Toronto, Clarkson Gordon Foundation, forthcoming, 1991.

Gordon, Roger H. "Taxation of Investment and Savings in a World Economy", *American Economic Review*, Vol. 76, 1986, pp. 1086-1102.

Grubert, Harry and John Mutti. "Financial Flows Versus Capital Spending: Alternative Measures of U.S.-Canadian Investment and Trade in the Analysis of Taxes", mimeograph, 1989.

Halpern, Paul and Jack M. Mintz. "Taxation and Industrial Structure", in *Taxation to 2000 and Beyond*, R. Bird and J. Mintz (eds), Toronto, Canadian Tax Foundation, forthcoming, 1991.

Harris, R. and D. Ravenscraft. "The Role of Acquisitions in Foreign Direct Investment: Evidence from the U.S. Stock Market", Darden School Working Paper, #89-27.

Hartman, David. "Tax Policy and Foreign Direct Investment", *Journal of Public Economics*, 26, 1985, pp. 107-121.

Hines, James R. Jr. "Taxation and U.S. Multinational Investment", *Tax Policy and the Economy*, Lawrence H. Summers (ed), Cambridge, MIT Press, 1988, pp. 33-61.

Hughes, J., D. Logue and R. Sweeney. "Corporate International Diversification and Market Assigned Measures of Risk and Diversification", *Journal of Financial and Quantitative Analysis*, November 1975, pp. 627-37.

Jacquillat, B. and B. Solnik. "Multinationals are Poor Tools for Diversification", *Journal of Portfolio Management*, Winter 1978, pp. 8-12.

John, K., L. Senbet and A. Sundaram. "Multinational Enterprise Liability and Cross-Border Investments" in *Pacific Base in Capital Markets Research*, Vol. 11, January 1991.

Kim, W. and E. Lyn. "Excess Market Value, the Multinational Corporation, and Tobin's q Ratio", *Journal of International Business Studies*, Spring 1986, pp. 119-25.

Kogut, B. and H. Singh. "The Effect of National Culture on the Choice of Entry Mode", *Journal of International Business Studies*, Fall 1988. pp. 411-32.

Leechor, Chad and Jack M. Mintz. "On the Taxation of Multinational Corporate Investment when the Deferral Method is Used by the Capital Exporting Country", Working Paper 9013, Toronto, University of Toronto, 1990.

Lessard, J. and A. Rubin. "Acquisition of U.S. Firms by Foreign Firms: Wealth Effects", Working Paper, Rochester Institute of Technology, October 1990.

Loveland, N. "Acquisition of a U.S. Business by Canadians - A Canadian Perspective", Canadian Tax Foundation, forthcoming, 1991.

Malach, D. "Cross-Border Acquisitions and Mergers - Canadian Tax Issues", Speech presented at CCH Canadian Limited, Business Mergers Seminar, 1990.

McKenzie, Kenneth J. "Essays on Taxation and Investment Under Uncertainty", Ph.D. Dissertation, Kingston, Queen's University, 1990.

McKenzie, Kenneth J. and Jack M. Mintz. "Tax Effects on the Cost of Capital: A Canada-United States Comparison", in *U.S.-Canada Tax Comparisons*, J. Shoven and J. Whalley (eds), Chicago, University of Chicago Press, 1990.

Mikhail A. and H. Shawky. "Investment Performance of U.S.-Based Multinational Corporations", *Journal of International Business Studies*, Spring/Summer 1979, pp. 53-66.

Mintz, J. "Corporate Tax Holidays and Investment", *The World Bank Economic Review*, Vol. 4, 1990, pp. 81-102.

Morck, R. and B. Yeung. "Why Investors Value Multinationality", Working Paper #5-89, University of Alberta, 1989.

Sadeque, Z. "Rational for Canadian Direct Investment Abroad", Annex #4, April 1990.

Schipper, K. and R. Thompson. "Evidence on the Capital Value of Merger Activity for Acquiring Firms", *Journal of Financial Economics*, Vol. 11, April 1983, pp. 85-119.

Scholes, Myron J. and Mark A. Wolfson. "The Effects of Changes in Tax Laws on Corporate Reorganization Activity", National Bureau of Economic Research Working Paper #3095, Boston, 1989.

Senchack, A. and W. Beedles. "Is Indirect International Diversification Desirable?", *Journal of Portfolio Management*, Winter, 1980, pp. 49-57.

Slemrod, J. "Effect of Taxation with International Capital Mobility" in *Uneasy Compromise: Problems of a Hybrid Income-Consumption Tax*, H.J. Aaron, H. Gelper and J. Pechmon (eds) Washington, DC, Brookings, 1988.

Steiss, C. "Acquisition and Disposition of a Canadian Business by Non-Residents", manuscript, 1990.

Tillinghast, D. "Acquisition of a U.S. Business by Canadians - A U.S. Perspective", Canadian Tax Foundation, forthcoming, 1991.

Ron Daniels
Faculty of Law
University of Toronto

7

Mergers and Acquisitions and the Public Interest: Don't Shoot the Messenger

INTRODUCTION

OVER THE LAST DECADE, the pace of merger and acquisitions activity in Canada and the United States has increased dramatically, sparking widespread and lively debate in policy and academic circles over its desirability. By and large, the issue of desirability of consolidation activity has been evaluated through the prism of shareholder welfare, particularly on whether or not mergers and acquisitions produce welfare gains that can be and are shared by both acquirer and target company shareholders. To the extent that the public interest is canvassed in this debate, it is usually examined in terms of the impact of consolidation activity on the structure and performance of product markets, the prospect of diminished tax revenue resulting from increased leveraging of corporate capital structures, and the danger of losses to national knowledge bases emanating from reduced research and development expenditure.

It is a perplexing feature of this debate that it has tended to overlook the effects of mergers and acquisition activity on the welfare of various individuals who have a non-trivial stake in the business and affairs of the modern corporation — namely, its employees, suppliers, customers, and creditors.[1] Recently, the significance of these interests has been given substantial, albeit belated, recognition in the form of various anti-takeover amendments to American state corporate statutes, which have allowed and, in some cases, required, corporate directors to consider the effects of mergers and acquisitions on non-shareholder constituencies.[2] Although these provisions have breathed new life into the simmering controversy over the capacity of corporate law to vindicate multiple and divergent interests[3], they have not yet resulted in a systematic examination of the case for protecting stakeholders from losses resulting from a merger or an acquisition event.[4] This paper attempts to redress this lacuna.

Although not numbered as such, this paper is divided roughly into six parts. Part one considers the various harms that stakeholders are alleged to suffer from mergers and acquisitions activity. By and large, these harms derive from the frustration of expectations that are alleged to be embedded in the various contractual or quasi-contractual relationships concluded between stakeholders and the corporation. Because the effect that an exogenous shock will have on a stakeholder depends on the underlying nature of one's relationship with the corporation, I canvass these effects by reference to different stakeholder groups.

Part two is a review of the relatively scant empirical literature available, dealing with the correlation between mergers and acquisitions and harm to stakeholders. This survey shows that, although such transactions are not inherently inimical to stakeholder interests, they often have the potential capacity to defeat stakeholder expectations.

Part three identifies, from first principles, the types of merger and acquisitions transactions that are most likely to hurt stakeholders. These transactions can be identified by considering the underlying motivation of a merger or acquisition transaction. In this section I also consider whether the introduction of a foreign acquirer changes the conclusions of the motivational analysis.

Part four contemplates the prevalence in Canada of transactions that can be characterized as potentially destructive to stakeholder interests. Part five discusses the rationale for intervention designed to protect stakeholders from the losses imposed by merger or acquisition activity in a neoclassical economic framework. I argue that defects in the bargaining environment provide a rationale for protecting certain classes of stakeholders in some contexts.

Finally, in part six, I evaluate possible instruments available to vindicate the interests of the various constituencies that deserve protection. In view of the fact that weaknesses in the present system of market contracting leave stakeholders vulnerable to a wide range of exogenous shocks — not just the harms occasioned by a merger or acquisition event — I argue that the central challenge for policymakers is to deploy instruments which are *not* confined to remedying the consequences of a narrow band of injurious events. Acknowledging, however, that fiscal pressures are likely to subvert the adoption of these more broadly based instruments, I then address the issue of instrument choice in a world in which the best available choice is often a second-best option.

HARM TO STAKEHOLDERS AS A CONSEQUENCE OF MERGER AND ACQUISITION ACTIVITY

IT IS ALMOST A CLICHE TODAY that somebody — in either or both the acquiring and target corporations — is likely to suffer an "injury", or will somehow be harmed as a consequence of a merger or acquisition event. Such harm can range from the loss of jobs by workers to financial losses by investors and creditors. In the main, the severity of losses sustained by stakeholders following the unilateral severance or modification of a contractual or quasi-contractual relationship with a corporation is a function of several factors, including the competitive vigour of local markets, the scope and magnitude of the severance, and the degree of asset-specific investment the parties have made in expectation of the continued existence of the relationship. Each of these issues is examined below in the context of an identifiable stakeholder group.[5]

EMPLOYEES

CONSIDER FIRST THE CASE OF A FEMALE WORKER who loses her job as a result of a merger or acquisition transaction. If it is assumed that the displaced employee was earning a wage equivalent to the value of her marginal productivity prior to severance, that labour markets are perfectly competitive in the region in which she is located, and that her layoff has not been accompanied by massive layoffs which depress local market wages, then it can be seen that the costs of dislocation are relatively trivial. By incurring search and retraining costs, the displaced employee should be able to secure comparable employment with a new local employer in a relatively short time. To the extent that losses are sustained in this setting, they are comprised of the difference between the present value of the anticipated earnings received from the old employer, and the present value of the adjusted earnings received from a new employer, taking into consideration any severance benefits and out-of-pocket adjustment costs. In a setting of rapid re-employment, it is unlikely that the worker will suffer any loss on her housing investment, nor should she suffer any loss of a psychic nature attributable to severed family or community ties, as there is no need for inter-jurisdictional migration.

Once, however, these assumptions respecting the operation of the local labour market are relaxed, the potential for severance to inflict serious losses on labour is enhanced. For instance, if local markets are beset by massive layoffs, then displaced workers searching for new employment will find that the market clearing price for their labour services has been reduced, causing losses on anticipated lifetime earnings. These losses reflect not merely the losses on future income tied to the performance of future services, but also include the losses on expected compensation for services performed for the previous employer. Deferred compensation arrangements are used as a means of bonding investments by employers in firm-specific human capital.[6] Such investments allow employers to increase the marginal productivity of their workforce by supporting the development of distinctive labour skills. Because of the danger that workers will leave an employer before the employer's investment in skills development is recouped, workers will bond their commitment to the firm by agreeing to accept wages below their marginal productivity today for wages in excess of their marginal productivity tomorrow. Since premature defection would jeopardize the ability of workers to gain deferred compensation, they will be loath to leave their employer prior to the full recovery of these deferred sums.

The predictable effect of a severe and unanticipated contraction in the level of expected lifetime earnings on workers and their families may be devastating. Initially, workers may be forced to default on long term credit obligations such as mortgage and automobile loans. This may spawn sales of secured assets at fire sale prices which, in turn, will quickly deplete the worker's long-term reserves. In cases where desirable employment opportunities can be obtained only by moving from the worker's current community, he or she must bear sundry mobility costs. These costs may be both monetary (moving costs, various transactions costs involved in selling an existing house and buying a new one) and non-monetary (psychic costs that result from severing community and family ties).

All of these costs are magnified in the event that labour market rigidities (i.e., an unwillingness on the part of workers to accept offers of employment at rates below those obtained from a previous employer) force workers to endure protracted spells of unemployment. Not surprisingly, as the period of unemployment lengthens, the differential between pre-layoff earnings and post-layoff receipts widens. This differential will be exacerbated by the termination of severance and unemployment benefits from the corporation and the state. Following in train, the more serious the loss in future expected earnings, the greater the likelihood of losses on housing and other investments[7]; and, most tragically, as these costs increase in severity, the prospect of family breakdown, mental collapse, criminal violence, and suicide becomes more likely.[8]

SUPPLIERS

SUPPLIERS' CONCERNS WITH MERGER OR ACQUISITION TRANSACTIONS arise from the prospect that corporations engaged in such transactions will sever or, at least, fail to renew contracts for supply of goods and services. The termination or non-renewal of such supply contracts may inflict losses on suppliers as a result of a high degree of asset-specific investment made by suppliers expressly in contemplation of the continuity of their relationships with a particular purchaser. Obviously, the more highly specialized the investment in assets peculiar to a particular purchaser, the more vulnerable the supplier is to loss on non-recoverable investments in the event of premature severance. In extreme circumstances, such losses may be so severe as to force the supplier into bankruptcy, thereby generating loss of employment for workers employed by the supplier. Such losses may also trigger a domino effect which may include the bankruptcy of other suppliers upon whom the initial supplier is dependent for intermediate goods. This, of course, leads to the layoff of workers employed by those other suppliers. Once individuals suffer bankruptcy or unemployment in this context, then many of the harmful effects enumerated earlier, with respect to workers laid off directly by companies, are sustained.

CUSTOMERS

THE PRIMARY THREAT TO CUSTOMER INTERESTS from a merger or acquisition is that an acquirer will attempt to rationalize production between existing and acquired plants by terminating certain product lines. If the product line to be terminated includes expensive goods that have a long life expectancy, then customers who have purchased those goods may well suffer losses on their investment from reduced market values. The reduction in value results from difficulties that purchasers may have in obtaining replacement parts or in accessing competent post-purchase service for those goods. Predictably, the severity of these problems turns on the distinctiveness of the good in question and on the capacity of competitive suppliers to offer adequate post-purchase support. If the goods are not manufactured through unique production processes, and are not protected through elaborate intellectual property safeguards, then it will be easier for a competitor to supply customized parts and services for the durable good. However, there is nothing inevitable about losses to customers from product line terminations, because even if there is not a robust market in after-purchase parts and services, the acquiring firm may decide that it can earn normal or, perhaps, even supra-normal returns on replacement parts and services. Moreover, even if the manufacturer were to face economic losses on the continuation of after-purchase support for customers, there may be strong incentives for the firm to maintain an inventory in these goods because the failure to do so may compromise the value of fixed investments in reputational capital. This concern will be greatest among acquirers who hope to lure customers to new product lines that are substitutes for the terminated good.

Communities

THE LOSSES FROM MERGERS AND ACQUISITIONS faced by communities are the direct result of the harm suffered by workers and suppliers who reside in the community. As bankruptcies and layoffs increase, the local tax base of the community will contract correspondingly. At the same time, because of increased utilization of publicly funded support programmes, the community's overall expenditures will increase. This financial pressure may result in cuts to so called "non-essential" services, which will lower the quality of community life. As the number of layoffs and bankruptcies increase, the younger, more mobile workers — the lifeblood of the community — will realize that the opportunities to prosper in the community are limited, and so will migrate to other communities, in the process, leaving behind family, friends, and co-workers. As this haemorrhaging continues, the community will be left with non-recoverable investments in infrastructure that will be under-utilized or abandoned altogether. This infrastructure takes the form of investment tied directly (e.g., roads, utility services, etc.) and indirectly (e.g., community recreational centres, schools, etc.) to the closed plant.

Creditors

FINALLY, FOR CREDITORS, the harm inflicted by a merger or acquisition may come in the form of depreciated debt instruments, which generate losses of real wealth.[9] Credit devaluation will result from any change in the circumstances that increases the risk that the debtor corporation will default on its obligations to the creditor (default risk). The same result will occur if the debtor corporation has insufficient assets available to secure the debt owed to creditors in the event of a default (liquidity risk). Assuming there are efficient and liquid capital markets, any increase in risk will precipitate an increase in the size of the discount necessary to entice other individuals to purchase the debt instrument. As the discount increases in value, so too will the losses to creditor wealth.

THE NEXUS BETWEEN MERGERS AND ACQUISITIONS AND DEFEATED EXPECTATIONS: THE EMPIRICAL CASE

ON THE BASIS OF THE FOREGOING DISCUSSION, it can be assumed that if stakeholders have clear and unequivocal contractual or quasi-contractual understandings respecting the existence or the continuing existence of a certain state of affairs, defeat of the expectations embedded in those understandings may harm the stakeholders. This much is clear. More complex, however, is the issue of whether, as an empirical matter, mergers and acquisitions activity systematically operates to inflict such losses on stakeholders. Despite the vigour with which this claim has been made, it is not self-evident why these transactions should be perceived as being intrinsically inimical to stakeholder interests. After all, from an economic perspective, mergers and acquisitions are construed simply as a means by which assets are moved to higher valued uses, thereby augmenting global wealth. Yet, despite fairly convincing evidence that ownership changes effected by a merger or acquisition transaction are in aggregate wealth increasing, there is a sufficient body of empirical evidence to suggest that in some circumstances some stakeholders may suffer wealth reductions as a result of these transactions — although such losses are not nearly large enough to offset the overall gains in wealth from the transaction. In other words, such transactions are only **potentially** *pareto superior*.

The task of correlating merger and acquisition activity with harm to stakeholder interests is confounded by several difficulties. The first reflects the problems that result when the effects of merger and acquisition transactions are evaluated without any sensitivity to differences in the underlying form or motive of transactions. Given that there is, as I argue *infra*, a correlation between different types of merger and acquisition transactions and the severity of consequences to stakeholders, the failure of empirical studies to differentiate stakeholder effects by underlying transaction will provide only partial validation for any *a priori* claim.

A second difficulty reflects the highly contingent nature of the empirical results on background legal and institutional arrangements, which vary from jurisdiction to jurisdiction and over time within a single jurisdiction.[10] The fact that empirical studies are contingent upon background institutional and market structures undermines, of course, the ability of Canadian policymakers to rely entirely on results derived from American studies. Although the legal/institutional regime in Canadian with respect to mergers and acquisitions is similar in many important respects to the American model,[11] the background capital market structure is fundamentally different.[12]

A third problem relates to the difficulties in controlling events prior to the consummation of a merger or acquisition which has greater causal bearing on stakeholder welfare than the actual ownership change. For instance, loss in product competitiveness attributable: to failed marketing or research and development initiatives; to exogenous changes in consumer tastes; or to the growing availability of import substitutes, may precede and, indeed, even increase the likelihood of a merger or acquisition. Arguably, such events will have considerable impact on the welfare of stakeholders irrespective of whether a change in ownership is ultimately effected. In this respect, studies that attribute all of the negative wealth effects, sustained by stakeholders following the event of a merger or acquisition, to the ownership change are likely to overstate the causal importance of the phenomena.

EMPLOYEES

STUDIES INVESTIGATING THE EFFECT ON LABOUR FROM MERGERS AND ACQUISITIONS activity show mixed support for the stakeholder harm thesis. Brown and Medoff[13] examined employment and wage data on over 200,000 Michigan firms over a 26-month period and found that, although mergers were associated with wage declines of four percent, employment in these same firms actually increased by two percent. Conversely, asset only acquisitions were associated with employment reductions of five percent but also with wage increases of five percent. The results led the researchers to conclude that "the common public perception that acquisitions provide the occasion to slash wages and employment finds little support".[14] Similar results were reported by Yago[15] and by Rossett.[16] Yago examined the correlation between layoffs and leveraged buyouts (LBOs) in the course of reviewing the effects of 43 large LBO transactions concluded between 1984 and 1986. He found that "on an average means basis, LBO firms reversed patterns of job loss prior to ownership change and increased employment after the buyouts".[17] In large part, these employment increases are related to systematic increases in productivity in the post-LBO period, as measured by input-output analysis.[18] Rossett analyzed the effects of mergers and acquisitions on union wage concessions following an ownership change, and observed that post-acquisition wage changes ranged from –.6 percent to +.3 percent. This led Rossett to conclude that the effects of mergers and acquisitions on wages activity pale in comparison to the benefits accruing to shareholders, as measured by econometric event studies. Under the most favourable assumptions to the stakeholder harm thesis, ownership changes result in worker wage losses equal to 12 percent of the combined premium. On assumptions least favourable to the harm thesis, however, ownership changes showed an increase equal to four percent of the combined premiums.

To the extent that job losses are sustained by workers following an ownership change, such losses are disproportionately concentrated at the level of non-production workers. Bhagat, Shleifer, and Vishny studied 62 hostile takeover contests between 1984 and 1986, and found that for those firms laying off employees (26 of 62 firms in the sample) most of the savings in labour costs were derived from white-collar layoffs (through head office consolidations).[19] Lichtenberg and Siegel also found that employment and wage losses were more — almost three times more — significant in administration and headquarters staff (middle management and white-collar workers) than in production units (blue-collar workers).[20]

Apart from the studies evaluating labour cost savings in terms of wage and employment reductions, other analysts have focussed on the effects of merger and acquisition activity on losses of other labour benefits. For instance, Pontiff, Shleifer and Weisbach examined reversion of excess pension fund assets both before and after a takeover, and found that such reversions occur more often after an acquisition event than before, and that there is a higher incidence of pension fund reversions following hostile as opposed to friendly takeovers.[21]

However, the researchers found that reversions occur relatively infrequently (i.e., in only 14 percent of all takeovers) and when they do occur, they account for only 10 percent to 13 percent of takeover premiums.

CREDITORS

THE DATA LINKING MERGERS AND ACQUISITIONS with injury to creditor interests are also somewhat equivocal. Early studies seem to indicate that mergers and acquisitions transactions do not have a deleterious impact on creditor wealth. Kim and McConnell studied monthly returns to non-convertible bondholders between 1960 and 1973 for 20 acquirer firms and 19 acquired firms and found that there were no significant gains or losses for either group upon an acquisition event.[22] The methodology used by Kim and McConnell to evaluate creditor losses has been criticized by Asquith and Kim on the basis of their reliance on monthly rather than daily returns data and merger consummation rather than announcement dates.[23] Nevertheless, after making the necessary corrections, Asquith and Kim reported results that paralleled those of Kim and McConnell. That is, over the period from 1960 to 1978, the researchers found no abnormal returns to bondholders in either acquirer or acquired firms. These results were echoed by Dennis and McConnell in 1986, in a study of 132 transactions executed from 1963 to 1980; here, too, the authors concluded that there were no losses to bondholders from merger activity.[24] In fact, the researchers found that some classes of senior security holders and bondholders gained from a merger.

Conversely, more recent studies, which parallel the rising incidence of more highly leveraged transactions, appear to support the claim that mergers and acquisitions can impose losses on creditors from defeated expectations.[25]

For instance, Amihud found that of the 15 large LBOs he examined, the outstanding debt of eight of 15 firms was downgraded, while the debt of the remaining seven was either placed on credit watch or considered for downgrading.[26] Lehn and Poulsen also found that creditors can suffer losses from LBOs.[27] From a sample of 92 LBOs from 1980 to 1984, they found that redistribution of wealth from bondholders to shareholders could not be an important motivation for these transactions as only 24 of the 92 firms involved in an LBO had outstanding debt. However, their examination of trading data close to the announcement date showed that bond prices in these firms *declined* by an average of 1.42 percent. Significantly, however, when the effect of these transactions is disaggregated by bond type (convertible and non-convertible) significant differences can be observed in the experience of different debt classes. That is, while the price of non-convertible bonds *decreased* by 2.46 percent on announcement of an LBO, the price of a convertible bond *increased* by .49 percent around announcement.[28] Differential effects on creditors, depending on conversion privileges, were also observed by Marais, Schipper and Smith, who evaluated the effect on creditors from *going private* transactions between 1974 and 1985, and found that while buyouts generated increased returns to convertible bondholders, they exerted no effect whatsoever on non-convertible bondholders.[29] The difference in the experience of convertible and non-convertible creditors stemming from a merger or acquisition event reflects the role that the provisions play in allowing creditors to participate in some of the upside gains from a merger or acquisition transaction, and which will overcome the losses these individuals would suffer were they confined solely to an interest in the debt of the corporation. These privileges can, therefore, be viewed as a device for attenuating endemic intra-investor conflicts.[30]

In summary, the empirical data derived from investigation of the wealth effects of merger and acquisitions transactions on employees and creditors (the only two stakeholder groups for which robust data are available) do not support a claim of systematic injury to stakeholder interests in every merger or acquisition transaction. Moreover, where these harms are manifest, they are not large enough to account for the gains to shareholders from a merger or acquisition transaction. In other words, the primary motivation for this activity does not appear to be redistributional in nature. Nevertheless, this survey does show that some classes of stakeholder can, in some circumstances, suffer harm from a merger or acquisition transaction. In the case of labour, employees have experienced wage and employment losses as well as loss of pension benefits as the result of some transactions. In the case of creditors, wealth losses from merger or acquisition transactions have become more common in the last decade and appear to be confined to creditors having foregone conversion privileges. On the basis of these data, it can be assumed that other stakeholders, i.e., suppliers, customers and communities, may also suffer some degree of harm as a consequence of a merger or acquisition event, although again, these harms do not appear to be large enough to motivate a transaction.

Once it is acknowledged that stakeholders can indeed suffer some harm as a result of a merger or acquisition transaction, rigid adherence to the claim that these transactions can never compromise stakeholder interests is rendered suspect. Even though such harms may be relatively small in relation to the total gain from these transactions as measured by the combined share premiums, the fact that these losses are imposed on a concentrated group of individuals, while other constituencies (shareholders) enjoy enormous windfall gains, bolsters the case for taking stakeholder harms seriously. Concern over this asymmetry is rooted in both pragmatism and ethics. In pragmatic terms, the fact that some constituencies will endure excessive hardship from a merger or acquisition transaction will cause them to invest resources in public lobbying against these transactions. Even if stakeholder objections do not prevail, (which would scupper the aggregate wealth gains that accrue from these transactions), efforts expended in lobbying consume scarce resources that could be used more profitably elsewhere. In ethical terms, it can be argued that the asymmetrical effects of a mergers or acquisitions transaction on members of the same community are ethically indefensible. That is, notions of distributive justice require sufficient compensation to injured workers such that they are at least in the situation they would have been prior to the initiation of the transaction. In contrast to the situation that would result if shareholders and stakeholders were each exposed to some level of harm (as in the case of the bankruptcy of the corporation) mergers and acquisitions produce glaring inequities in the same basic enterprise which are simply intolerable in view of the lengthy relationship of stakeholders to the corporation.

WHEN ARE MERGERS AND ACQUISITIONS LIKELY TO HARM STAKEHOLDERS?

THE CASE FROM FIRST PRINCIPLES

IT IS SELF EVIDENT that the harm to stakeholders from a merger or acquisition transaction derives from a change in corporate policy that is initiated by a change in firm ownership. In this respect, determining when corporate policy will work to impair stakeholder interests is a direct function of the underlying motivation of a merger or acquisition transaction. Scholars have identified four broad classes of motive for merger and acquisition activity: managerial displacement, synergies, monopoly power, and tax benefits. The impact of each class of motive on post-acquisition corporate behaviour and its implications for various stakeholder interests are assessed below.

MANAGERIAL DISPLACEMENT

INSPIRED BY MANNE'S GROUNDBREAKING STUDY on the market for corporate control, many law and economics scholars have argued that the motivation behind merger and acquisition activity is the prospect of displacing opportunistic corporate management in the target corporation with diligent individuals who will work harder to increase the overall wealth of the corporation.[31] The intervention of a third party is necessary to displace management as shareholders are themselves thought to be incapable of implementing this change owing to endemic coordination problems. This description applies most forcefully to corporations where ownership is relatively diffuse.

At first glance, mergers and acquisitions motivated by displacement of entrenched management appear to offer grounds for only mild concern over stakeholder welfare. The target of an acquisition event, after all, is usually the management of the acquired corporation, and it can be dislodged without affecting any of the other stakeholders in the corporation.[32] In fact, bringing in more responsible management may benefit a variety of corporate constituencies as it signals that the corporation will henceforth be run in a more efficient fashion. It may also effect improvements in the price and quality characteristics of goods and services produced by the corporation. Such gains can be expected to contribute to improvements in overall corporate performance.

Although this interpretation may be valid in relation to bondholder interests, its application to other stakeholders is less certain. For example, consider the case in which the displaced management is impervious to cost and quality considerations in employment and supplier appointment decisions. The propensity of unaccountable managers to focus more on the expansion of a corporation's assets — even at the expense of its profitability — is well documented in corporate finance literature.[33] If unchecked, such behaviour could result in the expansion of a company's workforce well beyond the levels mandated by pure efficiency or in the appointment of suppliers whose goods and services are not competitive in terms of price and quality. Accordingly, the appointment of new management following a merger or acquisition event can result in employee layoffs or in the termination of longstanding supplier relationships, generating losses for the community as a whole.

Another basis for concern with the impact of disciplinary motivated mergers and acquisitions on stakeholders has been raised by Shleifer and Summers.[34] They argue that *hostile takeovers* (not mergers and acquisitions, generally) are motivated by the gains shareholders can realize by severing implicit contracts (such as those involving deferred compensation) that exist between stakeholders — particularly employees — and the corporation. The removal of the management of the acquired company is necessary because, typically, these individuals are committed to safeguarding the interests of affected stakeholders and, therefore, refuse to divert wealth from these groups. Because the continued tenure of these individuals constitutes a threat to the implementation of a strategy based on opportunistic taking, acquirers will be anxious to oust target management soon after they take control of the corporation.

The difficulty with the Shleifer and Summers thesis derives from several different sources. First, the empirical data canvassed above does not support the claim that the principal motive for hostile transactions is the redistribution of wealth.[35] Stated simply, the gains from transactions, measured in terms of the combined premiums to shareholders, greatly exceed the losses suffered by various stakeholders.[36] Also, conceptual delineation of redistributive transactions from welfare-increasing transactions in the mergers and acquisitions area is difficult. Systematic renegotiation of contracts conducive to excessive shirking and perquisite consumption by the corporation's employees can, for instance, be justified on grounds of allocative efficiency, even though such renegotiation may inflict losses on employees. Finally, because the notion of implicit contracts is inherently amorphous, it is highly controversial. That is, it is difficult, perhaps even impossible, to know whether such a contract exists and what its content may be.

Synergies

ANOTHER MOTIVE FOR MERGERS AND ACQUISITIONS resides in the synergies that may be realized when the operations of the acquirer and the target companies are integrated. Essentially, synergy transactions are predicated on the gains realized when one company's firm-specific advantage can be fruitfully shared with another company, or when the integration of the operations of two companies creates new firm-specific advantages. In the main, there are three principal ways synergistic benefits can be realized from a merger or acquisition transaction: horizontal integration, vertical integration, and conglomerate diversification.

Horizontal integration involves the unification of corporations operating in similar lines of business. Ignoring the desire to enhance market power, horizontal integration is usually motivated by the prospect of achieving scale economies, i.e., reducing the cost of producing a given unit of output. Scale economies can be realized at the plant or multiplant level.[37] In the former case, production at a given plant is increased so that the fixed cost per unit of output is reduced. In the latter case, production of the same good is undertaken at a number of geographically dispersed plants, each of which is responsible for servicing the needs of a segmented market.

Although the realization of economies of scale at the plant or multiplant level can threaten stakeholder interests, it seems more likely that mergers motivated by single plant economies would be more inimical to stakeholder interests. Whereas the co-ordination of production across multiple plants may entail some degree of rationalization, probably concentrating on head office activities, the prospects for severed contractual and quasi-contractual relationships are likely to be greatest when production is shifted from multiple plants to a single plant. In this case, plants will be closed and employees will suffer job losses. Yet, depending on the nature of the collective agreement subsisting between the corporation and labour, and on the geographical proximity of the closed plant to the expanding plant, it may be possible for employees to retain their jobs. Further offsetting these deleterious effects, horizontal integration may nurture benefits in the form of shared product innovation activities resulting in increased demand for the goods and services produced by the combined corporation. These demands may, in turn, result in increased demand for factor inputs.

There is also the question of the future for the companies supplying goods and services to plants that are about to be closed. A supplier who is excessively dependent on the patronage of such a plant may find itself facing the prospect of bankruptcy. Of course, if the expanding (new) plant orders goods and services from the suppliers of the plant being closed, severe losses can probably be avoided. Compared to employees and suppliers, the impact of plant closures on creditors is less certain. On the one hand, closure may increase the operating efficiency of the corporation, resulting in gains to creditors. On the other, if the claims of creditors are secured by plants destined for closure, there is a danger that the underlying security interest of the creditor will be reduced.

Vertical integration is spurred by the savings that firms can achieve by substituting internal command over the allocation of goods and services for allocation based on market prices and processes.[38] Other things being equal, the internalization of functions previously executed through market interactions need not have an adverse effect on employees and suppliers. Indeed, both sets of stakeholders may benefit from the more stabilized set of interactions that are now nurtured and co-ordinated within a single firm. To the extent that there is scope for displacement, it will most likely be focussed on the senior management of acquired firms; they may be declared redundant because the acquiring firm already has its own managers in place. To a lesser extent, some workers who were previously responsible for marketing the goods and services produced by the acquired firm to multiple consumers may also be displaced. It is difficult to envision what injuries would result to creditors from vertical integration.

Internal diversification involves the least disruptive form of synergy transaction for stakeholders. By combining the cash flow of companies with zero or negatively correlated risks, the overall variance of the combined company's profit stream can be reduced.[39] Although a number of researchers argue that this activity is bereft of value to acquiring shareholders, (because they can achieve the gains of financial diversification at lower cost through effective portfolio construction) this activity is likely to confer gains on creditors as it decreases the overall risk of their investment.[40] The effect of diversification on employees and suppliers is less clear, although it can be argued that transactions motivated by diversification will exert a neutral effect on these constituencies because the acquirer may be anxious for target management to conduct its affairs exactly as it did prior to the transaction so that the anticipated pooling benefits can be obtained.

Monopoly Power

Another motive for merger and acquisition activity involves the realization of monopoly power. In this case, companies combine in an effort to achieve market power in the provision of certain goods, thereby obtaining monopoly rents. Conventionally, such rents are achieved through horizontal integration. The impact of these transactions on stakeholders is difficult to determine *a priori*. Although the welfare of creditors is likely to be enhanced by increased earnings, integration may, as in the case of synergies, result in a reduction in the amount of security available to safeguard a creditor's investment. Depending, therefore, on which effect is greater, a creditor may be better or worse off as a result of a monopoly-inspired merger or acquisition. The impact of these transactions on employees and suppliers is equally equivocal. In order for the benefits of market power to be realized, producers must cut back production of goods and services to a point below their competitive levels, so as to facilitate the appropriation of monopoly rents. These production cutbacks may reduce demand for labour and suppliers' services. Alternatively, the realization of monopoly rents may generate increased payments to the various factors of production.

Tax Benefits

Tax benefits from mergers and acquisitions activity are usually realized by increasing the amount of debt in a corporation's capital structure. Although leveraging benefits can be realized in the absence of a merger or acquisition transaction, target management's reticence to do so may reflect an unwillingness to be subject to the discipline of fixed interest payments.[41] In this respect, this motive overlaps with the managerial discipline motive. However, tax benefits can work to enhance the attractiveness of a merger or acquisition motivated by other factors because the cost of capital required to pay for the target company's shares is subsidized by the implicit tax shield obtained by substituting debt for equity in the firm's capital structure.

Standing alone, the tax motivation argument does not implicate a course of post-acquisition behaviour that is inimical to employee and supplier interests. Nonetheless, leverage-enhancing merger and acquisition transactions have been widely condemned for their effect on these constituencies. By increasing the debt load of corporations, leveraged transactions are believed to force corporations to engage in precipitous cost cutting in order to meet exacting interest payments.[42] Such cost cutting is thought to have a particularly harsh effect on employees and suppliers because it constitutes a variable cost in the merged corporation's production function. The difficulty with this claim, however, is that it is by no means clear that these relationships can be terminated without impairing the price and quality characteristics of a corporation's goods. Rather than enhancing a corporation's revenue stream, these cuts may cause the corporation to lose desperately needed sales, which will have the effect of further eroding its capacity to meet its interest obligation. Thus, it is not clear that leveraging transactions are hostile to employee interests.

While the impact of leveraging on employees and suppliers is somewhat ambiguous, its effect on creditors is much less so. By increasing the amount of debt in the corporation's capital structure that is equal or superior to existing claims, the wealth of creditors is reduced. This effect was powerfully demonstrated in the RJR Nabisco LBO, where the outstanding value of the corporation's debt diminished by 20 percent upon the announcement of the transaction.[43] This reduction reflects the dilution of the interest in the security of the corporation held by the corporation's creditors and the enlargement of the claim on the corporation's revenue stream.

This discussion has shown that the effect of mergers and acquisition transactions should not be approached generically when trying to assess the impact of these transactions on non-shareholder constituencies. Instead, it is important to evaluate these transactions on the basis of their likely effect on post-transactional behaviour, which can be predicted by identifying the underlying motivation of the transaction.

THE IMPACT OF FOREIGN ACQUIRERS ON THE MOTIVATIONAL ANALYSIS

TO ADDRESS THE IMPACT OF FOREIGN ACQUIRERS on the foregoing motivational analysis, it is useful to focus on the behaviour of the multinational corporation — the organizational form which is most frequently relied upon by foreign acquirers to hold assets outside the home country. The rationale for the rise of the multinational corporation is based on a myriad of natural and artificial market imperfections, including transactions costs, informational barriers, trade barriers, inadequate intellectual property safeguards that riddle international product, capital, and resource markets.[44] By internalizing production in the firm (i.e., substituting private for public markets) the distortionary impact of these imperfections can be overcome. The structure and performance of the multinational firm is a function of firm-specific factors (knowledge base in organizing production) and country-specific factors (proximity to local labour, resource, and customer markets, governmental stability, cultural system). A firm, for instance, with a lucrative production process that is unable to access inputs on price and quality-competitive terms in its home country, may decide to establish a branch in a foreign jurisdiction if that jurisdiction offers a more secure supply of these inputs on competitive terms.

How does the existence of the multinational firm change the motivation analysis used to assess stakeholder harms? For one thing, the fact of a multinational acquirer does not supply additional motives for a merger or acquisition transaction beyond those enumerated above in relation to domestic acquirers. To the extent that the multinational nature of the firm has any affect on the analysis, it is in terms of its more developed control and direction mechanisms, which enhance its ability to respond more effectively to rapidly changing patterns of country-specific comparative advantage reflecting, for example, increased local production costs or decreased political stability. Greater responsiveness implies a greater willingness to exit jurisdictions experiencing adverse effects. However, while this greater "adaptability" of corporations can enhance the survival value of the multinational corporation, this feature is troubling to stakeholders because it manifests both a capacity and a willingness to reduce or terminate production in a given jurisdiction in response to marginal changes in comparative advantage in favour of offshore plants and facilities, thereby inflicting harm on stakeholders in the home country.

Despite the plausibility of this claim, it has several defects. First, the linkage between factor mobility and foreign acquirers is by no means exclusive. There is, for instance, no reason why domestically controlled firms will not establish multinational holdings. Although these firms may be less likely to shift production activity out of the firm's home country, the inclination to indulge nationalistic preferences blindly by maintaining production at home — even though the home country's comparative advantage has eroded — is a luxury few multinationals can afford. As Ohmae has argued:

> "Most companies are still nationalistic down deep... But sooner than most people think, our belief in the "nationality" of most corporations will seem quaint. It is already out of date. Is IBM Japan an American or a Japanese company? Its workforce of 20,000 is Japanese, but its equity holders are American. Even so, over the past decade, IBM Japan has provided, on average, three times more tax revenue to the Japanese government than has Fujitsu. What is its nationality?"[45]

Even if a firm's production is concentrated entirely within a given country, there is still scope for intra-domestic migration, which may generate substantial dislocation costs. Although such costs may be less distressing, because they benefit other citizens in the country,[46] it is still not clear that this compensating benefit, especially when the beneficiaries are located in distant parts of the country, will be significant.[47]

Second, even if it is accepted that foreign acquirers are better able to adapt to shifting changes in national comparative advantage through migration, it is important not to overstate the ease with which this migration can be effected. Assuming that a firm has made an asset-specific investment in its plant and equipment, it will have difficulty recovering the full value of that investment if it decides to exit a given jurisdiction. The costs of its foregone asset-specific investment, when combined with the costs of transferring production to another jurisdiction, (transfer and set-up costs, and production losses), will temper the willingness of foreign acquirers to respond to relatively small marginal changes in national comparative advantage.

In this vein, once the role of costs is acknowledged in the calculus governing multinational firm behaviour, it can be seen that the concern — that the multinational acquirer will systematically wrest post-acquisition concessions from various stakeholder classes by threatening foreign migration — is overblown. In order for a foreign acquirer to deploy this strategy successfully, the acquirer must invoke credible threats of defection; that is, the acquirer must be able to signal stakeholders of its intent to move production off-shore if certain concessions are not made by stakeholders. Yet, such threats, especially when made soon after an acquisition, are unlikely to be credible. Why would a corporation acquire assets abroad, only to risk squandering them if stakeholders fail to make meaningful concessions? This is particularly unlikely when location-specific factors, i.e., proximity to local suppliers or markets, are considered. Stated simply, the decision to invest in a given jurisdiction implies "that the investing firm may see such facilities as a long-term and continuing asset".[48] Indeed, infrequent reliance on defection threats is exhibited in the empirical data which show that there is no correlation whatsoever between foreign ownership and diminished job security.[49]

To summarize, consideration of foreign, as opposed to domestic, acquirers offers scant grounds for modifying the conclusions respecting the threat to stakeholder interests in most types of merger or acquisition transactions. That is, the fact of foreign ownership neither ameliorates nor exacerbates the harms to stakeholders from most merger or acquisition transactions.

THE THREAT TO CANADIAN STAKEHOLDERS FROM MERGERS AND ACQUISITIONS ACTIVITY

THE PACE OF MERGERS AND ACQUISITIONS activity in Canada and the United States over the past decade has been dramatic. Whereas there were only 511 merger and acquisition transactions in Canada in 1979, by 1989 this number had increased by 113 percent to 1,091.[50] This rate of the increase in Canada appears to be roughly consistent with that observed in the United States.[51] Nevertheless, despite the surface similarity in the trends observed in the two countries, the mergers and acquisitions regimes are not identical. Specifically, close scrutiny of the types of merger and acquisition transactions occurring in the two countries indicates that Canadian transactions are usually consummated on a friendly, non-competitive basis, whereas American transactions much more frequently involve competitive or hostile bid situations. For instance, of the 1,148 Canadian mergers and acquisition transactions tracked by the Venture Economics database in 1989, only seven transactions could be characterized as involving competitive or hostile bidders; comparable data for the United States show this level to be much higher.[52]

Although it is tempting to construe the generally low level of hostile or competitive bid transactions in Canada as implying a lack of competitive vigour, it is difficult to identify specific entry barriers that limit the ability of acquirers to enter and operate in the Canadian market. By and large, the auction promoting features of the *Williams Act* in the United States, (minimum bid periods, disclosure levels, withdrawal privileges, etc.) have been faithfully reproduced in Canada and, therefore, do not confer special market power on Canadian acquirers. Further, the Canadian courts are no less defensive of target management in Canada than the American courts have shown themselves to be when reviewing American targets.

Yet, despite the similarity of the legal regimes in the two countries, scrutiny of the limited Canadian empirical data, which compares gains to acquiring and target shareholders as a result of an acquisition event, confirms that the American corporate control market is more competitive than the Canadian. For instance, Eckbo, in the most comprehensive Canadian study to date,[53] examined over 1,900 cases of corporate acquisitions occurring between 1964 and 1983, and found that on average bidding firms experienced cumulative average residuals of 4.31 percent and target firms experienced cumulative average residuals of 10.02 percent from a merger announcement during the 12 months prior to a merger announcement.[54] In contrast, American data show the gains to acquirers as smaller (ranging from 5 percent in the 1960s, 2.2 percent in the 1970s to zero or negative returns in the 1980s)[55] and gains to target shareholders as larger (ranging from 19 percent in the 1960s, 35 percent in the 1970s, to 30 percent in the first half of the 1980s)[56] than in Canada during the comparable period. In combination, these data suggest that acquirers earn supra-competitive returns in Canada compared to the United States.

The explanation for these differences probably resides in the higher level of share ownership concentration found in Canada in relation to the United States. Data from the Toronto Stock Exchange indicate that only 14 percent of the companies included in the 1990 300 Composite Index were widely held, whereas comparable data from the United States shows that 63.2 percent of the leading companies were widely held.[57] Higher levels of share ownership mean lower shareholder co-ordination costs, and imply that shareholders are more likely to supervise and discipline managerial opportunism without having to rely on the actions of third party bidders. As a consequence, the scope for hostile bids is reduced in Canada. High levels of concentrated share ownership may also explain the paucity of multiple-bid transactions in Canada. Because target shareholders can coordinate their responses to bids, much of the negotiation and bargaining that is conducted via the auction process in the United States can proceed prior to the formal announcement of a bid. By then, the majority shareholder may have agreed to sell its shares to a particular bidder, thereby discouraging a competitor bidder from launching another bid.

In Canada, the two most important motivations for mergers and acquisitions are synergies and monopoly power. Managerial discipline is less important in an economy characterized by high levels of share ownership, whereas tax motivated transactions have been hobbled by the lack of developed sources of speculative grade capital (especially compared to the junk bond market in the United States). In relation to the United States, the greater preponderance of synergistic transactions in Canada suggests a greater scope for stakeholder injury arising from a merger or acquisition.

Stakeholder Bargaining and Neoclassical Rationales for Intervention

HAVING IDENTIFIED THE POTENTIAL FOR MERGERS AND ACQUISITIONS activity in Canada to harm stakeholder interests in some narrowly defined circumstances, I now consider the issue of whether these harms can be anticipated by the parties and therefore dealt with on an *ex ante* basis through the bargaining mechanism. This framework is based on the assumption that since all of the corporation's stakeholders are linked to it through contractual or quasi-contractual relationships, any argument for *ex post* intervention must be supported by some evidence of market or transaction failure. That is, since parties voluntarily entered into their relationship with the corporation, why can we not reasonably assume that they knowingly assented to the risk of harm from a merger or acquisition transaction, and that this risk was compensated for through some *ex ante* concession conferred by the corporation? Creditors, for instance, might have obtained higher interest rate for debt, suppliers could also have received higher prices for their goods (especially if they were required to make non-recoverable investments in assets geared specifically to the needs of the corporation) and employees might have extracted a wage premium for their labour services.

Determining whether stakeholders had the opportunity to extract concessions from the corporation for assuming the risks that a merger or acquisition event would reap has special ethical significance. If the stakeholders received some *ex ante* compensation for this risk, then any interference with private ordering designed to confer *ex post* compensation on stakeholders for these events may constitute a form of double compensation. The provision of such compensation is perplexing not simply because of its undesirable equity effects, but also because of its distortionary impact on the incentive to undertake efficient care. As Kaplow has noted, by fully insuring individuals from the adverse impact of future events, governments will discourage beneficiaries from engaging in efficient risk reduction, which is simply the moral hazard problem that is endemic to private insurance markets.[58]

Review of the various grounds upon which relief from bargains is traditionally extended in a neoclassical framework reveals that there is a rich and determinate set of factors that can be used by government to support some classes of stakeholders who have suffered injury in the wake of a merger or acquisition transaction.

INFORMATION FAILURES AND NON-FORESEEABLE RISKS

PERHAPS THE MOST OBVIOUS IMPEDIMENT to parties entering into long term contractual relationships stems from difficulties in predicting future states of the world with any accuracy. Obviously, the longer the term of the contract, the more important it is for the parties to be able to form reasonable understandings as to future conditions which are likely to have an effect on their individual welfare. If parties overlook or dramatically misjudge some future contingency, then the allocation of risks embedded in a contract may be suboptimal. In the instant case, the question is whether various stakeholder groups have the opportunity to form reasonable judgments respecting the probability and the consequences of a future merger or acquisition and to impound these understandings into their contracts with the corporation.

To determine the capacity of parties to anticipate such future events, it is useful to invoke the distinction between uncertainty and risk developed by Frank Knight in 1921.[59] Whereas uncertain events are so remote as to be unpredictable, risky events are rooted in probability and can therefore be anticipated and allocated among contracting parties. Whether or not the wave of mergers and acquisitions that occurred in Canada and the United States over the last decade was so remote as to make it impossible for stakeholders to foresee (and therefore to impound the effects of this activity into their contractual bargaining) is unclear. On the one hand, it is highly improbable that parties could have accurately predicted the breadth and pace of the mergers activity that began in the early 1980s. Simply, it is unlikely that workers several decades ago would have predicted the myriad factors (diminished trade barriers, increased mobility of capital, development of a speculative grade investment bond market, telecommunications innovation, the ascendency of Japan and the newly industrialized countries) that combined to produce the wave of mergers and acquisitions. And, although mergers and acquisitions are cyclical phenomena, previous periods of consolidation were motivated principally by objectives of financial diversification, such as conglomeratization, which, as I argued earlier, poses the least threat to stakeholder interests. In these terms, it would have been difficult, if not impossible, for stakeholders to impound these events fully into their contracts.

A further difficulty for the bargaining paradigm is that, even if the risks could be anticipated, it is unlikely that they would have been adequately discounted. This phenomenon may be attributable to the so-called "availability heuristic" — "the probability assigned to a future outcome varies with the ease with which the individual can recall the event having occurred or can contemplate the circumstances of its occurrence in the future".[60] This means that a decision-maker who is not personally familiar with a law probability event, such as unemployment from a merger or acquisition, will discount the likelihood of that event occurring, even though there is no sound basis for doing so. As a consequence, the decision-maker's bargaining will be based on biased risk assessments, which will, predictably, have an effect on the nature of the bargains struck with the corporation.[61]

On the other hand, not all stakeholders entered into contractual relationships with the corporation several decades ago. Many will have concluded first-time contracts with the corporation immediately prior to or during the mergers and acquisitions wave and, consequently, had some capacity to anticipate the effect of these events on their future welfare and to incorporate this knowledge into their bargaining.

Further support for the claim that stakeholders were able to bargain for the risks of harm from mergers and acquisitions — even several decades ago — is furnished by the recent work of Triantis, who argues that, although individuals may have difficulty envisaging and bargaining for certain specific future risks, they may nonetheless be adept at predicting general categories of future risk that subsume these more particularized risks, even to the point of attaching accurate probabilities to them.[62] On this basis it can be argued that, although stakeholders may not have been able to foresee specific harm from a particular merger or acquisition, they could nonetheless have anticipated some rationalization and restructuring activity (of which mergers and acquisitions is simply a subset) and extracted appropriate *ex ante* protection and compensation from the firm. The difficulty, in this setting, is that the probability of even the general class of restructuring and rationalization risks has increased so significantly over the last decade as to render effective bargaining based on earlier probability estimates almost impossible.

Evidence for recent claims that stakeholders have been able to anticipate the harmful effects of mergers and acquisitions activity at some level, is growing. In the context of creditors, for instance, there is now considerable data to support the claim that broad conversion privileges are increasingly being relied upon to cover the risks of redistribution during a merger or acquisition. A failure, at least during the last decade, to negotiate specific contractual provisions against the risk of harm from a merger or acquisition, in the form of options to put the outstanding debt to the issuer for its face value on certain events (so called "poison puts") or in the form of conversion privileges, is indicative of a deliberate decision to run the risk of loss, which presumably must have been compensated for by other terms in the debt contract. This point was alluded to in the creditor litigation surrounding the RJR Nabisco transaction, where evidence was proffered demonstrating that Metropolitan Life Insurance Co., one of the company's largest investors, was aware both of the risks of LBO transactions and of the various covenants that could control these risks at the time the debt was purchased.[63]

In terms of employee bargaining, if it is assumed that harm from mergers and acquisitions activity could be anticipated at the time of contract formation, it might be expected that corporations vulnerable to this activity would offer higher wages to workers willing to assume the risks of making non-recoverable investments in firm-specific human capital or, alternatively, would extend credible guarantees that effectively insulate workers from the risks of this activity. These guarantees could take the form of commitments to maintain stipulated labour force levels, or to provide workers with generous retraining and severance benefits in the event that they are displaced following a merger or acquisition event.

Unfortunately, investigation of compensating wage differentials, which has been used to ascertain labour's capacity to identify other workplace risks, has not been undertaken in the context of mergers and acquisitions. There is, however, some anecdotal data from the United States which shows that collective agreements between labour and management are increasingly including terms that provide benefits to employees in the event of a merger or acquisition.[64] Although unable to identify provisions in Canadian collective agreements that pertain specifically to mergers and acquisitions, I did uncover evidence that collective agreements are increasingly including provisions that explicitly provide employees with severance benefits and notice upon a permanent layoff. For example, whereas in 1980 34.9 percent and 47.3 percent of collective agreements negotiated in Canada *did not* include provision for either severance or notice, by 1989, these percentages had dropped to 27.3 percent and 40.3 percent, respectively.[65] Of course, these data, although consistent with the claim that the risks of permanent layoffs have only recently been identified, cannot be construed as confirmation of that result.

In summary, the empirical evidence respecting the capacity of stakeholders to foresee the risks of harm resulting from mergers and acquisitions activity is simply too amorphous and conjectural to support robust conclusions. Clearly, as the time between contract formation and the commencement of mergers and acquisitions activity narrows, the capacity to foresee both the occurrence of the merger wave and its effects, increases correspondingly. For these stakeholders, there is a strong presumption in favour of the position that mergers and acquisitions activity was foreseeable. Other stakeholders, however, may have had less opportunity to anticipate harm from mergers and acquisitions in particular, and restructuring and rationalization in general. In any event, even in an ideal world of perfect information, other factors, which are considered below, may militate against the capacity of stakeholders to protect themselves against harm.

PREFERENCE PROBLEMS

EVEN ASSUMING THAT STAKEHOLDERS can ascertain the probability of harm from a merger or acquisition with some accuracy, it is not clear how this will influence actual bargaining. In large part this is attributable to second order preference formation problems.[66] These arise when an individual wants to obtain certain goods, but lacks the self discipline to make the sacrifices necessary to obtain these goods. In other words, individuals have strongly felt preferences about preferences. Second order preferences dictate that government limit the existing menu of choices available to workers so they will opt to consume more intensely desired goods. For example, a worker who wishes to achieve security of tenure may be unable to resist the temptation of trading off this security for increased current wages, and may, therefore, benefit from government intervention designed to coerce this consumption of increased security of tenure. Significantly, in contrast to unwarranted risk discounting, second order preference problems imply that individuals fail to bargain over risks of expected harm, not because of their inability to predict future expected risks accurately, but rather because of their unwillingness to act on this information.

Whether this constitutes a sufficient rationale for intervention is certainly controversial. The controversy derives from the potentially obtrusive role for governmental paternalism that is supported by this claim. That is, once governments are liberated from having to respond to and be disciplined by expressed preferences, the danger of unconstrained and oppressive state action is increased. Given that there are other more patent defects with the bargaining process in relation to mergers and acquisitions that do not involve the same concerns over unconstrained governmental action nor do violence to conventional notions of individual autonomy, this rationale should not be used as a basis for intervention.

COLLECTIVE ACTION PROBLEMS

EVEN IF STAKEHOLDERS ARE CAPABLE OF IDENTIFYING THE RISKS entailed by future mergers and acquisitions activity and, further, of impounding this information into their bargaining with the corporation, the existence of various agency costs may work to limit their capacity to harness this information. Specifically, if information is costly to obtain and no single stakeholder has the financial incentive to collect and analyze the information, then without governmental intervention, obtaining this information will require some other form of coordinated activity. However, owing to the existence of endemic collective action problems (free riding and rational apathy) this activity is not easy to coordinate.[67] Not only do collective action problems impair information-related activities, but they also undermine bargaining between stakeholders and the corporation.

The degree to which collective action problems undermine the capacity of stakeholders to negotiate bargains between themselves and the corporation varies considerably among constituencies. In the case of creditors, bond underwriters typically play a role in negotiating, and trustees in supervising restrictive covenants included in the bond contract. As the exclusive agents of creditors, they are well positioned to overcome collective action problems and would, therefore, also seem to be able to provide much of the information creditors need.[68]

The ability of employees to overcome collective action problems is, moreover, a function of whether or not they work in a union shop. In the former case, union representation should increase the likelihood that optimal investments in information are made. Nevertheless, whether the ability of unionized workforces to overcome collective action problems results in more efficient bargaining with optimally produced information is unclear.[69] Obviously, the prospects for non-unionized workers to overcome innate collective action problems is even less certain. The same holds true for customers and suppliers; although, depending on the size of their economic interest in the corporation, they may have a sufficiently strong incentive to undertake this activity themselves.

Finally, to the extent that a community's interest is not perfectly aligned with those of the employees and suppliers who are resident in it, local governments, by invoking powers over taxation, should be able to overcome problems of collective action relating to information generation and analysis. As a consequence local governments, compared to other stakeholders, should be better equipped to anticipate various contingencies that may trigger massive layoffs. Whether the community can extract credible commitments from the corporation that will protect investment in community infrastructure depends on the bargaining strength of the community government. In a setting characterized by intense competition among decentralized governments, a local government may be unable to extract these benefits because of its fear of losing the corporation to another jurisdiction.[70]

This discussion suggests, therefore, that, except for non-unionized workers, and perhaps a few customers and suppliers, collective action problems do not appear to be an important source of market failure.

RISK DIVERSIFICATION CONSTRAINTS

EVEN IF STAKEHOLDERS CAN FORESEE AND EXTRACT CONCESSIONS from the corporation for assuming the risk of a merger or acquisition, they may, because of insurance market failures, find themselves burdened with excessive risk. This concern is least forceful in relation to creditors. By simply constructing a well diversified portfolio of securities, creditors can reduce considerably the amount of firm-specific risk in their investment portfolio. In contrast, employees are not at all well equipped to diversify away the risks of merger or acquisition activity. Since firm-specific investments in human capital are largely non-diversifiable, self-help strategies are unavailable. This fact encourages employees to transfer the risks of mergers and acquisitions back onto employers. However, unless employers can re-insure those risks, employees should be dubious of an employer's ability to honour its commitments in the event of a merger or acquisition that affects stakeholders, and which may bankrupt the corporation.

A further difficulty with reinsuring risks assumed by employees or employers is that the risk of harm from mergers or acquisitions is rarely negotiated explicitly. Instead, these risks are dealt with as part of a general body of shocks that can create job losses. Since many of these shocks can be affected by employer conduct (layoffs in response to diminished product demand, for instance) re-insurers may be reluctant to accept an assignment of the insurer's initial obligation without substantial modification of the insurance contract. Such modification is necessary to avoid problems of moral hazard and adverse selection.

What impact does this analysis have on customers and suppliers? In the case of customers, one obvious strategy is for customers to patronize only those suppliers who have made credible commitments, in the form of non-recoverable investments in reputational capital, to operate over the long run. This foregone investment constitutes a form of insurance that will bond the supplier, irrespective of who owns it. Another way to reduce the risk of loss from premature termination is to purchase first party insurance directly. For suppliers, credible commitments aimed at bonding the survival of the relationship can be made in the form of reciprocal investment in assets that are specific to the relationship. Defection by either party to the relationship risks the loss of this investment for both parties. However, to the extent that an acquirer is willing to forego this investment, suppliers may be faced with non-insurable losses. Such losses may be uninsurable because of their moral hazard deriving from the potential of the supplier's conduct to contribute to the termination of the relationship — and, although some suppliers may be able to diversify these non-insurable risks through customer diversification, for suppliers in one-firm towns, diversification may be difficult to achieve.

EXTERNALITIES

WHEN NEGOTIATING PROTECTIONS against the risk of harm from a merger or acquisition, parties may fail to account for spillover effects on third parties. Although there is little scope for externalities in the contracts negotiated between a corporation and creditors, employees and suppliers may fail to account for the losses inflicted on the community when they are laid off or when their tenure with the corporation is terminated. A particular difficulty relates to congestion externalities. These arise when there are massive layoffs or contractual terminations, and the existing infra-structure of the community cannot cope with the demands placed on it.[71] As the number of workers requiring social assistance and searching for jobs increases, the welfare of other unemployed workers or underemployed suppliers is commensurately reduced. These externalities are likely to be modest in large communities with a number of corporations. In smaller communities dominated by single employers, the effects are likely to be much more serious.

The discussion so far suggests that intervention designed to protect stakeholders from the harms of a merger or acquisition transaction can be justified on the basis of a number of bargaining defects. For virtually all stakeholders, the ability to foresee or anticipate problems provides strong justification for intervention, although this argument collapses when applied to those bargains most recently consummated. On this basis, at least for stakeholders who entered into first-time contracts with the corporation in the last decade, the force of the claim alleging inadequate information is undermined. The arguments related to collective-action concerns have the greatest force in the context of non-unionized labour, although it is important to recognize that unionized workers may not be adequately protected because of agency conflicts between workers and their representatives. Risk diversification constraints and externalities provide the strongest justification for worrying about workers (unionized or not) and suppliers.

INSTRUMENT CHOICE

BEFORE CONSIDERING POLICY OPTIONS in this area, several key findings made earlier in this paper warrant review:

- mergers and acquisitions are wealth increasing events;
- mergers and acquisitions activity is not motivated principally by redistributive objectives;
- while mergers and acquisitions can, in some circumstances, give rise to stakeholder harm, this harm is by no means a principal or central feature of these transactions;
- when mergers and acquisitions do cause harm, one cannot be confident that this harm would not have occurred but for the transaction;
- defects in the bargaining environment account for harm to stakeholders, and review of these factors reveals the strongest support for employee and, in some cases, supplier interests.

In light of the foregoing, the challenge for policymakers is to prove that there is something distinctive about the source and magnitude of the injury sustained as a result of mergers and acquisitions activity and that such injury deserves special relief for stakeholders. That is, in the absence of proof demonstrating unique injury, why would we not simply subject corporate stakeholders to the same protections ordinary individuals have from other exogenous economic shocks? What, for instance, makes the injury resulting from a merger or acquisition substantively different from the losses a stakeholder may suffer as a result of rising interest rates, adverse currency movements, increasing penetration of foreign imports, or even uninspired or inefficient management? Perhaps, the strongest argument in favour of intervention has to do with the ethical undesirability of allowing some groups in the corporation to profit from a merger or acquisition while others suffer hardship — especially when full compensation to injured stakeholders will still leave the winners with substantial, although smaller, residual profits. In contrast, the other shocks enumerated imply losses, although not of equal magnitude, to all stakeholders in the corporation.

Assuming that the argument in favour of special protection for stakeholders in the context of a merger or acquisition transaction is not uncontroversial, the first/best policy prescription is to call for the creation of generic adjustment programmes aimed at reducing the private costs of adjustment faced by dislocated employees and suppliers. As Trebilcock, Chandler and Howse[72] argued in relation to employees in the context of trade liberalization, these programmes would not differentiate among injured stakeholders on the basis of the source of injury; rather, the fact of injury would be enough to justify public support. Such support would be forward-looking, and aimed at salvaging a displaced worker's human capital by reintegrating him/her into the labour pool as soon as possible.

In view of daunting fiscal pressures, governments may, at present, be reluctant to implement such ambitious and sweeping programmes. At the time the Free Trade Agreement with the United States was negotiated, the Canadian government undertook a commitment to such programmes but, unfortunately, two years after the conclusion of that agreement, the promise remains unfulfilled. In this setting, other "second-best" options, must now be considered. The option of deliberately restricting or prohibiting mergers and acquisitions activity is not seriously examined, however. Stated simply, the ability to transfer existing assets efficiently from one owner to another so as to maximize national wealth is too important a goal to abandon, especially in the ferociously competitive global markets of the '90s.

MANDATORY SUCCESSORSHIP RIGHTS

ONE WAY TO ENSURE THAT STAKEHOLDERS are not harmed by a change in control is to insist that legal obligations assumed prior to the change in control are binding on the new owners of the firm after the change in control is completed. For some types of ownership changes, amalgamation, for example, corporate law already provides protection to creditors in the form of statutory provisions requiring directors of a corporation to furnish creditors with advance notice of such transactions and permit them to file their objections in the event that their interests are believed to be prejudiced.[73]

Protection under corporate law may not be sufficiently broad, however, to protect workers' interests under a collective agreement. To remedy this defect, labour legislation offers protection to *unionized* workers for opportunistic changes to collective agreements resulting from an ownership change. For example, s. 63 of the Ontario *Labour Relations Act* ("OLRA")[74] binds a successor employer to the terms of any collective agreement executed by its predecessors. The provision states that "where an employer ... sells his business, the person to whom the business has been sold is ... bound by the collective agreement as if he had been a party thereto".

In *Marvel Jewellery*,[75] the Ontario Labour Relations Board stated that, in order to provide permeance, the "obligations flowing from those rights are not confined to a particular employer, but become attached to a business. So long as the business continues to function, the obligations run with that business, regardless of any change in ownership." The safeguard set out in section 63 has been construed purposefully and liberally, and has been applied to myriad transactions, including mergers and acquisitions.[76]

Successorship obligations constitute one of the most effective ways to address the harms occasioned by merger and acquisitions activity. By stipulating that there is a statutory obligation upon acquirers to respect the entitlements of stakeholders obtained from prior owners, the potential for opportunistic severance of contractual relationships is reduced. The difficulty with these instruments is their lack of breadth. That is, protections are strongest in the context of unionized labour, but weak in relation to non-unionized employees and other deserving stakeholders such as suppliers and customers.

MANDATORY BARGAINING OVER CLOSURES OR LAYOFFS

MANDATORY BARGAINING PROVISIONS require union and employer representatives to bargain in good faith over certain specific issues. In principle, these provisions can apply when the entire collective agreement is negotiated or at some other time during the life of the collective agreement. In Canada, the protection of employees following a plant closure or layoff tends to be subject to good faith bargaining at the time an agreement is negotiated.[77] It is, however, less clear whether the duty arises during the life of the collective agreement if/when a closure or massive layoff is announced.[78] In the United States, the decision of the Supreme Court in *First National Maintenance*[79] has left limited scope for the duty to arise during the course of a collective agreement.[80]

The case for mandatory bargaining over these issues at the time of initial negotiation of the collective agreement is incontrovertible. Consistent with the tenets of the neoclassical paradigm, parties should be encouraged to anticipate deleterious future events and plan for them in their contractual relationships. To the extent that an employer is disinclined to negotiate these events in good faith, the law should compel that employer's cooperation. The case for bargaining during the course of an agreement is, however, more complex. Langille has argued that by limiting the negotiation of plant closure and layoff issues to the time at which the collective agreement is negotiated — the so-called "statutory timetable" — the law encourages

> "employers not to *implement* changes, but the further incentive ... not to reveal possible or actual decisions upon changes. Rather, the incentive to the employer is to remain silent (during negotiations), lock the union into the agreement, and then reveal the plans or act upon them. It is a system geared to nondisclosure."[81]

With inadequate information, labour representatives are hobbled in their capacity to bargain effectively, and this increases the likelihood that bargaining outcomes may deviate from arrangements that would otherwise have been concluded in a setting of equal bargaining power and full information. Presumably, by insisting that unions have the right to negotiate these issues during the life of a collective agreement, the quality and fairness of bargaining outcomes will be improved.[82]

There are, unfortunately, several difficulties with the argument favouring mandatory bargaining rights respecting plant closures and layoffs during the course of a collective agreement. First, even assuming management has some strategic motive for refusing to make valuable information available to labour when an agreement is first negotiated, it is unclear that this will seriously handicap labour's ability to bargain. The access of union representatives to information provided by affiliates in other firms in the same industry may equip labour with important information about industry trends that can powerfully mitigate information asymmetries. Such "pooled" information may endow labour with the capacity to make reasoned judgments respecting the severity of job dislocations that are on a par with or, indeed, even superior to management's.

A second difficulty with conferring bargaining rights respecting plant closure on labour during the course of a collective agreement relates to disincentives for long-term private planning. By introducing opportunities for the parties to deal with dislocations when they arise, there is the danger that cost-effective risk reduction strategies in advance of a plant closure will not be employed. Rather, labour representatives may decide to eschew these strategies in favour of more costly solutions at the time of actual closure.

Finally, the efficacy of mid-term bargaining is itself suspect. Once a corporation decides to reduce its productive capacity through either layoffs or plant closures, the bargaining climate between the union and management is altered in a way that is inimical to labour's interests. Unlike the forward-looking nature of bargaining when a collective agreement is first negotiated, a decision to reduce productive activity signals an end to any commitment management may have had to the maintenance of long-term relationship; it also signals the beginning of debilitating "final period" problems. In this setting, the bargaining power of labour will be severely eroded, and the likelihood that management will make meaningful concessions to employees is relatively remote. Therefore, conferring such bargaining rights may offer no significant protection to unionized employees, and none whatsoever to non-unionized workers.

EXPANSION OF CORPORATE LAW DUTIES

ONE FREQUENTLY ARTICULATED METHOD for protecting stakeholder interests is to expand the ambit of fiduciary duties of directors under corporate law, which are conventionally believed to be limited to shareholders, to encompass direct responsibility to creditors, employees, suppliers and communities. One of the earliest proposals of this nature was made by Merrick Dodd in the 1930s. He claimed that since public opinion had grown to view the corporation as an "economic institution which has a social service as well as a profit-making function", corporate directors should be made responsible to constituencies other than shareholders.[83] Although modified somewhat, Dodd's proposal has been put forward frequently since then.[84] Most recently, calls for expanded directorial duties have been welcomed by several state legislatures, which have moved to expand the duties of directors through their state corporate codes. Section 23-1-35-1 (d) of the Indiana Business Corporation Law is instructive:

> "A director may, in considering the best interests of a corporation, consider the effects of any action on shareholders, employees, suppliers, and customers of the corporation, and communities in which offices or other facilities of the corporation are located ...."

In large part, such measures provide target management with more latitude in responding to a hostile takeover bid.

These proposals have met with considerable resistance from mainstream legal scholars. For instance, the Committee on Corporate Laws of the Section of Business Law of the American Bar Association concluded that the constituency statutes may

> "radically alter some of the basic premises upon which corporation law has been constructed and create opportunities for misunderstanding and thus pose the potential for mischief ."[85]

The basis for this discomfort is rooted in Berle's classic response to Dodd:

> "[Y]ou can not abandon emphasis on the view that business corporations exist for the sole purpose of making profits for their stockholders' until such time as you are prepared to offer a clear and reasonably enforceable scheme of responsibilities to someone else."[86]

In other words, without clear legal obligations owed to one set of principals (e.g., shareholders) it will be difficult, if not impossible, to monitor the performance of corporate management effectively.

The consequences of adopting constituency statutes into corporate codes are easy to see in the context of mergers and acquisitions. By introducing multiple and potentially irreconcilable objectives into corporate legislation, agents of the corporation are empowered to exercise additional discretion in mapping corporate objectives. This discretion may be so broad as to render managers virtually unaccountable to any stakeholder group, and therefore leave them free to engage in self-serving behaviour. Indeed, such statutory amendments are particularly useful to target management in imparting legislative sanction to conduct which, although superficially aimed at protecting stakeholder welfare, is really a ruse to prevent their own ouster from the management of the corporation.

One way to address the potentially unlimited discretion conferred on managers is to recast the governance apparatus of the modern corporation. Through extensive institutional re-ordering, managerial duties to stakeholders can be formalized, and subjected to direct monitoring. Most of these recommendations are aimed at restructuring the board of directors. One option focusses on the direct inclusion of special interest representatives on the corporate board.[87] That is, seats on the board for identifiable stakeholder representatives would be specified in a corporation's constating documents. Most options are, however, marred by concern as to the quality and nature of decision-making that would result from the introduction of disparate interest groups on the board. With divergent and incompatible interests enshrined on the board, the directors' ability to impart strong leadership to the affairs of the corporation would be undermined. As in pluralist legislative models, decision-making is likely to be governed by consensus-building exercises, which subvert the capacity of the corporation to react effectively to challenges. Moreover, because of the fears surrounding the use of information in such an environment, management may deliberately reduce the flow of information to the board.

Despite the air of noble minded intention, such statutory amendments offer only crude protection to stakeholder interests. At best, they are a panacea to delay painful, though inevitable, corporate restructuring. As such, they can confer only modest short-term benefits on stakeholders. However, they can also prevent the corporation from making the changes necessary to ensure its survival in a world of heightened competition. In these terms, thwarting mergers and acquisitions activity may condemn the corporation and its stakeholders to far more serious consequences — plant closure and/or bankruptcy — than any upheaval triggered by rationalization. At worst, however, such amendments may be a device to enable target management to extort personal benefit from acquirers in order to secure their acquiescence to a merger or acquisition. Once the bribe has been extracted, target management may drop all opposition to the transaction, leaving stakeholders to fend for themselves. For all these reasons, any expansion of duties under corporate law to encompass stakeholder interests in a merger or acquisition should be eschewed.

PLANT CLOSING LEGISLATION

PLANT CLOSING LEGISLATION typically requires employers to give employees advance notice of impending plant closures and to confer severance payments on those workers who suffer permanent job losses. Advance notice enables workers and communities to prepare for the harm occasioned by a layoff. Employees may start modest job searches and make necessary financial adjustments. Communities can also use this time to prepare for additional demands on their infrastructure. Empirical evidence substantiates the claim that workers are significantly assisted by such legislation.[88] Severance payments represent a form of compensation to workers for the losses they sustain from premature termination, particularly on the firm-specific component of their human capital. For older workers, such compensation is especially important as it reduces the losses they will sustain on foregone future payments of deferred compensation related to investment in firm-specific human capital.

Despite its efficacy and ethical force, plant closing legislation is still criticized for its tendency to hobble the corporation's operations prior to closure and for its unwarranted intrusion on the rights of management. Specifically, critics assert that the legislation increases union demands, causes customers to cancel orders, and constrains the corporation's ability to secure needed credit. Cipparone has argued that most of these concerns are unwarranted,[89] and that plant closing legislation creates an environment more conducive to cooperation between labour and management. Instead of embroiling corporate management in protracted brawls with labour over the prospect of closure, management can pay attention to appropriate adjustment schemes. Cipparone also doubts that plant closing legislation is likely to have any disruptive effect on the company's relationship with major customers. In only very limited circumstances will pre-notification precipitate any cancellation of customer orders,[90] Finally, creditors will not refrain from extending credit to a corporation if closing a plant is construed as a way to enhance overall corporate productivity.

From the perspective of protecting workers from the dire effects of mergers and acquisitions, plant closing legislation appears to be particularly well-suited and responsive to the ethical case for protection for workers. One difficulty with the legislation is its failure to protect suppliers who may sustain serious losses in customer-specific investments in their plant and equipment. Another difficulty has to do with the capacity of plant closing legislation to deter efficient transactions. At some point, a tax on exit can become a tax on entry; and prospective acquirers will not invest in a corporation that contains these sleeping liabilities. Whether or not the current level of notice and severance benefits are adequate to stymie an acquisition in a specific industry depends on the elasticity of the demand for corporate control in that industry.

CONCLUSION

I HAVE ATTEMPTED, in this paper, to make a strong case for refraining from restricting or prohibiting mergers and acquisitions transactions on grounds of stakeholder protection. My message is that although these transactions often upset expectations, they nonetheless yield consequences that benefit the entire economy. Mergers and acquisitions are simply the manifestation — not the source — of inevitable restructuring and rationalization. On this basis it is incumbent upon policy makers not to shoot the messenger.

What role should Investment Canada play in regulating mergers and acquisitions activity in this setting? Although foreign investment review processes may be invoked to protect stakeholder interests, there is no consensus for subjecting foreign acquisitions to a distinctive review process. As discussed earlier, there is no empirical evidence to support the claim that foreign acquirers are intrinsically more inclined to impose hardship on stakeholders following an acquisition than domestic acquirers. Furthermore, the process involving a review of foreign investment applications seems particularly ill-suited to identifying threats to stakeholder interests. Because information at this stage is limited, predicting the future effects of an acquisition on stakeholders is necessarily a highly speculative exercise and prone to error. Although binding commitments to safeguard stakeholders could be extracted by requiring certain production or employment levels to be maintained, for instance, these undertakings, if honoured, could preclude the realization of efficiencies that would otherwise be derived from shedding excess labour.

In the past, the administrators of the Canadian investment review process frequently relied on employment and production undertakings in the course of approving applications by foreign acquirers.[91] Reliance on these measures was largely an outgrowth of the Foreign Investment Review Agency's (FIRA) statutory mandate, which required the agency to evaluate the desirability of foreign investment on the basis of several substantive considerations, which, inter alia, included employment benefits. Spence and Rosenfeld have noted that because employment effects were one of the more quantifiable criteria and because of their political significance, they were given substantial weight by FIRA.[92] Indeed, scrutiny of the record of cases approved by FIRA in the period from 1982 to 1984 shows that approximately 70 percent of the cases, where transactions had employment effects, generated a net benefit to Canada. Although information concerning the basis for approvals is more sparse for FIRA's successor agency, Investment Canada, it appears that the combination of procedural and substantive reforms introduced by the Investment Canada Act have resulted in a process less committed to employment maintenance, and more to global competitiveness.

Nevertheless, in a second best, or even third best world, Investment Canada may find itself to be one of the few government agencies capable of offering real protection to stakeholder interests. Although there is a risk that intervention by Investment Canada may create undesirable distinctions in the treatment of stakeholders subject to foreign as opposed to domestic mergers and acquisitions, it is hoped that the political fallout from widespread recognition of this differentiation will be to spur the legislature to adopt more generalized adjustment schemes. Following the earlier discussion, Investment Canada's role should not be to restrict these transactions but rather, to emulate the forward-looking adjustment policies that would assist in moving both human and capital resources to their most highly valued uses.

ENDNOTES

1. In the United States, the AFL-CIO has claimed that mergers and acquisitions activity has resulted in the loss of over 500,000 jobs. (Hostile Takeovers: Hearings Before the Senate Committee on Banking, Housing and Urban Affairs, 100th Cong., 1st Sess. 262, March 4, 1987, [statement of Thomas P. Donahue, Secretary Treasurer, AFL-CIO.) As well, numerous politicians and academic commentators have catalogued harms sustained by other stakeholders in the corporation. (See Lipton, "Corporate Govern-ance in an Age of Finance Capitalism", 1987, 136 *University of Penn. Law Review*, p. 1; Proxmire, "What's Right and Wrong About Hostile Takeovers?", 1988, *Wisconsin Law Review*, p. 353.) Long term suppliers of the corporation, either of goods or of services, have had their contracts with the corporation severed or not renewed. Customers are unable to access parts or obtain service for expensive durable goods. Creditors of the corporation have found their claims on the corporation diluted by extensive corporate restructuring and refinancing. Finally, in communities excessively reliant on the fortunes of a single corporation, the reduction in plant activity or, even more seriously, its shut-down threatens the value of non-recoverable community infrastructure, which may signal the death of the community.

2. For a review of the effect of state anti-takeover statutes on shareholder welfare, see Romano, "The Political Economy of Takeover Statutes", 1987, 73, *Virginia Law Review*, p. 111; and "The Future of Hostile Takeovers: Legislation and Public Opinion", 57 *University of Cincinnati Law Review* 1988, p. 457.

3. See Berle, "Corporate Powers as Powers in Trust", 44, *Harvard Law Review*, 1931, p. 1049; Dodd, "For Whom Are Corporate Managers Trustees?", 45, *Harvard Law Review*, 1932, p. 1145; Berle, "For Whom Corporate Managers Are Trustees: A Note", 45, *Harvard Law Review*, 1932, p. 1365; and Dodd, "Is Effective Enforcement of the Fiduciary Duties of Corporate Managers Practicable?", 2, *University of Chicago Law Review*, 1935, p. 194.

4. See for instance Carney, "Does Defining Constituencies Matter?", 59, *University of Cincinnati Law Review*, 1990, p. 385.

5. This discussion defers until later difficult questions concerning the strength and exclusivity of the linkages between these putative harms and merger and acquisition transactions, the capacity of stakeholders to invoke *ex ante* arrangements to protect themselves adequately from harm, the legitimacy of stakeholder expectations regarding their treatment following a merger or acquisition transaction, and the form in which these expectations are enshrined (i.e., explicit or implicit contracts).

6. For an elaboration of the role of deferred compensation arrangements, and its impact on collective bargaining and labour law, see Wachter and Cohen, "The Law and Economics of Collective Bargaining: An Introduction and Application to the Problems of Subcontracting, Partial Closure, and Relocation", 136, *University of Pennsylvania Law Review*, 1988, p. 1349.

7. Shleifer and Summers, in "Breaches of Trust in Hostile Takeovers", *infra.*, report that the takeover of Youngstown Sheet and Tube resulted in the loss of 6,000 jobs between 1977 and 1979. Bankruptcies rose from 769 in 1977 to 1,948 in 1981; and the value of housing in a one-year period dropped by 23 percent, generating a community wide loss in housing from the takeover of $1 billion.

8. See Bluestone, "In Support of the Deindustrialization Thesis", ch. 4 in Staudohar and Brown, *Deindustrialization and Plant Closure*, 1987.

9. McKee has argued that there is anecdotal evidence that bondholders are adversely affected by takeover related activity. (McKee, D. "Managerial Behaviour and Takeovers" in *Hostile Takeovers*, D. McKee, [ed], 1989.) Support for this contention is derived from two newspaper articles.

10. Evidence respecting the distribution of the control premium between acquirer and target shareholders in American control transactions, for instance, indicates that the nature of this distribution has changed significantly over time in accordance with legal/institutional changes, such as the adoption of auction-based regimes, and market based changes, such as the entry of more bidder companies. See Jarrell and Bradley, "The Economic Effects of Federal and State Regulations of Cash Tender Offers", 23, *Journal of Law and Economics*, 1980, p. 371.

11. MacIntosh, "Poison Pills: Noxious Nostrum for Canadian Shareholders", 18, *Canadian Business Law Journal*, 1989, p. 57.

12. Daniels and MacIntosh, "The Distinctive Features of Canadian Capital Markets and their Impact on Corporate Securities Regulation", *Osgoode Hall Law Journal*, forthcoming, 1991.

13. C. Brown and J. Medoff, " The Impact of Firm Acquisitions on Labour" in Auerbach, *Corporate Takeovers: Causes and Consequences*, 1988.

14. Brown and Medoff, *supra* at 23. Support for the claim that mergers do not result in across the board wage reductions for employees is furnished by the results of a recent study undertaken by Fust and Peoples, "Merger Activity and Wage Levels in U.S. Manufacturing", 10, *Journal of Labour Research*, 1989, p. 183. By examining 1981 micro data, the researchers found that, while some forms of merger activity (conglomerate mergers) resulted in wage reductions for workers in the affected industry, most mergers (horizontal, vertical or product extension mergers) resulted in wage increases to workers employed in the affected industry.

15. Yago, *Junk Bonds: How High Yield Securities Restructured Corporate America*, ch. 7., 1991.

16. Rossett, "Do Union Wage Concessions Explain Takeover Premiums? Evidence on Contract Wages", National Bureau of Economic Research Working Paper # 3187, 1989.

17. Yago, *supra* p. 135. These results are consistent with earlier work done by Yago and Stevenson, "Employment Impacts of Mergers and Acquisitions", Working Paper, Economic Research Bureau, W. Averell Harriman School

for Management and Policy, State University of New York at Stony Brook, 1987. They are also consistent with studies undertaken by the Bureau of Labor Statistics, 1989, (Yago, p. 136) which found that of 2,020 large plant closings and layoffs in 29 states, only 6.6 percent of the total jobs lost could be attributed to the ownership change.

18. Yago found that, in the period between 1981 and 1986, the cumulative productivity growth of plants involved in LBOs was 2.8 percent higher than plants not involved in LBOs (p. 163).

19. Interestingly, the comparatively higher costs of white-collar (as opposed to blue-collar) layoffs were accomplished by laying off fewer workers. The reason for the higher total costs of these layoffs derives from the higher wages these laid off employees received prior to termination.

20. Lichtenberg and Siegel, "The Effect of Takeovers on the Employment and Wages of Central Office and Other Personnel", First Boston Working Paper Series, Graduate School of Business, Columbia University, FB-89-05, January 1989.

21. Pontiff, Shleifer and Weisbach, "Reversions of Excess Pension Assets After Takeovers", University of Chicago, Graduate School of Business, Centre for Research in Securities Prices, Working Paper #267, 1989 quoted in Romano, "Theory of the Corporate Form". Case materials prepared for a course taught at the University of Toronto, Faculty of Law, January 1991, pp. 299-300.

22. Kim and McConnell, "Corporate Mergers and the Co-Insurance of Corporate Debt", 32, *Journal of Finance*, 1977, p. 349.

23 Asquith and Kim, "The Impact of Merger Bids on the Participating Firms' Security Holders", 37, *Journal of Finance*, 1982, p. 1209.

24. Denis and McConnell, "Corporate Mergers and Security Returns", 16, *Journal of Finance and Economics*, 1986, p. 143.

25. Crabbe, *infra*, observes that the losses that creditors suffered on the announcement of the mammoth RJR Nabisco leveraged buyout ($1 billion) constituted only a small fraction of the gains accruing to target shareholders ($12 billion).

26. Amihud, "Leveraged Management Buyouts and Shareholders' Wealth", in Amihud, *Leveraged Management Buyouts: Causes and Consequences*, 1989, pp. 11-12. In a similar vein, see Crabbe, "Event Risk: An Analysis of Losses to Bondholders and 'Super Poison Put' Bond Covenants", Draft working paper, Federal Reserve System, February 1990. In this study, bondholders experienced losses of 12.33 percent in the value of their bonds following a capital restructuring. However, these results are only crudely applied in this setting as there is no necessary link between capital restructuring and mergers and acquisitions activity.

27. Lehn and Poulsen, "Leveraged Buyouts: Wealth Created or Wealth Redistributed?", in Weidenbaum and Chilton, *Public Policy Toward Corporate Takeovers*, 1988.

28. Even more strikingly, the price of outstanding preferred shares (not market adjusted) increased by an average of 23.37 percent on announcement, with the most notable increases experienced by three non-convertible issues (40.67 percent).

29. Marais, Schipper and Smith, "Wealth Effects of Going Private for Senior Securities", 23, *Journal of Finance*, 1989, p. 155. They also found that "there are only 19 buyouts, which together account for less than two percent of the total dollar gains to stockholders, for which plausible debtholder losses — on the order of 10 percent of book value — can account fully for stockholder gains".

30. The divergence in interests between shareholders and creditors in responding to certain types of proposed transactions (the "agency costs of debt") is discussed in Barnea, Haugen and Senbet, *Agency Problems and Financial Contracting*, 1985, chs 3 and 4; and in Klein and Coffee, *Business Organizations and Finance: Legal and Economic Principles*, 4th ed., 1990, ch.4.

31. Manne, H. "Mergers and the Market for Corporate Control", 73, *Journal of Political Economy*, 1965, p. 110. Manne argues that because of various defects in the markets that control managerial behaviour, i.e., the product, labour, and capital markets, the takeover market is essential to protect the interests of widely dispersed shareholders.

32. Empirical support for this claim is furnished by Lichtenberg and Siegel, *supra*.

33. There are several leading works in this genre, including: Baumol, *Business Behaviour and Growth*, 1959; Marris, *The Economic Theory of 'Managerial Capitalism'*, 1964; and Williamson, "Managerial Discretion and Business Behavior", 53, *American Economic Review*, 1963, p. 1032.

34. Shleifer and Summers, "Breach of Trust in Hostile Takeovers", in Auerbach, *Corporate Takeovers: Causes and Consequences*, 1988.

35. See the conclusion respecting the minimal role of diversion among creditors and shareholders in Dennis and McConnell, *supra*.

36. Although, as noted above, changes in ownership do appear to provide opportunities for opportunistic redistribution.

37. Scherer, *Industrial Market Structure and Economic Performance*, 2nd ed., 1980, pp. 81-104.

38. See Coase, "The Nature of the Firm", 4, *Economica.*, 1937, p. 386.

39. See Levy and Sarnat, "Diversification, Portfolio Analysis and the Uneasy Case for Conglomerate Mergers", 25, *Journal of Finance*, 1970, p. 795.

40. See Amihud and Lev, "Risk Reduction as a Managerial Motive for Conglomerate Mergers", 12, *Bell Journal of Economics*, 1981, p. 605. See also Mason and Goudzwaard, "Performance of Conglomerate Firms: A Portfolio Approach", 31, *Journal of Finance*, 1976, p. 39.

41. For a complete exposition of this claim, see Jensen, "Agency Costs of Free Cash Flow, Corporate Finance, and Takeovers", 76, *American Economist*, p. 323 (Papers and Proceedings, May 1986).

42. See, Lipton, "Corporate Governance in the Age of Finance Corporatism", 136, *University of Pennsylvania Law Review*, 1987, p. 1.

44. The outstanding "A" rated RJR-Nabisco bonds plunged in value by an estimated 20 percent or $1 billion on the announcement of the management buyout. See Crabbe, "Event Risk: An Analysis of Losses to Bondholders and 'Super Poison Put' Bond Covenants", Working Paper, Capital Markets Section of the Division of Research and Statistics, Board of Governors of the Federal Reserve System, February 1990, p. 1.

44. See Caves, *Multinational Enterprise and Economic Analysis*, 1982.

45. Ohmae, *The Borderless World*, 1990, p. 10.

46. A similar claim has been made by Sykes in the trade setting. He argues that, although increasing imports derived from trade liberalization increases national wealth, the fact that foreign workers displace domestic workers is ethically significant. See Sykes, "GATT Safeguards Reform: The Injury Test", in Trebilcock and York, *Fair Exchange: Reforming Trade Remedy Laws*, 1990.

47. Because the losses from intra-domestic migration are offset by benefits realized within the country whereas the costs of international migration do not yield such compensating benefit, this activity may be of less concern to domestic policymakers. From an ethical perspective this differentiation may be suspect as it implies a heavy discount on the welfare of foreign citizens. The ethical significance of nationality is considered in a symposium issue on Duties Beyond Borders in 98 Ethics 647, July 1988.

48. Enderwick, "Labour and the Theory of the Multinational Corporation", *Industrial Relations Journal*, Summer 1982, pp. 32 at 36.

49. See Warner, "The Comparative Measurement of Industrial Relations in Multinational Firms", in Tudyka (ed), *Multinational Corporations and Labour Unions*, 1973; McAlesse and Counahan, "Stickers or Snatchers? Employment in Multinational Corporations During the Recession", 41, *Oxford Bulletin of Economics and Statistics*, 1979.

50. See Khemani, "Recent Trends in Merger and Acquisition Activity in Canada and Selected Countries" in this volume.

51. See data in Khemani, *supra*.

52. See MacIntosh and Daniels, "Capital Markets and the Law: The Peculiar Case of Canada", 3, *Canadian Investment Review*, 1990, p. 77.

53. B. Epsen Eckbo, "Mergers and the Market for Corporate Control: The Canadian Evidence", 19, *Canadian Journal of Economics*, 1986, pp. 236-60.

54. Eckbo also found that there was no statistically significant difference between the returns experienced by bidding and target shareholders from horizontal as opposed to vertical mergers.

55. See G. Jarrell and A. Poulsen, "Bidder Returns", working paper referred to in "The Market for Corporate Control: The Empirical Evidence Since 1980", G. Jarrell, J. Brickley, and J. Netter, 2, *Journal of Economic Perspectives*, 1988. See also M. Jensen and R. Ruback "The Market for

Corporate Control: The Scientific Evidence", 11, *Journal of Financial Economics*, 1983, p. 5. and M. Bradley, A. Desai and E. Kim "Determinants of the Wealth Effects of Corporate Acquisitions", working paper, University of Michigan, 1984.

56. Jensen and Poulsen, *supra.*

57. See MacIntosh and Daniels, *supra*, p. 44.

58. L. Kaplow, "An Economic Analysis of Legal Transitions", 99, *Harvard Law Review*, 1986, p. 511.

59. Knight, *Risk and Uncertainty*, 1921.

60. Triantis, *infra*, p. 14.

61. The role of risk discounting in distorting worker bargaining is exhibited most clearly in the context of occupational health and safety, where workers tend to dismiss serious risks of contracting diseases with protracted latency periods in bargaining with management. For instance, see Tuohy and Trebilcock, *Policy Options in the Regulation of Asbestos-Related Hazards*, Study for the Royal Commission on Matters of Health and Safety Relating to the Use of Asbestos in Ontario, 1982. But *contra*, see Gunderson and Swinton, *Collective Bargaining and Asbestos Dangers at the Workplace*, Study for the Royal Commission on Matters of Health and Safety Relating to the Use of Asbestos in Ontario, 1981, ch. 5; and Dworkin, Feldman, Brown and Hobson, "Workers' Preferences in Concession Bargaining", 27 *Industrial Relations,* 7, 1988. Study of United Steelworkers Union contractual negotiations found a consistent preference for health, pension, and job security items over other benefits.

62. G. Triantis, "The Management of Unknown Risks and the Doctrine of Excuse", Paper delivered at the Canadian Law and Economics Association, October 26 and 27, 1990. Triantis draws on the work of Fischoff, Slovic and Lichenstein, "Fault Trees: Sensitivity of Estimated Failure Probabilities to Problem Representation" 4, *Journal of Experimental Psychology: Human Perception and Performance*, 1978, p. 330, who found that the probability estimates fashioned by individuals who were exposed to complete fault trees as to why a car would not start, were similar to those estimates fashioned by individuals who had access to pruned fault trees.

63. *Metropolitan Life Insurance Company and Jefferson-Pilot Life Insurance Company v. RJR-Nabisco and R. Ross Johnson*, p.716, F.Supp. p. 1504 (S.D.N.Y. 1989), at pp. 1511-1514. After surveying the internal documentation that showed that investor risk awareness, Walker, District Judge, stated: "the documents ... highlight the risks inherent in the market itself, for nay investor. Investors as sophisticated as MetLife and Jefferson-Pilot would be hard-pressed to plead ignorance of these market risks." (1514)

64. E. Kassalow, "Concession Bargaining: Towards New Roles for American Unions and Managers", 127, *International Labour Review*, 1988. Kassalow reports that the merger mania occurring in the United States has exerted a profound effect on union behaviour. Not only have unions bargained for

various notice and successorship clauses, but have also played an important role in the restructuring process, even to the point of arranging employee buyouts and identifying white knight acquirers.

65. Data from *The Current Industrial Scene in Canada*, 1989. An example of the specific type of contractual commitments extracted by labour from management in response to a plant closure can be observed in the merger of Carling O'Keefe and Molsons. Since the merger was expected to entail the loss of 1,400 to 7,000 jobs, the unions negotiated for a series of benefits for displaced employees, including generous severance pay, early retirement pension benefits for older employees, continuation of health and dental benefits, and career counselling. See "Facts and Trends", Canadian Labour Views Co Ltd. Reports.

66. These problems are discussed in C. Sunstein, *Disrupting Voluntary Transactions*, ch. 10.

67. Agency costs are discussed at length in M. Jensen and W. Meckling, "Theory of the Firm: Managerial Behaviour, Agency Costs, and Ownership Structure", 3, *Journal of Finance and Economics*, 1976, p. 305; E. Fama, "Agency Problems and the Theory of the Firm", 88, *Journal of Political Economy*, 1980, p. 288; and Robert Clark, *Corporate Law*, 1986, pp. 389-400.

68. For a thorough discussion of the various mechanisms protecting creditors from abuse by corporations, see M. McDaniel, "Bondholders and Corporate Governance", 41, *Business Lawyer*, 1986, p. 413.

69. It is unlikely that the preferences in a union will be sufficiently homogenous across the entire membership to force the union to choose from among competing preferences in the course of negotiating a collective agreement with management. (See B. Kaufman and J. Martinez-Vazquez, "The Ross-Dunlop Debate and Union Wage Concessions: A Median Voter Analysis", 8, *Journal of Labour Res.*, 1987, p. 291; P. Cappelli and W. Sterling, "Union Bargaining Decisions and Contract Ramifications: The 1982 and 1984 Auto Agreements", 41, *Industrial and Labour Relations Review*, 1988, p. 195). This selection process invariably means that the preferences of some workers will be discarded in favour of the preferences of other workers. Typically, therefore, union representatives focus on the preferences of the median voters, as their support (and the support of *infra* marginal voters) is necessary to ensure ratification of a collective agreement under a simple majority voting rule. (See B. Howard, "The Interpenetration of Voting in the Allocation of Economic Resources", 58, *Quarterly Journal of Economics*, 1943, p. 27).

70. This concern relates to the efficacy of the competitive federalism model. See R. Prichard with J. Benedickson, "Securing the Canadian Economic Union: Federalism and Internal Barriers to Trade" in Trebilcock, Prichard, Courchene and Whalley (eds), *Federalism and the Canadian Economic Union*, 1983.

71. See M. Gunderson, "Alternative Mechanisms for Dealing with Permanent Layoffs, Dismissals and Plant Closings" pp. 125-27 in Riddell, *Adapting to Change: Labour Market Adjustment in Canada*, 1988.

72. Trebilcock, Chandler and Howse, *Trade and Transitions*, 1990.

73. See s.177 of *Ontario Business Corporations Act, 1982*, S.O. 1982, ch. 4.

74. OLRA, R.S.O. 1980, c.228.

75. OLRB Report, September 1975, p. 733.

76. In *Thorco Manufacturing Ltd.*, 65 CLLC, p. 16, 52, the Board stated that it was "impelled to give the section a large and liberal rather than a narrow and restrictive construction" and that it was "constrained to believe that the section does comprehend transactions including gratuitous dispositions or otherwise which operate to dispose of the employer's business or a discernable part or parts thereof". Although the Board can exempt successors from the section 63 obligation when it is shown that the successor employer has "substantially changed the character of the business", this relief has been given infrequently. As the Board stated in *Vaunclair Meats Ltd.*, [1981] OLRB Rep. May 581: "Both the language and the context suggest that this exception to the general rule is intended to be an exceedingly narrow one .... (The relief) will only be applied in to exceptional situations in which a person purchases a business organization then turns it into something quite different operating in an entirely unrelated labour and product market "

77. B. Langille, "Equal Partnership in Canadian Labour Law", 21, *Osgoode Hall Law Journal*, 1983, p. 496.

78. Langille, *supra* citing *Pulp and Paper Industrial Relations Bureau and Canadian Paper Workers Union* [1978] 1 Can. LRBR 60, Weiler.

79. *First National Maintenance v. N.L.R.B.* (1981) 452 U.S. 666.

80. The Court stated that "bargaining over management decisions that have a substantial impact on the continued availability of employment should be required only if the benefit, for labour-management relations and the collective bargaining process, outweighs the burden placed on the conduct of business". Analysis of the case can be found in D. Kuhn and C. Zech, "Plant Closings and Public Policy: Achieving an Optimal Level of Plant Closings", 1988, 10, *Law and Policy*, 63 (respecting the United States), and J. Hedlund, "An Economic Case for Mandatory Bargaining over Partial Termination and Plant Relocation Decisions", 96, *Yale Law Journal*, 1986, p. 949.

81. Langille, *supra* p. 517.

82. See also Hedlund, "An Economic Case for Mandatory Bargaining over Partial Termination and Plant Relocation Decisions", 95, *Yale Law Journal*, 1986, p. 949. He argues that mandatory bargaining during the life of the collective agreement will alleviate labour's concern that management is not sincerely committed to plant closures, and is simply trying to extract wage concessions from workers by threatening layoffs and closures. The procedural protections triggered by mandatory bargaining, (e.g., the duty to disclose, penalties for misrepresentation, good faith duties) all combine to increase the likelihood that credible information will be disclosed and

increase the prospect that labour and management will be able to effect a value maximizing agreement.

83. Dodd, "For Whom Are Corporate Managers Trustees?", 45, *Harvard Law Review*, 1932, pp. 1145, 1148.

84. See R. Nader, M. Green and J. Seligman, *Taming the Giant Corporation*, 1976; and E. Weiss, "Social Regulation of Business Activity: Reforming the Corporate Governance System to Resolve an Institutional Impasse, 28, *UCLA Law Review*, 1981, p. 343.

85. Committee on Corporate Laws, "Other Constituencies Statutes: Potential for Confusion", 45, *Business Lawyer*, 1990, p. 2253.

86. A. Berle, "For Whom Corporate Managers Are Trustees: A Note", 45, *Harvard Law Review*, 1932, pp. 1365, 1367.

87. For a discussion of this and other proposals designed to give expression to the stakeholder model of corporate governance, see R. Romano, "Metapolitics and Corporate Law Reform", 36, *Stanford Law Review*, 1984, p. 923.

88. E. Lazear, "Job Security and Unemployment" cited in Ehrenberg and Jakubson, *infra* (advanced notice provisions of greater than 60 days increased the employment/population ratio by .003 and increased average weekly wages by .07); N. Folbre, J. Leighton, and M. Roderick, "Plant Closings and Their Regulation in Maine, 1971 - 1982", 37, *Industrial and Labour Relations Review*, 1984, p. 185, (voluntary provision of one month's notice to displaced workers significantly diminished the impact of plant closings on local area unemployment in the month of closing); J. Addison and P. Portugal, "The Effect of Advance Notification of Plant Closing on Unemployment", XLI, *Industrial and Labour Relations Review*, 1987, p. 3, (advance notice is associated with unemployment durations that are 35 percent shorter than expected); and Ehrenberg and Jakubson, "Advanced Notification of Plant Closing: Does it Matter?", 28, *Industrial Relations*, 1989, p. 60 (advanced notice provisions significantly reduced the probability but not the duration of unemployment suffered by displaced workers). But, *contra*, see M. Howland (little benefit from advanced notice found); Podgursky and Swaim (advanced notice only exerted a positive impact on white-collar females with respect to duration, not probability) (cited in Ehrenberg and Jakubson).

89. J. Cipparone, "Advance Notice of Plant Closings: Toward National Legislation", 14, *University of Michigan Journal of Law Reform*, 1981, p. 283.

90. These circumstances include: where production of a particular goods is ending, alternative suppliers are readily available, other companies do not manufacture spare parts for the terminated product line, and future sales to present customers do not concern the business closing the plant. See Cipparone at p. 298.

91. See, for instance, *Canadian GE - Pirelli Cables* (80-81); *Amdahl Corporation - Tran Communications Ltd.* (81-82); *Prudential Insurance Co. - Bache Halsey Stuart Canada and Halsey Stuart Corporate Services* (82-82); and

Hewlett Packard - Panacom Automation Inc. (83-84). These cases, however, typically involved a commitment by the acquirer to increase the amount of employment, not to maintain employment levels following rationalization. One approved application, *Canadian General Electric - Camco Inc.* (83-84), involved a commitment by the acquirer to invest a substantial amount of money, $50 million, in the modernization and rationalization of plant activity. No explicit employment undertakings were negotiated as these development plans "were viewed favourably as improving Camco's prospects and thus the job security of its employees" (FIRA Annual Report 1983-84 at p.3).

92. Spence and Rosenfeld, *Foreign Investment Review Law in Canada*, 1984, p. 183.

ACKNOWLEDGEMENT

I WISH TO ACKNOWLEDGE the superb research assistance provided to me for this paper by Mark Crawford, Andrew Green, Gord Haskins, Sue Hutton, Mike Kovacevic and Tim Lewis. As always, I relied heavily on the creative and efficient services of Debra Forman, the International Business and Trade Law Librarian at the Faculty of Law, University of Toronto. Extremely useful comments were provided by David Beatty, Bruce Chapman, Robert Howse, Lawson Hunter, David Husband, Roberta Romano, Ian Stewart and Len Waverman. My greatest debt of gratitude is owed to Michael Trebilcock, who gave generously of his time and ideas frequently throughout the writing of this article. I am deeply in his debt. Of course, the usual disclaimer applies.

A. E. Safarian
Centre for International Studies
University of Toronto

Rapporteur's Comments

STUDIES OF FOREIGN DOMESTIC INVESTMENT AND MULTINATIONAL FIRMS have been a growth industry for at least 20 years. Research on mergers and acquisitions (M&A) has also accelerated in recent years in response to the wave of takeovers in the United States, Canada and some other countries during the 1980s. The papers in this volume explore a topic which has been little researched independently of foreign direct investment (FDI). Cross-border M&A, as distinct from greenfield investment, have dominated such direct investment since the 1980s and perhaps earlier.[1]

Each of the papers is summarized here. We turn then to two related policy questions. One is an issue now attracting some attention from governments: the fact that, quite apart from foreign investment policy restrictions *per se*, national markets for M&A are quite unevenly accessible. The other question is the implications of these papers for public policy aimed at reviewing both inward and outward M&A activity.

SUMMARY OF THE STUDIES

THE PAPER BY KHEMANI DESCRIBES RECENT TRENDS in M&A activity in Canada and compares them with trends in several other industrialized countries. The comparisons are limited to the number of M&A transactions or announcements. The data for Canada indicate increased M&A activity over the 1980s both in the number of cases and the incidence of transactions exceeding $100 million. Since 1981 the number of foreign transactions has generally exceeded those by domestic firms. These data portend increased levels of foreign ownership and aggregate concentration in Canada, some of which is already evident.

Trends in M&A activity in Canada tend to parallel those in the United States and United Kingdom, but not those in the other industrial countries examined. M&A activity relative to that in the United States, adjusted for differences in the size of real GDP, is highest in Sweden followed by Canada and the United Kingdom. Two qualifications Khemani notes are worth underlining in interpreting these measures. They are based on numbers, hence dominated by acquisitions of smaller firms. There are also differences in the definitions of numbers of M&A, with those for Australia and France yielding measures whose scope is relatively limited. Khemani also notes that while there are some common factors affecting M&A activity across countries, there are also important institutional differences, such as review of foreign takeovers and differences in the concentration of share ownership.

The paper by Knubley, Krause and Sadeque is the only one that concentrates on Canadian acquisitions abroad. The first part uses data on direct investment abroad and on cross-border M&A to highlight some important changes in such activity abroad. In the last two decades Canadian direct investment abroad has increased steadily relative to inward investment. The more even relation which has developed between inward and outward investment is typical of major industrial countries except Japan. Along with a strong upswing in Canadian acquisitions abroad, especially from 1986 to 1990, Canada, like other small countries, shows a relatively high tendency to invest abroad in relation to GDP. Two-thirds of the firms investing abroad are small- or medium-sized, most with only one affiliate. However, 39 larger firms, most of which are Canadian controlled, accounted for almost 40 percent of the transactions and a much larger share of the value. About 70 percent of the value of Canadian direct investment abroad is in the United States.

The second part of the paper reports the results of an Investment Canada survey of 23 larger Canadian-controlled firms with direct investment abroad. Some of the factors that significantly influence investment abroad, such as trade and transportation barriers, are consistent with other studies. However, some may find it surprising to note that Canadian taxes and regulations ranked as the least significant motivation on a long list of "push" factors. Four case studies supplement the paper's findings.

Rugman and Waverman examine cross-border acquisitions from the perspective of some questions about Porter's model, particularly the treatment of foreign direct investment.[2] That model traces the competitive advantage of nations to four endogenous variables (factor conditions, demand conditions, supporting industries and firm strategy) and two exogenous variables (government and chance). Dunning has argued that this model downplays the role of multinational firm activity, and suggested that such activity be considered a third exogenous variable influencing all four endogenous determinants.[3] To test these issues, Rugman and Waverman use an internalization approach in which country-specific assets interact with firm-specific assets. Their data was obtained from Investment Canada and covers all foreign acquisitions of Canadian firms from 1974 to 1990 classified by sectors and home countries. They find acquisition patterns by resources, manufacturers and services to be broadly similar for Japan, the United States and the European Community, particularly if an allowance is made for Japan as a latecomer to direct investment in Canada. Hence, they conclude that opportunities in Canada largely drive the pattern of inward acquisitions, while Porter's analysis suggests different patterns driven by home-country variables.

The authors go on to examine the pattern of inward acquisitions and greenfield investments in the periods covered by the Foreign Investment Review Agency and Investment Canada. The main impact of the former agency was most likely on smaller scale acquisitions by American firms that could not cope with the transaction costs of the review process. However, neither agency appears to have disturbed the patterns of inward direct investment as between Japan, the United States and the European Community. The authors add that studies of the overall economic impact of such agencies require fuller models of the determinants of M&A. They also point to some data improvements that would sharpen analysis, such as the need to separate the many indirect acquisitions subject to review only because ownership of the parent has changed.

In an earlier study Caves noted that entry abroad by acquisition of an established firm rather than a greenfield investment tends to yield a lower but less uncertain expected rate of return.[4] The paper by Baldwin and Caves in this volume analyses the effects of mergers and other changes in control using the full data set of Statistics Canada for manufacturing establishments in 1970 and 1979. A major objective is to sort out the effects on M&A performance of domestic and foreign control of the establishment, in relation to such matters as productivity and plant size. One question that arises with such tests is how to control for other aspects of industry structure, such as concentration of industry, that might attract multinational enterprises. Their method was to rank industries in 1970 by the percentage of shipments due to foreign-controlled establishments, then divide these into thirds with high, medium and low foreign shares.

Over this period the proportion of establishments subject to changes in control increases with the importance of foreign ownership. Also, greenfield entries by new firms and close-down exits by existing firms fall significantly with foreign ownership. In effect, where high foreign ownership exists it is characterized by changes in control rather than by product-market competition which exerts the larger pressures for efficiency. The favourable effects of control changes increase as the industry's foreign ownership rises, but favourable effects also occur in shifts between nationality of ownership. The one area where a number of negative effects occur is in domestic-to-domestic control changes in the low foreign ownership sector.

Baldwin and Caves also note that industries with high foreign ownership offer greater opportunities for gains from changes in control through the deployment of lumpy and intangible assets. However, the nationality of the acquirer does not systematically affect performance across the entire set of industries if one allows for the opportunities offered by market structure for productive changes in control. There is some division of labour in that domestic control favours cost containment while foreign control leads to more resource reallocations that can involve synergistic gains.

The paper by Patry and Poitevin examines ten hostile takeovers of larger firms in Canada between 1985 and 1989 for which sufficient data could be found to assess the reasons for the (estimated) large premiums paid to sellers. Their assessment of post-takeover performance suggests the premiums cannot be attributed in large measure to cost savings from layoffs, cuts in investment, or tax savings. Strategic factors appear to account for most of the premiums, particularly if the sell-offs of assets by the initial acquirer are traced. Virtually all of the foreign acquisitions and sell-offs fall into the strategic category.

These findings are similar to those reported in comparable studies in the United States, except for layoffs. It should be noted that the authors define "strategic" quite broadly, to include horizontal and vertical mergers, with the former dominant in this study. These types of mergers, it is argued, are more likely to allow for cost savings due, for example, to economies of scale and scope or integration of various functions of the firm. These potential sources of gain are not separately identified in the present study but, rather, are derived as a residual after the likelihood of the other sources are assessed.

Halpern and Mintz analyze how tax differences between Canada and the United States affect cross-border transactions. Their detailed examination of the nature of the two tax systems suggests that: 1) in most cases, higher effective Canadian tax rates on capital favour location in the United States; 2) the rules on tax-free rollovers and the transfer of pre-acquisition tax losses tend to favour M&A over greenfield entry if both firms are incorporated in the same jurisdiction; 3) tax rules tend to favour the subsidiary over the branch form of organization with some exceptions; 4) such rules also favour share-for-share exchanges over cash-for-share exchanges; and 5) it is usually preferable to issue more debt in Canada where the statutory corporate tax rate and inflation rate are higher.

It is difficult to believe that the differences in tax systems they describe do not affect these issues, assuming the supply of tax lawyers and accountants in Canada and the United States has not dried up. Yet, it is not possible with present data to test directly the influence of taxation on various aspects of cross-border M&A, as distinct from foreign direct investment. The indirect evidence, summarized in the paper, consists of studies of the ways in which foreign acquisitions improve the after-tax profitability of multinationals. Some of the indirect evidence is consistent with the impact of taxation on cross-border M&A, although the authors note that non-taxation issues also affect most of the results. Their tentative conclusions include a number of questions on taxation and cross-border M&A that could be tested with the generation of suitable data.

In contrast with the frequent emphasis on shareholder welfare, Daniels examines how M&A affect the interests of stakeholders, especially employees, suppliers, customers and creditors. He argues that, while harm can be done to such interests in some cases, *a priori* reasoning and the available empirical studies do not suggest this is the principal or central feature of the transactions.[5] Nevertheless, some stakeholder interests are harmed at times. Also, stakeholders are frequently unable to protect their interests in advance because of non-foreseeable risks and the costs associated with such protection. Daniels argues that intervention is justified, preferably in the form of adjustment programs aimed especially at reducing private costs faced by dislocated employees and suppliers. He also examines the desirability of a number of second-best policies, such as mandatory bargaining over closures or layoffs, and the expansion of the duties of directors under corporate law.

Daniels also asks how the existence of multinational firms responding more directly to international conditions might affect stakeholder interests. He argues that foreign ownership "neither ameliorates nor exacerbates the harms to stakeholders" from most M&A, but the evidence cited is not extensive enough to support a strong conclusion either way.

SELECTED PUBLIC POLICY ISSUES

THIS SUMMARY CONCENTRATES ON CERTAIN THEMES, which recur throughout most of the papers, notably the determinants of M&A and their impact on shareholders and other private interests. Although some of the papers involve substantial empirical testing, there was considerable emphasis, especially during the discussion periods, on the need for improved data on M&A and related cross-border transactions.

While public policy is not the main focus of the papers, some of them do comment on substantive policy issues. Several papers note that the literature is somewhat ambivalent on the social welfare effects of M&A.[6] Some of the findings in the literature suggest that competitive market forces prevail in that resources may be reallocated to higher valued uses. Other findings in the literature point to motivations such as speculation, managerial utilities, or monopolization, which may harm shareholder and broader interests.

Three papers explicitly deal with the public policy implications of cross-border M&A. Their positions on the effects of such transactions range from benign to inconclusive. The Baldwin-Caves conclusions are largely in the former category, in that their statistical measures suggest that changes in control usually affect productivity and efficiency favourably. The presence of both domestic and foreign enterprises is considered desirable because of the different skills they bring to the market for corporate control. The one sector with an inferior record is large mergers by domestic firms, but this may reflect the limited scope for improvement in the sector rather than a limited ability to bring about improvements. Baldwin and Caves note that industries with high foreign ownership are also highly concentrated and less subject to competitive pressure. They question, therefore, the public review of foreign acquirers "unless the procedure embraces recognition of the value of control changes" (p. 116).

The Patry-Poitevin position on welfare appears to be inconclusive in the sense that the key variable they identify — strategic behaviour — can lead to either positive or negative social welfare outcomes. The analysis of rationales and instruments for intervention leads Daniels to the conclusion that protection of stakeholder interests through restrictive policies on M&A cannot be justified. He favours protection of stakeholder interests through generalized adjustment schemes; he also sees the role of Investment Canada in that context.

Obviously, a great deal more could have been said on public policy issues if the conference had focussed on them. From the perspective of one who is more familiar with the literature on direct investment than that on M&A as such, I offer a few further reflections on this topic.

In the 1980s there was a shift in government policies towards inward direct investment. Since then, inward review agencies have been either dismantled or made less restrictive. Although some countries still impose significant obstacles to some types of inward investment, incentives to investment in general and multinational investment in particular have been increased, and targeted more precisely by sectors. Firms or industries restricted in varying degrees to domestic ownership have been at least partially opened to foreign ownership as deregulation and privatization have increased.

Some view these changes as a liberalization of policies on foreign investment, a claim with some justification. They can also be viewed as an attempt to focus policy on a more targeted and international approach to multinational firms — to assure that foreign-owned subsidiaries take advantage of the international market, and that domestically owned multinationals are encouraged.[7]

My comments here centre on two points of policy: one is the meaning of restrictiveness of cross-border acquisitions once an M&A viewpoint is adopted; the other is the appropriate policy stance in the context of the 1990s.

On the first point, we are used to the idea that governments impose restrictions on inward direct investment. All countries continue to restrict foreign ownership in some sectors or they discriminate against such firms after they are established; some countries still review foreign-controlled firms on entry and subsequent merger. Such restrictions, it may be noted, have always been larger for cross-border acquisitions than for greenfield investments. Every review agency with which I have had direct experience in the developed countries has favoured the latter and has imposed more tests on the former in principle. Investment Canada, for example, usually requires only notification for greenfield investment, but may review acquisitions.

The trend toward openness noted above has highlighted other notable limitations on M&A. The ease of merging or acquiring is highly uneven by country because of differences in state holdings of shares, private concentration of shareholdings and a variety of restrictions on takeovers. While there is, for example, an active and even aggressive market in M&A for smaller Japanese firms, the larger companies are protected by the fact that the majority of their shares are held by banks, suppliers and customers, and also by a tradition (encouraged by governments) opposing hostile takeovers of such firms. Close holdings by governments and banks also exist in Germany and some other European countries. These situations stand in contrast with those of the United States and United Kingdom. Canada occupies an in-between position, with the result that hostile bid situations are less common in Canada than in the United States.[8] In addition, during the 1980s, we in the United States and Canada have become familiar with the measures firms now take to make hostile takeovers difficult. It is of interest that such measures were adopted by many firms in the 1960s and 1970s in countries such as Germany, Switzerland, Sweden and Holland, often supported by legal changes to encourage their defence. For example, a recent study of shareholders' rights ranked countries under four headings: disclosure of corporate information, voting rights, shareholder rights to introduce resolutions, and notification to shareholders of meetings and proxy rights. This is a limited set of issues, but it helps to point up the differences between countries. If one places the United States at 100, Canada ranks at 80, the United Kingdom and Australia at 73 and 65, France, Japan and West Germany each rank at 48, Italy and Holland at 40, and Switzerland at 18.[9]

Care must be taken in making a case against some of these and other barriers to cross-border (and domestic) mergers. One hears much these days about the potential advantages of "patient capital", although those who examine the welfare aspects might also consider the "patient consumer" to be at least as worthy of attention. If some harmonization of such policies is favoured, there are several important issues at the international level.

One issue has to do with the difficulties in using an approach based on reciprocity as against one based on national treatment. Reciprocity would require that firms from country A have the same acquisition rights in country B as B's firms have in A — a much more difficult criterion than prohibiting discrimination on the basis of nationality in each country. Another more specific issue is how to deal with state ownership of acquiring firms, given anticompetitive and other problems due to implicit state guarantees on loans, the takeover protection such firms enjoy, and other forms of state intervention involved. Again, how far should states go in standardizing the shareholders' rights noted above as an aspect of encouraging cross-border M&A?

Such national differences in the treatment of M&A have already become an issue between countries and can be expected to grow in importance. As the European Community has moved to regulate larger mergers, for example, the harmonization of some of these matters within the Community and, with regard to M&A from outside the Community, have become important questions. The ease of cross-border acquisition of larger firms has also become an issue in the talks on structural impediments between the United States and Japan. The issue is only partly one of cross-border acquisition, of course, since similar restrictions may apply internally, but the insistence on reciprocity in some sectors by some countries makes it a potentially difficult international problem.

The second policy issue has to do with the appropriate stance on changes in the nationality of ownership as such. In Canada and elsewhere this issue has usually been couched in terms of a choice between foreign or domestic ownership and control, and drawing various welfare conclusions depending on what one thinks of the evidence on the economic and political consequences of each type of ownership.[10] If one believes that the performance of foreign-owned firms is inferior, either generally or in only a few significant cases, a review mechanism for foreign takeovers is one way to address the issue. Clearly, it is not the only way. Various government departments and agencies will address many particular aspects of performance, such as competition and environmental effects, in any case. Also, many countries manage to review occasional sensitive foreign takeovers with a minimum of both law and organization. Even Investment Canada, which has explicit review functions as well as other responsibilities, monitors a relatively limited and defined set of restricted sectors, and has negotiated undertakings in only 11 percent of the number of acquisition proposals it has reviewed.

Of the many points that might be made on the policy issues, two seem pertinent in the context of globalization through M&A. One is to emphasize the significance of *outward* direct investment and the related cross-border M&A; the other is to be clear about the impact of the welfare issue involved. On the first point it is important to note that Canada's stock of outward direct investment is now two-thirds the value of that on the inward side. Even in absolute terms, Canada easily ranks among the ten largest direct investors abroad. While there are many comprehensive studies of the effects on the inward side for Canada, there are few on the outward side. Two of the papers in this volume, those by Knubley et al, and by Halpern and Mintz, deal to a significant extent with issues involving outward M&A.

The literature on the significance of the concerns of home countries with regard to their direct investment abroad raises issues very similar to those on the inward side, such as which country captures tax gains or employment effects.[11] Such questions about welfare effects lead to our second point. The performance of domestic firms which do not have multinational investments clearly has an impact on social and group welfare, whether in an M&A setting or otherwise. It is difficult to see why the welfare effects covered in the various studies in this volume are any less important for shareholders or stakeholders simply because the source of the M&A is a domestic firm rather than a Canadian multinational or a foreign multinational. Substantial layoffs of workers, in circumstances where alternative employment is limited or requires retraining or other support, can hardly be dismissed because it is from one source rather than another. If it is perceived that one of these three types of firms tends to a particular form of behaviour, the issue is surely capable of testing. And even then, there is the question of dealing with particular cases, whatever the averages suggest.[12]

To the extent that there is a case for policy applicable to all firms, wherever owned, so as to assure desirable outcomes from M&A, some important issues remain. One is that of implementation costs and appropriate instruments, which may well differ for cross-border M&As in either direction compared with domestic firms. An example is the extra-territorial aspects of policy or, in current terminology, conflicting requirements among governments.

The question of appropriate instruments is not resolved if one decides to aim at the consequences of M&A rather than ownership issues *per se*; a significant debate would still remain between two groups. One group would favour generalized public policy approaches which can deal with harm from a variety of sources, and which would also put much emphasis on improving private-sector devices to anticipate and respond to such harm. The other group would argue the need for specific government interventions in specific circumstances. They believe such circumstances cannot be fully anticipated or provided for in advance, and also that the more generalized policy approaches would be inordinately expensive in terms of free-rider problems and the like. I have stated the issue in terms of harm but it can easily be put in terms of gain. For example, the advocates of strategic trade and investment would point to the potential for capturing oligopoly rents and other gains by a timely and credible intervention by the state in support of some types of domestically owned or domestically located firms operating at a world level. This is not the place to survey the literature on the potential for different types of governments to realize welfare gains from strategic policies.[13] In fact, as noted above, many governments have converted their direct investment policies to such a task, and are now encouraging mergers or consortia to capture high-technology sectors in particular. Even in those instances were privatization and deregulation have occurred, governments have usually been careful to retain a veto on some of the ownership and structural changes through "golden shares" and other means.

All of this underlines an important policy issue. Increased globalization has raised awkward questions in a world where governments often appear to be doing two contradictory things: developing their own multinationals through various subsidies, protected local markets, public ownership and the like, while insisting they must also have access to other countries' markets through the acquisition of firms as well as through trade. It is not difficult to see why other countries resist such subsidized competition or why they are concerned about the impact of state-owned firms. It is also not difficult to envisage the damage to foreign trade and investment such policies can bring — indeed, have already brought — through a welter of new or extended trade- and investment-distorting measures. The usual method for dealing with such problems is through mutually-restraining international agreements. Canada has already taken out a good deal of insurance in this respect for both her trade and her direct investment through the Free Trade Agreement with the United States. The scope of the approach to some of these problems goes well beyond that market.

ENDNOTES

1. See United Nations, *Transnational Corporations in World Development: Trends and Prospects*, New York, United Nations, 1988, pp. 54-66.
2. Michael G. Porter, *The Competitive Advantage of Nations*. New York, Free Press Macmillan, 1990.
3. John H. Dunning, "Dunning on Porter: Reshaping the Diamond of Comparative Advantage." Paper to the annual meeting of the Association for International Business, Toronto, October 1990, mimeo.
4. Richard E. Caves, *Multinational Enterprise and Economic Analysis*, Cambridge, Cambridge University Press, 1982, pp 81-85.
5. In arriving at this conclusion it is assumed that M&As are generally wealth increasing, a point on which other authors in this volume are more ambivalent.
6. For a summary of this literature, see the "Symposium on Takeovers" in *Journal of Economic Perspectives*, Winter 1988, pp. 21.
7. I have dealt with these changes more fully in "Firm and Government Strategies in the Context of Economic Integration", in B. Burgenmeier and J.L. Mucchielli (eds), *Multinationals and Europe 1992*, London and New York, Routledge, 1991.
8. Several authors, including Daniels in this volume, have noted Canada's relatively high concentration of shareholdings. Abe Tarasofsky's research for the Economic Council of Canada indicates that a dozen large conglomerates account for 20 percent of the Canadian corporate sector, a figure which rose from 10 percent during the 1980s when such conglomerates fell out of favour in the United States. Also, there is a relatively high degree of foreign ownership of Canadian industry, much of it in firms where the parent holds 100 percent of the equity, making hostile takeovers impossible except as the result of events in the country of the parent firm.
9. Data from Investor Responsibility Research Centre as noted in *Economist*, 29 April 1989, p. 76.
10. Policy, of course, is often made for reasons that go well beyond such welfare issues, ranging from electoral influences to views about the role of large firms and to the interplay of group interests.
11. See, for example, C. Fred Bergsten, Thomas Horst and Theodore H. Moran, *American Multinationals and American Interests*, Brookings Institution, Washington, DC, 1978 and J. E. Vahlne, "Foreign Direct Investment: A Swedish Problem", in W. J. Goldberg (ed) *Governments and Multinationals: the Policy of Control versus Autonomy*, Cambridge, MA, Oelgeschlager, Gunn and Hain, 1983.
12. It was suggested at the conference that discrimination against foreign-owned firms derives from the fact that there is no general recognition of the right to establishment in international law, although some agreements limit state powers in this area. This simply leaves open the question of why

one would discriminate against firms on the basis of their nationality, rather than their failure to perform in socially desirable ways.

13. See Safarian, *Firm and Government Strategies*, for a review of the literature and a viewpoint on this.

ACKNOWLEDGEMENT

I AM GRATEFUL to Leonard Waverman for a number of helpful suggestions.

About The Contributors

John Baldwin is Professor of Economics at Queen's University, now on leave as Research Fellow at Statistics Canada and the Economic Council of Canada. His research interests in industrial economics have concentrated on the relationship between trade flows and market structure, the evolution of the regulatory process, and the effect of firm adjustment on labour markets.

Richard Caves is Professor of Economics and Business Administration at Harvard University.

Ron Daniels is Assistant Professor in the Faculty of Law at the University of Toronto and Director of the International Business and Trade Law Program. His research interests are in the capital markets area and have focussed on corporate law, financial institutions, and securities regulation with a special emphasis on international issues.

Paul Halpern is Professor of Finance and Economics at the Faculty of Management and Faculty of Law at the University of Toronto. He has published in the areas of corporate finance, mergers and acquisitions, and investments. His current research interests, in addition to the impact of taxation on corporate restructurings, are in the corporate governance area, including poison pills and the role of institutional investors, and management buyouts.

Shyam Khemani is Adjunct Professor, Faculty of Commerce and Business Administration at the University of British Columbia, where he teaches courses in competitive strategy. He has held various positions in the Bureau of Competition Policy and has published articles on corporate concentration, barriers to entry and mergers.

John Knubley is Director of Investment Canada's research program. He was an economist in the Federal-Provincial Relations Office, with responsibilities relating to trade, agriculture and fiscal arrangements; he was also an executive/research assistant to the Chairman of the Economic Council.

William Krause is a Senior Economist at Statistics Canada, on assignment to Investment Canada analyzing investment issues. He has written extensively on foreign control, concentration, and international labour affiliations.

Jack Mintz is Professor of Business Economics in the Faculty of Management at the University of Toronto. He has been a special advisor in the Tax Policy Branch of the federal Department of Finance and has consulted on taxation issues for numerous organizations, both in Canada and abroad.

Michel Patry is an Associate Professor at the Institut d'économie appliquée of the École des Hautes Études Commerciales in Montreal.

Michel Poitevin is an Assistant Professor in the Département de sciences économiques at the Université de Montréal. His recent articles have dealt with the subjects of financial signalling, managerial compensation and debt financing.

Alan Rugman is Professor of International Business at the University of Toronto and Research Director of the Ontario Centre for International Business. He has published numerous articles and books dealing with the economic, managerial and strategic aspects of multinational enterprises and with trade and investment policy.

Zulfi Sadeque is Senior Investment Economist at Investment Canada (Research and Policy Sector). His areas of interest include international corporate merger and acquisition activity and trends in Canadian direct investment abroad. A recent working paper for the Agency dealt with Canadian minority equity participation in foreign-controlled subsidiaries.

A. Edward Safarian is Professor of Economics at the University of Toronto and holds appointments at Trinity College, Massey College and the Institute for Policy Analysis at the University of Toronto. Professor Safarian's main teaching and research interests are in Canadian public policy and have focussed on foreign ownership, economic integration and multinational corporations and various policy questions in international economics.

Leonard Waverman is Director of the Centre for International Studies and Professor of Economics at the University of Toronto. He writes and teaches in the areas of industrial organization and public policy, energy and resource economics, and public utility and public entreprise economics. His forthcoming publications will deal with pricing, access and the regulation of telecommunications services and with an international comparison of costs and productivity in the automobile industry.